TED WILLIAMS

TED WILLIAMS

A PORTRAIT IN WORDS AND PICTURES

Edited by
DICK JOHNSON

THE SPORTS MUSEUM

Text by
GLENN STOUT

WALKER AND COMPANY
NEW YORK

First published in the United States of America in 1991
by Walker Publishing Company, Inc.; first paperback edition published in 1994.
Published simultaneously in Canada by Thomas Allen & Son
Canada, Limited, Markham, Ontario

The Library of Congress cataloged the hardcover edition as follows:
Ted Williams : a portrait in words and pictures / edited by Dick
Johnson ; text by Glenn Stout.
p.   cm.
Includes index.
ISBN 0-8027-1140-5
1. Williams, Ted, 1918– . 2. Baseball players—United States—
Biography. 3. Williams, Ted 1918– —Pictorial works. 4. Baseball
players—United States—Pictorial works. I. Johnson, Dick, date.
II. Stout, Glenn, date.
GV865.W5T43   1991
796.357'092—dc20
[B]   90-43425
CIP
ISBN 0-8027-7434-2 (paper)

Book design by Circa 86

Frontispiece photograph courtesy of Brian Interland

Printed in the United States of America

4 6 8 10 9 7 5 3

To Mom and Pop, Mary, and Bobby with much love.
In memory of Tom Warner and Kevin Aylward.
—DJ

To Anne, Harold, Gary, and Lisa Stout,
Bill Gavin, Doc Kountze, and Donette Calhoon.
—GS

CONTENTS

Acknowledgments

As a native New Englander I became aware of Teddy Ballgame at an early age while listening to Curt Gowdy broadcast his heroics on hot summer afternoons many years ago. It has since been my pleasure to make the acquaintance of Mr. Williams through my position with the Sports Museum. It is safe to say that Williams is still the most fascinating and original athlete in Boston sports history, not to mention the fact that no mortal ever whacked a baseball in anger with more grace, power, and authority.

The idea to create a volume celebrating his career came as the result of my continuing hope to mount an exhibition chronicling the same. It is my sincere hope that this book stands as the definitive work on Ted Williams and that those who didn't see him play get some measure of his majesty from its pages.

I am grateful to Will Thorndike and the staff at Walker for making this project a reality. Likewise, Glenn Stout performed above and beyond the call of duty in crafting a text that is both insightful and sensitive as well as exhaustive in detail.

The staff and volunteers of the Sports Museum are my continual inspiration. In particular, Steve Garabedian and Harvey McKenney proved invaluable with their many hours of picture research. The Harold Kaese statistical appendix would have been an impossibility without the skilled editing of Mark Shreve. Thanks also to Brenda Cook, Jeff Craig, Brian Codagnone, Sports Museum founder Vic Caliri, and Sports Museum Chairman Dave Cowens. They are all .400 hitters who have made great sacrifices to make the museum a place where young and old can learn valuable lessons from the likes of Ted Williams.

I am also grateful to a multitude of individuals and institutions who opened their collections for this project. The print department of the Boston

Public Library provided access to the Leslie R. Jones Archive, which showcases the work of Boston's greatest photojournalist. Department chief Sinclair Hitchings was of particular help, as were library staff members Gunar Rutkovskis, B. Joseph O'Neil, Charles Longley, Katherine Dibble, Joe St. George, John Dorsey, Sean Andrew Heaney, Allison Cook, and Ralph Montilio. Dennis Brearley of the Brearley Collection of Rare Negatives couldn't have been more supportive or generous. Dick Bresciani and Debbie Mattson of the Boston Red Sox shared a wealth of material as did Don Skwar and George Collins of the *Boston Globe*. Fellow SABR member Luke Salisbury wrote a splendid essay and did double duty editing the narrative text. Brian Interland and Fay Ruby flattered me with their generosity and enthusiasm, as did Joe Ofria, Dick Darcy, George Joe, Rick Dunfey, Ted Lavash, Susan McKeon and family, Siobhan Silag, Harold Paretchan, Stu Thornley, Dick Beverage, Louie Plummer, Carolyn Whitaker, Frank Kern, Al Coulthard, Bob Walsh, Steve Gietschier of *The Sporting News*, and the ever-cheerful Pat Kelly of the National Baseball Hall of Fame.

—DICK JOHNSON
June 18, 1990

•••••••••••••

INTRODUCTION

•••••••••••••

Is Ted Williams the greatest hitter who ever lived? Williams sought that label, to the exclusion of almost any other. Any treatment of his career must, at some point, ask this question. In Williams's own terms it answers what is really a second, even more interesting question. Who is Ted Williams?

Ted Williams discovered the value and meaning of his life on the baseball diamond, between the thin chalk lines that separate fan from professional ballplayer. In that timeless arena Williams lived, wholly and completely, as he did nowhere else. Off the field, in the clubhouse, in his hotel, or even fishing along the Miramichi River in New Brunswick, Williams was only marking time until his next at bat, trying at all costs to preserve the special concentration he brought to the field.

When Ted wasn't hitting he wasn't Ted Williams, the world's greatest hitter. For one so wrapped up in that goal, all other experiences were lacking. Without the focus that came only at the plate, Ted came unbound. The parts and pieces of his personality could come unleashed, and sometimes go out of control, in a series of disconnected feelings and emotions, roaring by in a headlong lurch toward that next moment when he could pick up the bat, look at the pitcher, and *know*. He was Ted Williams, greatest hitter.

When Williams stepped to the plate he became a different being. Of all the controversy in his career: the gestures, the expectorations, the feuds with writers, the challenges he threw at the world, none ever took place at bat. Williams never charged out to the mound after a pitcher, never argued with an umpire, never lost focus, never did anything, anything but hit. In the confines of the batter's box Williams knew, better than most of us, precisely who he was and what he was supposed to do.

As soon as he left the box, that changed, and the bat could fly from his hands into the sky or Ted could storm into the dugout steaming at some slight or failure and once again wrestle with the question of what the world's greatest hitter does when he is not hitting; and whether or not what he does even matters. *Who he is* forms the larger question: for Ted Williams and for those who watched him.

There are answers to these questions. During his career, Ted Williams was probably the most scrutinized human being in the world. There were more photographs taken of Ted Williams, and more words written about Ted Williams, than any other man of his time. World leaders and politicians rose to power only to be deposed. Williams ruled for over twenty years. Entertainers and movie stars did not have 9,725 official performances, or the thousands of unofficial appearances he made each spring and in batting practice.

For twenty-one years America was in pursuit of Ted Williams. His five years in the service were relative vacations in comparison with his service in baseball. While playing, Ted was watched at each moment: at each instant he was judged. Whatever he said was written down. Whatever he did was written about. What he looked like was captured on film and sent around the world. Years after Ted's retirement, Detroit sportswriter Joe Falls randomly asked one hundred people on the street, "Who is Ted Williams?" All one hundred knew.

How could Williams stand it? The answer is he loved to hit, and that made the rest of it bearable.

Williams followed Ruth as Rome followed Athens, but Ruth, despite his immense popularity, was never the object of study that Williams was. Ruth lived in a different time. Sportswriters didn't pay much attention to what Ruth really said. They preferred to make up his quotes. In his first five or six seasons, he was rarely photographed. Most newspapers at the time rarely used photographs. Little film of Ruth remains. He predated, by an instant, the Golden Age of Hollywood. Ruth's career exists, most appropriately for the creature of legend he is, primarily in the imagination.

Ted Williams is no fable. Timing, circumstance, and his undeniable talent combined to make him the most public figure of his era. Williams's big league career spanned the age of Hollywood to the age of television. By 1939 photographs were a staple of the American press. Between two wars the communications industry expanded and matured. Baseball writers grew tired of fairy tales and turned to fact. The America that glimpsed Williams as a raw rookie in 1939 was radically different from the one that watched in awe as he homered in his last at bat in 1960.

For most of Williams's career there were seven daily newspapers in Boston. They followed the Red Sox but usually wrote about Williams. Another six or eight papers from surrounding communities did the same. The national and visiting press added to the crush. Every day for eight months each season Ted Williams was written about, at-length and in-depth, by twenty or more writers whose livelihood depended on their ability to keep pace with the public's insatiable appetite for Ted. Each writer was usually paired with a photographer who took hundreds of photographs. If Ted was written about twenty times a day, he was probably photographed a thousand. Williams was Hollywood-handsome, and in attics all across New England are photo albums containing shots of Ted taken by blushing bobby-soxers who preferred mooning over Williams to swooning over Sinatra.

In the beginning, this didn't bother Ted. He was young and brash, refreshingly unaware. After his first season in the major leagues he heard his first boo and started paying attention to all those who were paying attention to him. He wanted everyone to see things the way he did. He learned that the view from beneath the microscope is radically different from the one above. Ted dug in his heels, squared off with the press, and never blinked.

But he hit, he swung the bat, and that spoke volumes. For a while the press and public were more concerned, not with what Ted did at the plate, but how he could do it acting as he did. If the press thought Williams was obsessed with hitting to the degree his behavior suffered, the press was equally obsessed with Williams to the degree their objectivity suffered. But they wrote. Williams once estimated he'd swung the bat several million times. And each of those swings resulted in a written word.

Season by season, Ted's accomplishments as a hitter are undeniable. No other hitter, not even Ruth, has ever been so good, so consistently, for so long a time. If Ted Williams didn't win quite as many individual honors as some other players, and if the Red Sox did not win as many pennants as some other teams, each set records for coming close.

Thirty-four years after he retired as a player, fifty years after becoming the last man to hit .400, it is possible today to survey the results, scan the photographs and box scores, and try to determine who Ted Williams is, and whether he is the greatest hitter who ever lived. One of the great ironies, in a career marked by irony, is that these questions can be answered today because of the attention lavished on Williams by the press. Prior to this book no one has attempted, to any depth or degree of certainty, to step back, sift through the mountain of Williams material, and try to put together as completely as possible a portrait of this "greatest hitter."

In telling his life story, one cannot fully explain why Ted Williams became who he is, but can find influences and locate moments when the Ted Williams known by the public first made his presence known. From the playgrounds of San Diego, to Nicolette Park in Minneapolis, from Fenway Park to the Florida Keys, Ted Williams never seemed like anyone else. He had no loose ends, no inexplicable traits. He had personality to burn and the talent to match it.

Writers of Williams's era tended to take his record for granted and concentrated on the question of his character. Those who came later have tried to consider his record apart from the personality. Williams's own book, *My Turn at Bat*, does a fine job in both areas but leaves significant gaps and contains more than a few errors of fact. Some great myths exist about the Williams we think we know, and some remarkable achievements have gone unnoticed. Now, at a time when half the population of the United States was either not yet born or too young to see Williams play, this portrait is an attempt to set down the facts of his life and provide material for an accurate appraisal of his career. The greatest hitter deserves as much.

The essays included herein attempt to provide what the text cannot: a more personal and emotive response to Ted Williams by some of the best contemporary observers of both Ted Williams and the game of baseball. The writers were free to choose their own topic and have responded with a fascinating array of anecdotes and impressions. Like Ruth, whatever more we learn about Williams only increases his stature. Ted is never diminished. He only becomes more remarkable.

The text of this portrait is chronological and narrative. The scope of the book precluded any in-depth interviews with either Ted, his teammates, friends, family, or opponents. Fortunately, through the efforts of literally thousands of other writers, their comments and unique perspective were available through a thorough survey of previously published material. In writing this book, virtually every published monograph and magazine article concerning Ted Williams was consulted and compared to separate fact from anecdote, and embellishment from fact. Likewise, a number of valued friends and fellow writers checked the text, offering their unrestrained comments and opinions.

The bulk of information making up the text was culled from the daily newspaper reports from the Boston press over the course of Williams's career. At one time or another, microfilm from nine different newspapers at the Boston Public Library was consulted and compared in order to compile the most accurate and balanced record possible.

The archives of Harold Kaese, also retained by the library, made a particularly important contribution. Kaese's columns, clip file on Williams, unpublished stories, and notes, laid the groundwork for this portrait, allowing me to quickly determine the path of Williams's career, its significant moments, and its ultimate direction and meaning.

When first approached about this project I recalled an instance several years ago when I was asked, by one of the people *not* stopped on the street by Joe Falls, "Who is Ted Williams?" I hope the reader finds that answer here. Far more important, however, is that in the consideration of another's life, one learns about one's own.

Is Ted Williams the greatest hitter who ever lived? My answer to this question also answers the question, "Who is Ted Williams?"

Simply put, the greatest hitter who ever lived is who Ted Williams is.

• • • • • • • • • • • • • •

SAN DIEGO BOYHOOD TO
MINOR LEAGUE
APPRENTICESHIP

• • • • • • • • • • • • • •

On September 11, 1918, the Boston Red Sox defeated the Chicago Cubs in the World Series to become the world champions of baseball. Although the Red Sox have failed to win another championship in the seventy-three seasons that have since passed, that accomplishment is only the second most significant Red Sox event in 1918. Two weeks before the World Series banner was last lifted at Fenway Park, on August 30, 1918, Ted Williams was born in San Diego.

More than any other player in Red Sox history, Ted Williams, over thirty years after his retirement, defines what it means to play baseball in the city of Boston. His career is the story of one city's ongoing love affair with the game of baseball. And as in most love affairs, that relationship has passion and pain, heartbreak and joy.

Of all of baseball's most legendary figures, Ted Williams is perhaps the most human. While his on-field accomplishments test the boundaries of belief, they are tempered by Williams the human being; a man who has, almost to a fault, been nothing but himself. Williams never acted the part of baseball superstar: he *was* the part.

Ted Williams had but one goal in life, as he put it himself, "To walk down the street and have people say, 'There's the greatest hitter who ever lived.'" Williams's struggle for that goal took place in public, in full view of an entire city. When the demands of the challenge made Ted happy, you could tell. When it made him mad, he let you know. When he failed, it was written all over his face. When Ted succeeded, his happiness was shared.

By turns, he was both loved and hated, usually at the same time by the same people, for Ted was more than just a ballplayer. He was everyman: someone who seemed as vulnerable and as mortal as we are, but who could do remarkable things. When Ted Williams walks down that street today, he walks with millions. Those who saw him play, cheered him, booed him, wrote about him, all know what it means to want to be the best at something. Williams actually did it. When the question is asked, "Who is baseball's greatest hitter?" the answer inevitably includes only two men, Williams and Babe Ruth. Given that the two men played in different eras, the difference is infinitessimal; the ranking meaningless.

Yet unlike Ruth, Williams was not a god, never remote or mysterious, hardly the creature of legend Ruth was—half fact, half fairy tale. Ted Williams was a man, undeniably real and human, replete with all the weaknesses of the species. Yet somehow he achieved grandness.

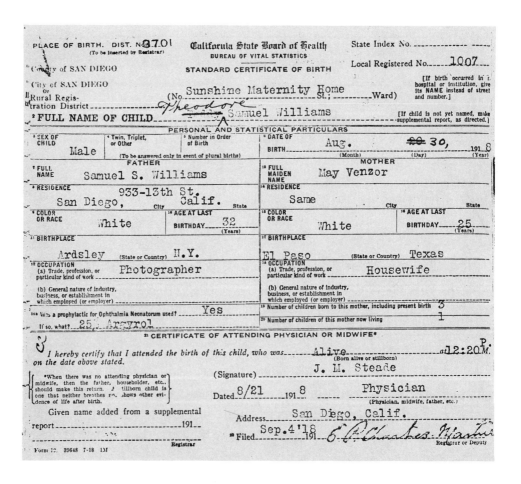

Ted Williams's birth certificate lists his name as Teddy, as he was named by his father after Teddy Roosevelt when he was born on August 30, 1918. Williams later changed his name to Theodore—it's his own handwriting on the certificate. (Courtesy of Brian Interland)

Ted at age 6 in 1924, at left, shown with mother May Williams and brother Danny, age 4. (The Sporting News)

His birth certificate reads "Teddy Samuel Williams." Named after his father, Samuel, and Teddy Roosevelt, Ted Williams was the first child of Sam and May Williams.

Sam Williams was born in Mount Vernon, New York, of Welsh and English extraction. At age 16 he ran away from home and joined the United States Cavalry. In 1908 and 1909 he served in the Philippines, and later bragged he served with Teddy Roosevelt's old unit.

In Hawaii, on his way back to the states, Sam Williams met, and later married, May Venzer, a commissioned lieutenant in the Salvation Army. Of

Williams's childhood home, 4121 Utah Street, San Diego. (The Sporting News)

Mexican and French descent, May Venzer joined the Army in 1904 and remained an active member until her death in 1961. The Army, best known for its work in social services, is actually a creed unto itself, adopting the trappings of the military in its battle for the salvation of souls. By marrying outside the Army, May Williams lost her commission.

Sam and May Williams settled in San Diego, purchasing a small home on Utah Street in the North Park section of town. Sam worked as a commercial photographer. It was not a lucrative career, but there was plenty of work in the growing port city, taking passport, souvenir, and portrait shots for the growing population of servicemen. May Williams spent the bulk of her time proselytizing for the Salvation Army, hawking the group's recruitment magazine, *War Cry,* playing cornet in the Salvation Army band, and administering to the down-and-out in San Diego and across the border in Tijuana.

A selfless woman of strident beliefs, May Williams gained a measure of local notoriety for her efforts on behalf of the Army, earning the monikers "Salvation May" and "the Angel of Tijuana." The restrictiveness of her religion clashed with the less restrictive lifestyle of her husband. Sam Williams saw himself as a bit of an adventurer and raconteur. He smoked a pipe and, to

May's horror, was not averse to an occasional drink. Sam felt the time May gave to the Army gave him the right to do as he pleased. Their pairing was less than ideal.

The birth of "Teddy," and, several years later, his younger brother Danny, had little effect on the family. May still devoted herself to helpless causes, and Sam Williams worked his photography business. Family life was never a priority. Once the boys entered school they were on their own, often waiting until well after dark before either parent returned.

The North Park neighborhood was a close-knit community. Neighbors kept an eye out for the Williams boys. Besides, Ted, as he preferred to be called, had found an antidote to the loneliness and isolation of home.

At about age eight or nine, while attending Garfield Grammar School, Ted Williams discovered baseball. At nearby North Park, young Williams embarked on what was to become a lifelong obsession: hitting. Naturally right-handed, when Ted first picked up a baseball bat he swung from the left side. On the playground at North Park, playing a succession of baseball-type games, young Williams developed the skills and learned the life lessons that eventually would carry him to Cooperstown.

Enthralled with baseball, Ted started going to school early so he could get the bat and ball and find someone to play with before school, sometimes even bribing kids with his lunch money to pitch or shag flies. At lunch he'd race home, grab something to eat, and charge back to school so he could get in a few licks before the bell sounded. After school it was off to North Park again.

The playground made Ted Williams. And he remained, in some sense, a playground player for his entire baseball career—not on the level of performance, but in style and personality. Williams loved to hit, and in order to get that chance on the playground, he developed, by necessity, a personality to match his ability. Being the best is not always enough on the playground. It's a Darwinian, adolescent world where the kid who talks the longest, yells the loudest, cries the hardest, and is the most stubborn most often succeeds, whether the game is baseball, tag, or marbles. The meek don't get to play, and Ted wanted to play more than anything. Lacking a sense of self-esteem at home, Williams made up for what he missed at the playground. He wanted to play, he wanted to be best, and he was never shy about saying so. His later approach to the game never varied. What some would interpret as selfishness was actually this adolescent braggadocio—the law of the playground, extended into the major leagues. This was Williams's secret. He had to be the best, and it didn't matter whether he was in North Park or Fenway Park.

Ted's unbridled passion for the game drew attention. Older boys and men in the neighborhood took an interest. A neighbor told him stories about Joe Wood, Walter Johnson, and the Negro Leagues. Rod Luscomb, the playground director at North Park, fed Ted's growing enthusiasm and interest in the game

At San Diego's Herbert Hoover High School, Williams won All–Southern California honors as a pitcher in 1935, and outfielder in 1936. (Courtesy of the San Diego Hall of Champions)

by playing with him for hours. Hitting all day, to the exclusion of practically everything else, Ted quickly became better than his peers. He and Luscomb would compete as equals in a game of their own invention, "Big League," batting a softball against a backstop, playing whole games based on where the ball hit. At home, Ted was just a boy, a little lonely and completely average. At the playground he was any ballplayer his imagination allowed him to be—the object of thunderous cheers from imaginary crowds, the best pitcher, the most feared hitter in the world. It was always two outs, two on, and the bottom of the ninth. Ted always hit the home run and became the hero.

For Ted Williams, hitting was an outlet and escape into another world, but it did not come easy. Williams still recalls one particular day, "one of those ten days you remember in your life," he discovered he could hit any pitch thrown by his friend Wilbur Riley. Despite later raves about Williams's eyesight and lightning reflexes, he was never physically gifted. His overall coordination was poor and running was difficult. His eyesight and reflexes became remarkable through hours of practice hitting a baseball. "They never talk about the practice," Williams said years later. "Practice, practice, practice. Damn it, you've got to practice. . . . There's never been a kid who hit more baseballs than Ted Williams."

Although Ted would later write a book entitled *The Science of Hitting,* his approach was anything but scientific. While his philosophy of hitting is deceptively simple, on the order of "get a good pitch to hit, swing with a slight uppercut, and be quick," his method shares more with the artisan than the scientist. Science uses measurement and results can be exactly duplicated. Hitting is the ability to adjust to change. No two pitchers, no two pitches, are ever precisely alike. Williams hit like the jazz musician, who only after countless hours of learning scales and mastering technique, can begin to play the most tentative solo. Ted perfected his technique and then developed this other side of hitting. In the batter's box he was no machine, but a master craftsman.

At around this time, Williams developed a second, parallel interest; one that would eventually supplant baseball as the most important activity in his life. A neighbor named Chick Rotert, a game warden, took Ted bass fishing. Another man from the neighborhood, Les Cassie, introduced Ted to the wonders of surf casting at nearby Coronado Beach. Ted's mother bought him a shotgun, and on Saturdays he would walk the canyons around San Diego in search of small game. When Williams was growing up, the city was still small and just beginning to push from the sea into the surrounding country. Within an hour or two he could be in virtual wilderness.

Hunting and fishing provided the same challenges hitting did: technique and practice. Like baseball, the two pursuits allowed Ted to explore another world. Outdoors, alone with his own thoughts, away from the house on Utah Avenue, Ted Williams could be himself. Hunting and fishing became Ted's

The 1935 Hoover High School varsity team — Ted Williams is in the bottom row, far left. Coach Wos Caldwell (upper right) exhorted his players by hitting them with a wooden switch during practice! (Courtesy of the San Diego Hall of Champions)

other great escape, and as his baseball career blossomed, Ted came to appreciate his time outdoors even more. Hunting and fishing provided the challenge he craved while leaving him free from the notoriety and pressures of major league baseball.

In school Ted felt no pressure from baseball. He played on his grammar school team, then the team at Horace Mann Junior High, the American Legion Padre Serra "Fighting Bob" Post team, and eventually the school team at Herbert Hoover High. While at Hoover, Ted carried his bat to class, where he was an average student, preferring shop and home economics to English or arithmetic. After school he was back at the playground, hitting.

At Herbert Hoover Ted began to attract the attention of professional scouts. A few "bird dogs" had seen the eager youngster on the sandlots. In high school, Ted pitched and played outfield. His junior year he hit .583, before "slumping" to .406 as a senior. On the mound he was just as impressive, once striking out 23 batters, and compiling a 16–3 record as a senior. Ted's legion team reached the sectional finals in the California state tournament, and Ted was named All-Southern California.

By this time, the scouts were serious, and Ted's parents, suddenly aware that he was going to make money playing baseball, took an interest. Ted attended a tryout for the Cardinals, and was scouted by Detroit's Marty Krug in his last high school game. Krug thought Ted, six feet three and 145 pounds, was too skinny for professional ball. He suggested Ted try to put on weight before thinking of pro ball.

The Yankees' Bill Essick was more positive. He offered $200 a month to sign with the Yankees. But May Williams, who had to sign all Ted's contracts until he turned 21, didn't want her 17-year-old son sent away to a far-off city in the minor leagues. Ted, whose high school eligibility ended in June of 1936, wasn't scheduled to complete high school until January of 1937, so signing with the Yankees was out of the question.

In the meantime Ted played semi-pro ball for three dollars a week. May Williams refused to allow him to play for five dollars for the Texas Liquor House team. Anything to do with liquor was strictly forbidden.

The Pacific Coast League Los Angeles Angels showed interest in Ted, but to Williams's good fortune, there was a new PCL franchise in San Diego, the Padres. The team had moved from Hollywood to San Diego for the 1936 season. The growing city, with a population of nearly 200,000, rallied around the team and the Padres became a source of city pride. The club lacked a local draw. Ted was San Diego's best high school player, and civic leaders pushed for owner Bill Lane to tender young Williams a contract. It was good business, and besides, Ted was a prospect.

Ted is shown with high school coach Wos Caldwell in a 1955 reunion at Fenway Park. (Photograph by Leslie Jones, courtesy of the Jones family)

In 1936, Williams made his debut with the San Diego Padres of the Pacific Coast League, batting .271 in 42 games. (Courtesy of the San Diego Hall of Champions)

Frank Shellenback, shown here as a Red Sox coach in 1941, was Williams's manager with the Padres. (Boston Public Library)

In the summer of 1936, while still enrolled in high school, for the princely sum of $150 a month, Ted Williams became a professional ballplayer.

The transition from high school ball to the Pacific Coast League was baseball's version of the transition from adolescence to adulthood, and Ted was forced to do both at the same time. The PCL was perhaps the strongest of all minor leagues. The San Diego club was well stocked with tough, veteran ballplayers accustomed to the grueling 176-game season. The league supplanted the majors on the West Coast, and many players spent their entire career in the circuit. San Diego manager Frank Shellenback pitched in the PCL for two decades and racked up 295 wins. In 1936 Williams was, quite simply, out of his league.

All arms, legs, and enthusiasm, Williams had his San Diego teammates scratching their heads in wonder. Everyone could see that Ted could hit, but no one was quite sure if he could do anything else but talk. Williams spoke before he thought, and responded to wisecracks from veteran ballplayers with his own. Standing in the outfield, he spent more time swinging an imaginary bat than shagging real fly balls. Chasing after hits he sometimes slapped his own rump and yelled, "Hi, ho, silver!" It was hard to believe.

Shellenback took his time with Williams. The club had a veteran outfield featuring Vince DiMaggio, Joe's brother, and there was no way for the rookie to crack the starting lineup. Shellenback let Williams pinch-hit, play the late innings, and occasionally start against right-handed pitching. In his first professional at bat, against Sacramento's Henry Pippen, Williams struck out. The Padres were curious about Ted's pitching ability and allegedly Ted made one mound appearance for the club, although PCL records inexplicably fail to record this appearance. Ted relieved at the end of a blowout and set down the side in order in his first inning, but in the second he gave up four consecutive hits, culminating with a home run, before Shellenback came to the mound.

"Look," quipped Ted, "there's no one on base." As the exasperated Shellenback tried to sputter a reply, Williams added, "Skip, as a pitcher I think I'm a pretty good outfielder. You've got me in the wrong position." This ended the career of Ted Williams, pitching ace.

It was all for the best. Padres outfielder Ivy Shivers retired in midseason and Ted began to get some playing time. The Red Sox had a working agreement with San Diego and were interested in a couple of prospects, infielder Bobby Doerr and pitcher George Myatt. Red Sox general manager Eddie Collins made a rare scouting trip to San Diego to check out the two players.

Williams as a seventeen-year-old Padre rookie in 1936. (Courtesy of the San Diego Hall of Champions)

Red Sox general manager Eddie Collins, shown here with Williams and Red Sox manager Joe Cronin, secured options on both Williams and Bobby Doerr on the one and only scouting trip of his career in 1937. (Photograph by Leslie Jones, courtesy of the Jones family)

Never has a trip been more successful, as it eventually resulted in the Sox acquiring two Hall of Fame ballplayers. Collins, a Hall of Fame second baseman himself for Connie Mack's Philadelphia Athletics, had been Red Sox owner Tom Yawkey's GM since Yawkey purchased the club in 1934. In those first few seasons, Yawkey broke the bank trying to buy a pennant. Frustrated, the Sox decided to change strategy and concentrate on prospects. Collins went to San Diego with his eyes wide open.

While Collins picked up an option on Doerr and Myatt, he was most impressed with a certain gawky young outfielder. He was raw, but Collins saw the swing. There was nothing raw about that.

Seeing Williams swing was like spotting a virtuoso in a Salvation Army band. Ted had all the tools; he just needed time. Although he was young, undisciplined, and lacked power, the hours of practice had paid off. The swing was classic. Moreover, it was obvious Williams loved to hit. There was every reason to expect improvement.

Collins convinced a disbelieving Lane to give him an option on Williams. Padre owner Lane agreed, but felt Collins was making a mistake. As far as he could tell, all Williams could do was eat. Lane even docked Williams's pay when he went above the $2.50-per-day meal allowance. Lane refused to accept money from the Red Sox for Williams until the Sox actually took Williams. He valued the working agreement and was afraid one sour option deal would botch things up.

Williams finished the year with a .271 average without a home run in only 42 ballgames. Still, it was an impressive beginning for so young a player. When the Padres sold Vince DiMaggio to the Boston Bees after the season, Williams's spot in the San Diego lineup was secure.

Williams added another inch and some ten pounds in the off-season, and graduated from high school in January 1937. Although a much-improved ballplayer, he showed no similar signs of growing up. During the 1938 season, he had the audacity to lobby Lane and Shellenback for a two-week, midseason vacation. When his request was granted, Ted didn't take it, stating, "It's the principle of the thing. It's amazing what you can get when you ask for it."

PCL pitchers would have preferred that Williams take a vacation for the entire 1937 season. Ted wore them out. His whiplike swing now delivered both long balls and line drives. Ted homered in every PCL park and finished with 23 home runs. San Francisco manager Lefty O'Doul, a career .349 hitter including a mark of .398 for the 1929 Phillies, told Williams, "Don't let anybody change you." A San Francisco paper heralded Ted as the greatest hitter since Paul Waner. It was heady stuff to be hearing at age 18.

In December the Red Sox purchased Ted's contract for $25,000 and four ballplayers—Dom Dallessandro, Al Niemiec, Bunny Griffiths, and Spencer Harris. Williams was signed to a two-year contract worth $3,000 and $4,500, and told to report in March to Sarasota, Florida, for spring training.

In 1937, Williams whacked 23 homers while driving in 98 runs. His next stop was the Red Sox camp in Sarasota. When chided by veteran Red Sox outfielders Doc Cramer, Ben Chapman, and Joe Vosmik for his demotion to the minors, he informed them that he'd be back before they knew it and would soon be making more money than all three combined.
(Courtesy of the San Diego Hall of Champions)

As a Minneapolis Miller, Williams won the American Association triple crown, batting .336 with 43 homers and 142 RBIs. The cozy confines of Nicollet Park contributed to his impressive numbers. (Minnesota Historical Society)

Due to floods in California, Ted was late in arriving in Sarasota. When he did, however, he made an immediate impression. Williams treated his Red Sox teammates no differently than he did those in San Diego. He led with his mouth and then let his bat do the rest of his talking. Posing before newsreel cameras, he responded to a quip from catcher Moe Berg with the flippant reply, "Looks like there's at least one agitator in camp," and then proceeded to call Berg "Adge" for the remainder of camp, driving the multilingual backstop batty with questions like, "Can a man marry his widow's daughter?"

The veterans responded in kind, dubbing Williams the "California Cracker" and "San Diego Saparoo" among other, less delicate nicknames. Youth was not something much admired in 1938, and Williams had a hard time. Rookies were cut little slack in training camps of the day, but Ted didn't behave any differently than he did in the playground at North Park. He made sure he got his cuts in the batting cage, even telling the older players their time was up and informing them they could see some real hitting.

And they did. For despite Williams's youthful gaffes, his swing caused players to stop and stare. Ted enjoyed the attention and spewed forth a running commentary on his performance.

Williams made his Red Sox debut on March 13 in an exhibition game against Cincinnati, batting third, and going 0–4 against three Cincinnati pitchers. One newspaper noted prophetically, "Williams was noisy on the bench and enjoyed himself thoroughly, was loose at the bat, and merely because he did not hit safely, you must not conclude he is not impressive as a batter."

Big league pitching was a cut above the PCL and gave young Williams trouble. Veteran pitchers learned to take advantage of his eagerness and soon had him leaning over the plate, flailing at curve balls just out of reach. Meanwhile, Sox veterans, particularly outfielders, were relentless in their ribbing of Ted. He was out to take their job, and it was obvious the Red Sox were counting on Williams. Ted wasn't ready, and the constant kidding got under his skin. He started to press and worry. As much to protect his confidence as anything else, on March 21, Williams was optioned to Minneapolis.

Ted took the cut hard, as Joe Vosmic, Doc Cramer, and Ben Chapman afterward cruelly inquired, "Where are you going, California?"

"Someday," Williams vowed, "I'm gonna come back and make more money than those three put together." In Minneapolis, he would take giant strides in that direction.

In camp with the Millers, Williams was much more relaxed, but still the same young Ted. The *Minneapolis Star* reported, "Williams is tickled to death to be with the Millers, especially under the tutelage of [manager] Donie Bush, talks a blue streak, wants to know all about Minneapolis and Minnesota, when the duck-hunting season opens, the fishin', and would like to get his hands on the guy that started 'this second DiMaggio business.'" Although he again went hitless in his exhibition game debut on March 23, on April 1 the great Rogers Hornsby temporarily joined the club as a batting instructor.

Under Hornsby, Williams worked on the other side of hitting, the mental part that turns technique into success. Hornsby was hard as nails in his approach to hitting and refused to give pitchers any credit for ever getting a man out. It was all a matter of the hitter not executing. Williams and Hornsby engaged in hitting contests; Ted watching in wonder as Hornsby hit line drive after line drive. Williams questioned the Rajah tirelessly about hitting, taking from him the lasting advice to "get a good ball to hit."

Just as it had in San Diego, hitting still distracted Williams from other aspects of the game. On April 3, Williams failed to run out a ground ball he thought was foul and it cost the Millers a run. In the next half-inning, brooding over the mistake, he dropped an easy fly ball. He was still practicing his swing with his glove, and it was hard to tell if Williams even cared about the rest of his game. Ted was like some strange, slugging idiot savant: hitting was everything.

On April 16, the Millers opened their season in Indianapolis. Williams, wearing number 19, batted third and played right field. In the first three games, Ted went hitless, a cumulative 0–11.

On April 19, in Louisville, Ted put Hornsby's advice to get a good ball to the test. Determined to wait for a ball he could hit, Williams singled and walked five times in six plate appearances, tying the league record. The next day, he gave Louisville fans a preview of the remainder of the season.

In the fourth inning Ted belted a line drive over the center fielder's head, the ball coming to rest 470 feet from the plate as Ted circled the bases with an inside-the-park home run. In the sixth, with the center fielder back another 50 feet, Ted duplicated the effort, this time the ball flying 450 feet on the fly and rolling to a stop against the fence a full 512 feet from home. Williams couldn't wait to get to Minneapolis. The right field fence in Nicollet Park was only 279 feet 10 inches from home plate.

Had the fence been 379 feet away, it wouldn't have mattered. Most of Ted's home runs in Nicollet cleared not only the fence but Nicollet Avenue as well, bouncing off the roofs of buildings across the street. (American Association pitchers were powerless against Ted. He won the league triple crown with a .366 average, 43 home runs and 142 RBIs. Williams didn't depend on Nicollet. Twenty-one of his home runs were hit on the road.

While Ted drove the opposition batty, he also drove manager Donie Bush nuts. Ted was still playing baseball as if it were "Big League," practicing his swing in the field, ignoring the occasional fly ball, sitting down between hitters, and talking to fans. Things came to a head on September 4. After fouling out to first, Williams threw his bat skyward, "even with the grandstand roof," according to one report. He stormed back to the bench, saw the water cooler, and gave it a vicious swipe. The cooler broke and Ted narrowly missed serious injury to his hand. Referring to his bat toss, Ted quipped to the press, "It's all in the wrist."

Williams made Bush so distraught he went so far as to go to Minneapolis owner Mike Kelley and tell him that if Williams stayed on the team, Bush would leave. The manager, however, wasn't hitting .360 and Bush realized that if it came down to a question of Williams or Bush, Ted would be the one to finish the season in Minneapolis.

Despite Williams's spectacular year, the Millers finished sixth at 78–74. In an instance of foreshadowing, Williams finished second, by five votes, in league MVP balloting. Still, for 20-year-old Ted, it was a successful year. Apart from baseball, he found the hunting and fishing to his liking. And, for the first time in his life, Ted Williams had a girl friend.

The Red Sox were already counting on Williams. They finished second in 1938, 9½ games behind New York, and were hoping to trade for a pitcher. Williams gave them the luxury of dealing a starting outfielder, each of whom had hit over .300. Ben Chapman went to Cleveland for pitcher Denny Galehouse. For Ted Williams, there was now a clear path from "Big League" to the real thing.

WILLIAMS THE ARTIST:
A CERTAIN ALIENATED MAJESTY

BY LUKE SALISBURY

Nowhere in team sports is man so nakedly pitted against man, with no help from teammates or clock, as when batter faces pitcher. This has led to a breed of athletes which has no equivalent in sport: the high average hitter. He is the consummate artist in that most individual game: pitcher versus batter—within that most individual game: baseball. Baseball has produced only a handful of these maestros. Ty Cobb and Rogers Hornsby have the highest numbers; Tony Gwynn and Wade Boggs are the most recent; Ted Williams may have been the best. These men do what all hitters do, but they do it more consistently—much more constantly. Only four men who played their whole careers against the live ball have lifetime averages over .340. Fourteen men hit 500 home runs. Only one did both: Ted Williams.

In *My Turn at Bat,* Williams says, "I was and am too complex a personality, too much a confusion of boyish enthusiasm and bitter experience to be completely understood by everybody." In this excellent book, in characteristically straightforward

fashion, Ted Williams tells his story: the neglected boy in San Diego who developed an obsession with hitting, dreamed of being a big leaguer and "the greatest hitter who ever lived," made the big leagues, loved and hated every minute of it, feuded, spat, endlessly perfected his swing, hit .400, never won a World Series, battled with the press, held center stage in Boston for over twenty years, ended with a majestic flourish immortalized by John Updike, and forever will be mentioned when people discuss the great hitters. In forthright Williams style, he blames himself ("I was impetuous, I was tempestuous") the club for not shielding him from reporters who discovered how easy Williams was to rile, and the meanness of particular writers ("I can *still* remember the things they wrote, and they still make me mad"). This isn't quite T. E. Lawrence's "Some of the evil of my tale may have been inherent in our circumstances," but it is an admission playing wasn't easy.

Ted's story is many stories. The most compelling, and least recognized, is that his story is

an artist's story. The high average hitters are artists. They do not hit so high because they have physical gifts others don't. They hit so high because they have mental gifts others don't. Ty Cobb was not the best natural hitter of his time. He was the smartest. Joe Jackson had more ability. So did George Sisler and Babe Ruth, who, had he concentrated on average, might have hit .450. The high average hitters taught themselves. They practiced constantly. They adjusted constantly. They watched pitchers constantly. They taught themselves to think. For them, hitting was a discipline and an art, like writing for Flaubert. They developed the mental part of the game. For them, sitting in the dugout meant studying a pitcher's sequence of pitches. As Ted said, "Pick your nose, scratch your ass, and it all goes by."

Williams, Cobb, and Hornsby were all notoriously difficult personalities. Cobb fought with opponents and teammates. His autobiography, written many years after he finished playing, was called *My Life in Baseball: The True Record,* as if by talking,

Cobb could change people's opinion of him. Hornsby was traded four times. His autobiography is *My War with Baseball*. Williams was the mellowest of the three, which is saying something.

With the obsessive devotion that made them great, came the dark side of the artist. They were, as each repeatedly says in his autobiography, their own man, and lived exactly as they wanted to. These men were driven. They were intense loners, frequently disliked by teammates and writers, and vilified by home and opposing fans. What they did required so much work, so much thinking, so much seriousness, they just weren't "good ole boys"—those athletes the public perceives as joyous adolescents who make youth flesh again for spectators. Cobb was so at odds with the world, he carried a gun. Hornsby was so obsessed with his eyes, he wouldn't read a book or view a movie during the season. Williams required the solitude of fishing to restore his spirit. These men were artists, for good and bad. They were accused of playing for themselves, for their stats. In a way, they were. Hitting was their lives.

We expect writers, composers, and painters to exhibit the idiosyncrasies associated with extraordinary talent. We don't expect them to create in public. It's amusing to think of Hemingway trying to craft those enormously concentrated stories while a gallery of critics called him a bum, questioned his talent, intelligence, or masculinity. One might argue hitting a baseball is more like performing in a symphony orchestra, but here too the audience doesn't usually offer on-the-spot commentary. When Ted Williams says hitting a baseball is the hardest thing in sports, he is understating the case. Hitting a baseball, the way he hit it, in front of a critical audience, whose emotional lives are enmeshed in the ritual, is one of the most difficult tasks on earth.

Williams was too obviously an artist. In *My Turn at Bat,* he addresses the complaint he walked too often when the game was on the line, by reiterating Hornsby's dictum, "Get a good ball to hit!" What Ted really meant was that if he broke his discipline, he would interrupt the game he played with the pitcher. What fans were objecting to was this demonstration that the game between Williams and pitcher transcended the game between Boston and opponent. This is clearly a battle between the fans' ego and Williams's. How dare a player so obviously choose his game over ours? The fan wants to beat New York. Ted Williams wanted to beat all the other hitters who ever lived. Hitting is a solitary business. Winning is not. When Williams took that pitch a half-inch outside with the tying run on second, he set himself apart. The world was willing enough to whip him for it.

My Turn at Bat tells a painful story. Williams's early years read like the biography of a writer. His Salvation Army mother felt morally superior to his ne'er-do-well father. "The Angel of Tijuana" spent all day in the streets soliciting money, chiding drunks, and doing "good." Like Dickens's Mrs. Jellyby, who worried about the natives of Borrioboola-Gha while her children went hungry, Mrs. Williams came home late and tired. Sometimes Ted stood on the front porch casting with a fishing rod in the dark waiting for her. Other times he had to march with a Salvation Army band through the streets of San Diego while his mother begged alms. Like so many writers, Williams knew shame. He knew loneliness. He must have wondered who loved him. His mother never saw him play in the big leagues. His father got interested in Ted's baseball career when his son was going to sign a professional contract. Of home, Ted said, "The house was dirty all the time."

Like so many artists, Williams did what he had to do on his own. Baseball filled his hours. Baseball gave him friends. Baseball provided father figures. It was his life.

The autobiography makes it clear that Ted Williams was not born a star. He was not the best player in his neighborhood or in high school. Ted was awkward ("All arms and legs flailing"), but he had the supreme desire to hit, to practice, to never stop

The artist with his tools. (Courtesy of The Brearley Collection)

trying to get better. He lived in San Diego where he could play all year, frequently until late at night. In the minors and the first years in Boston, Ted carried hitting into the outfield where he would practice his swing while playing right. He practiced in front of mirrors, with towels, constantly talked hitting, analyzed pitchers. Ted said he could tell you the count, location, type of pitch, and describe the flight of each of his first 300 major league homers. He drove people crazy but he became one of the greatest hitters who ever lived.

Baseball is as obsessed with its past as Williams was with hitting. Fans love quantifiable greatness and baseball is the most quantifiable of games. Its artistry is calibrated. Winning the batting title, the triple crown, leading in home runs, hitting .400, are contests of their own, and owing to the individual nature of the game, can be sought without automatically ruining a club. For sheer beauty of numbers, no post–Second World War player can compare with Williams. Ted mastered the "little game between the pitcher and the batter," as he called it, as no one since Hornsby. His rookie year he hit .327 and set the rookie record for RBIs with 145. The next year he hit .344 and led the league in runs. In '41 he hit .406 (Ted has a way with words—"I think hitting .400 is a big deal, but not *that* big a deal"—Every year no one does it, the deal gets bigger). His

fourth year he won the triple crown. Fans must have gone crazy. What else could this guy do? It must have seemed he could dominate like no one since Ruth. Then, as if fate had been too sorely tempted by a man who had done everything in his first four years, Williams went into the service for the first of his two celebrated hitches. This was more artistry, though not of Ted's making ("Fate also is an artist," Emerson said), but the tantalizing mystery of potential. What else could this man do? When he returned from the Navy, he led the Red Sox to the pennant.

Now the story becomes more interesting. Williams's discipline and personal system—the very art around which he organized his personality—were used against him. The shift was diabolical. It went at the heart of everything he perfected. It challenged him where he was least likely to refuse a challenge. In the '46 Series, Ted took a swollen elbow up against the shift and some good left-hand pitching, and was hamstrung. Now the accusation he couldn't hit in the clutch was supported by failure in baseball's greatest showcase. Cobb hit .200 in his first Series, Hornsby .250: they played in more; Williams never did. In '47 Ted won the triple crown again, making him the only man besides Hornsby to win it twice. Williams and Hornsby are the only men to hit .400 and more than 19 homers. Hornsby, incredibly, hit 42 and

39 HRs while hitting .401 and .403. Ted hit 37. Then came the two lost pennants in the last games played in '48 and '49. (The tragedy that year, as I've said elsewhere, is Williams losing a third triple crown as George Kell got two singles that final Sunday, and beat Ted by .0002 for the batting title—had Ted won three Triple Crowns, he would forever be the triple crown king, but his career was destined to be more complicated.) In 1950, he broke his elbow. The Red Sox were never contenders again. Williams's arena was personal after '50, and in that arena, as always, Ted was amazing.

His career is fabulous. The numbers, the military service, the might-have-beens of the career totals, the Achillian wrath, the outspokenness, the unswerving quest for perfection, make Ted Williams the most interesting, if not greatest, hitter who ever lived. Williams did something more difficult than hitting a baseball. He was an artist in front of America. To quote Emerson: "In every . . . genius, we recognize our own rejected thoughts; they come back to us with a certain alienated majesty."

Luke Salisbury is the author of The Answer Is Baseball *and a contributor to* Baseball and the Game of Life. *Currently an assistant professor of communications at Bunker Hill Community College, he is working on a novella about Ty Cobb.*

THE ROAD TO
FENWAY PARK

. . . .

In 1939 Williams was again late arriving at the Red Sox spring training camp in Sarasota. Driving from San Diego with his friend, Lou Cassie, Williams contracted a bad case of the flu and was ordered to bed by doctors in New Orleans. The Red Sox worried while Ted rested; he'd neglected to notify the club he'd be held up. As yet he had no idea of his importance to the club.

Ted finally arrived on March 7 and received an immediate lecture from player/manager Joe Cronin. "You're in a great city working for the best man in baseball," said Cronin. "You've got a lot of ability and had enough schooling. This is serious and there is no place in the game for clowning. I hope you take advantage of the chance you've got." Williams nodded in agreement. The Sox were fully aware of the consternation Williams had caused Donie Bush the year before. Cronin hoped to steer Ted in the right direction.

Unfortunately Cronin's tutelage stopped with the speech making. He shared the same dismay at Williams's behavior as the other club veterans. As player-manager, Cronin could not yet separate his feelings as player from those of manager. He worked with Ted on his hitting, and delivered lectures, but otherwise left him to find his own way.

Williams displaying the batting style that made him the 1939 American League Rookie of the Year. (The Sporting News)

As a 20-year-old rookie, Ted stood six feet four, and weighed 172 flu-weakened pounds, which reminded one sportswriter of "a human clothespin." Everyone knew what Williams had done in Minneapolis. The right-field job was his for the asking. His spring buildup, while modest by today's standards, was the greatest any Boston rookie had yet received. Virtually every spring report featured Williams's progress. Daily either his photograph or cartoon likeness garnished the sports page.

Williams was important to the Sox. Sox fans were growing impatient, despite Yawkey's monetary extravagance. Rookie Bobby Doerr had given them a glimpse of the future in 1938. In 1939 the Sox expected the same from Williams.

Donie Bush was in camp to ease Williams's and rookie third baseman Jim Tabor's transition to the majors, and Ted got off to a quick start. In an intra-squad game on March 10 he tripled and went 2–5. Installed into the third slot in the Red Sox batting order, Williams hit well, but not spectacularly, for much of the spring before breaking loose with a home run against minor league Louisville. Off the field he was the same irrepressible character he'd been the year before.

The Sox broke camp on March 30, working their way north playing a series of exhibitions. All spring long writers had been wondering when they were going to see the real Ted Williams, the wild, undisciplined kid they'd heard about from Minneapolis and thus far only listened to all spring. On April 1, in Atlanta, they got the chance.

After a bases-clearing triple in the sixth, in the seventh inning Ted let a ball roll between his legs, leading to an Atlanta score. In the eighth an Atlanta batter hit a towering foul fly to right. Ted raced over into the unfamiliar foul territory, then heeded the crowd's warning and pulled up. The ball dropped at his feet.

The partisan crowd jeered the rookie. He'd fallen for their ploy. Incensed, Ted bent over, picked up the ball and fired it over the right-field fence, breaking a fourth-story window in the process. Cronin immediately replaced Ted with Fabian Gaffke, and Williams trotted off the field while the crowd howled.

"I've got to take the busher out of him and make him a big leaguer," snapped Cronin, and fined Williams fifty dollars. Williams was unimpressed and didn't understand all the fuss. "I'll pay you fifty dollars," he told Cronin, "for every one I throw out if you'll pay me fifty dollars for every one I hit out."

Joe Cronin said of his star rookie, "I've got to take the busher out of him and make him a big leaguer." (Photograph by Leslie Jones, Boston Public Library)

April 15, 1939—Williams's Boston debut against the cross-town rival Braves in the pre-season city series. Hall of Famer Al Lopez was the catcher, George Magerkurth was the umpire. Williams went hitless in four times at bat. (Courtesy of Brian Interland)

Ted made amends the following day, smacking the game-winning home run in a 3–0 Sox win. This set a career-long pattern. Each time Ted got in trouble he'd come back the next day and do something spectacular with the bat to make up for it. Over the course of his career it happened too many times to be coincidence. Somehow, Williams was able to use such moments to his advantage, increasing his concentration toward the task at hand. In fact, it almost seems as if there were times Williams purposefully got himself in trouble, just to give himself a wake-up call. Whatever the reason, it worked.

The Sox opened the season at Yankee Stadium in New York. Ted was in awe. He was in the House that Ruth Built, and Ruth was in attendance. Gazing at the outfield facade, Williams wondered out loud whether anyone had ever hit the ball over the third deck. Williams's teammates just shook their heads and laughed. They knew by now "the Kid," as he'd been dubbed by clubhouse boy Johnny Orlando, might say anything.

In his first at bat Williams, hitting sixth in the Red Sox lineup and wearing number 9, struck out on a high fastball from Red Ruffing. As teammate Jack Wilson gave Ted the needle, Williams lashed back. "Screw you," he said. "This is one guy I know I'm going to hit." The next time up, he doubled off the wall.

Opening at Fenway on April 21, Williams could manage only a single in four times up. Two days later, on the 23rd, Williams gave Red Sox fans a glimpse into the future.

In five at bats against the A's, Ted homered, doubled, and singled twice. His first-inning home run off Luther Thomas into the right-field bleachers was a magnificent shot some 400 feet from home. Not only was it Ted's first major league home run, but Ted became only the sixth player *ever* to homer to that part of Fenway Park. Only Ruth, Gehrig, Bill Dickey, Charlie Gehringer, and Hal Trosky had previously homered into the bleachers. Before the season was half over, Ted would do it six more times. Pitchers had to learn to keep the ball away.

The Boston crowd loved him. Each time Ted ran into right field they stood and applauded. He grinned widely, and bantered back and forth with the fans. With the A's leading 9–2, much of the crowd stayed until Williams came to bat in the ninth.

All season long Ted and the fans in right field were like a young couple learning to fall in love. Each put the other on a pedestal neither would ever approach again. The cheers were real. Each Williams base hit or routine outfield grab brought raucous response, and when Ted came onto the field he

Max West, Doc Cramer, and Ted Williams (left to right) at Braves field, April 15, 1939, prior to Williams's Boston debut. (Courtesy of The Brearley Collection)

Ted arrives in Boston for the first time, at Back Bay Station, April 1939. (Courtesy of Brian Interland)

Bobby Doerr was starting his second full season with the Red Sox when his former minor league teammate arrived on the scene. (Photograph by Leslie Jones, Boston Public Library)

didn't just tip his cap, but pulled it from his head by the button and waved it madly, all the while smiling like the kid he was. Even the playground had never been this much fun. Ted and the fans were mutually smitten with each other.

Boston sportswriters were similarly taken. They were used to dealing with either the taciturn Collins or the smoothtalk of Joe Cronin. Most Sox players simply replied to their questions with a few brief words punctuated with language that sent the reporters to a thesaurus. Williams was different. There was hardly any need to ask a question. Ted talked the way he hit; incessantly. As a result he attracted press clippings all out of proportion to his considerable talents. In turn, when Williams erred in the field or choked in the clutch, the press went sideways not to criticize him. He was "the Kid," their kid, and they protected him.

In some ways the Red Sox did the same thing. Williams was already Tom Yawkey's favorite, and although Cronin stubbornly insisted that Jim Tabor was the better ballplayer, he wasn't about to cross Yawkey. The Sox put up with Williams's occasional adolescent outbursts. It would not have been tolerated in any other player.

As Williams himself later wrote, "I can't imagine anyone having a better, happier, first year in the big leagues." And with good reason. He was tearing the league apart. According to Ted, there were only five pitchers in the league who gave him trouble.

On his first visit to Detroit, Williams homered off the roof of the press box atop the stands in right field, 120 feet above the ground. His next time up, with the count 3–0, Tiger catcher Rudy York muttered to Williams, "You wouldn't swing at the next one, would you?" Williams replied, "I sure as hell am." Nonetheless, York called for the cripple. This time Williams hit it *over* the press box.

At the All-Star break Williams received a few days off. Even though he led the league in RBIs, for the only time in his career he was not named to the team.

Only twice in 1939 did Cronin have real trouble with Williams. During a close game in June, Williams missed a sign. Ted was busy talking to the catcher and umpire and blew the play. Then on August 8 came a more serious gaff. In the midst of a mild slump, his first time up Ted grounded out, and barely jogged to first. His next time up he sliced the ball off the wall and loafed a possible triple into a stand-up double. Cronin blasted him. "Don't you want to play?" he asked. Williams responded that he did.

In the sixth, with the bases loaded, Ted lofted a fly ball to center. He threw his bat down, disgusted, and started to the bench, not even bothering to run until Cronin told him to. The ball fell in. Williams barely made first. Cronin pulled him from the game, replacing Ted with Lou Finney. As Cronin put it later, "He was taken out because he did not hustle on the fly, because he had not been hustling all afternoon, and because he had not been hustling for about a week." Now batting cleanup, Williams was too important to the Sox to give anything but his best effort.

Properly chastised, Williams returned to the lineup for a doubleheader the following day. Although Ted went hitless in game one, in game two his ninth-inning smash off the left-field wall scored Bobby Doerr and broke a 5–5 tie to give the Sox a doubleheader sweep over Philadelphia. Ted's slump and problems were over for the time being. A week later all was forgotten, as Ted's ninth-inning grand slam—his first—beat Washington 8–6.

Williams finished the year with a .327 average, leading the league in RBIs with 145 and smacking 31 homers. Although there was no official "Rookie of the Year" award, Ted collected every unofficial award available, including one from the Boston Baseball Writers Association.

1939 had been a learning experience for Ted, a wonderful, thrilling initiation to big league baseball. He was impressed, but he hadn't been intimidated. He told one interviewer, "This baseball, it's not as easy as it looks. It's one of the arts."

Jimmie Foxx and Ted Williams provided ample muscle to the 1939 Red Sox, slugging for a combined 66 home runs and 250 runs batted in. (Courtesy of The Brearley Collection)

Fishing provided the perfect escape for the young superstar. (Courtesy of the Boston Globe)

After the season Ted returned to Minneapolis. His parents finally had broken up and Ted wasn't anxious to get caught in any cross fire. Besides, everyone knew him in San Diego. While Williams enjoyed being famous, he hated being a celebrity. In Minneapolis he'd be anonymous.

His girlfriend, Doris Soule, the daughter of a fishing guide in Princeton, Minnesota, was nearby. Ted visited with her, took a five-dollar-a-night room at the King Cole Hotel, and explored Minneapolis, teaching himself to ice skate and taking in movies. He enjoyed the quiet.

Being fitted for his first dinner jacket prior to the 1940 Boston Baseball Writers' Banquet. (Courtesy of The Brearley Collection)

A rare image, sharing a laugh with the writers at the 1940 writers' dinner. (Photograph by Leslie Jones, courtesy of the Jones family)

In February he returned to Boston to accept the Tim Murnane Trophy award at the annual writers dinner. Decked out in his first dinner jacket, Williams was the hit of the evening, grinning and speaking with his characteristic exuberance. "I started in baseball with a sports shirt," Ted told the writers. "Last summer Joe Cronin got me to wear a tie. Now he's got me in this thing. What's next?" The *Herald*'s Bill Cunningham reported that Ted "looked something like a young movie star." He did, and thousands of bobby-soxers had already taken note.

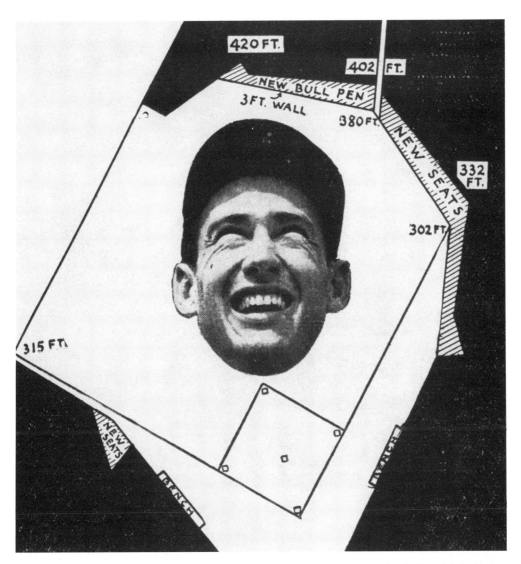

Following the 1939 season, the Red Sox constructed new seats in right field and a bullpen, prompting sportswriters to dub the new power alley "Williamsburg." The field dimensions remain unchanged to this day. (Courtesy of Osborn Engineering Company)

Great things were expected of Williams in 1940. In the off-season the Red Sox, impressed by Ted's 7 home runs into the bleachers, decided to move the bull pens into right field. Distance down the right-field line went from 325 to 300 feet, while in right center it went from 402 to 380 feet, still a prodigious poke. In this new configuration the Sox thought Ted might be good for at least another 10 or 12 home runs. He might even challenge Babe Ruth's home run record.

In spring training Ted was moved from right field to left. While his arm was strong, Williams was never a fast runner and his play in right field at Fenway Park exposed his weakness. In left, he had the wall behind him. Besides, right field in Fenway Park is a notorious sun field, and the Sox didn't want a hitter like Williams to have to stare at the sun all day.

Ted checks out the construction in right field, February 1940. (Courtesy of The Brearley Collection)

Joking with workers at the "Williamsburg" construction site. Throughout his career Williams enjoyed the company of "his people," namely the cops, carpenters, and bellhops of Boston. (Courtesy of The Brearley Collection)

In 1940, Williams moved from right to left field. He mastered the Green Monster for eighteen seasons. This posed photograph shows the old left field wall in intricate detail. (Courtesy of The Brearley Collection)

The first sign of trouble came just before the start of the season, when the Sox hosted the crosstown Braves in an inter-city exhibition. When Williams was introduced to the crowd, the cheers were sprinkled with a surprising amount of boos. The honeymoon between Ted and the Boston fans was officially over.

The fans thought Ted was receiving special treatment. After all, Tom Yawkey had Williams change positions and even moved the fences to help the young slugger. They weren't sure Williams deserved such treatment yet. In an era in which youth was not greatly admired, they resented Williams's favored status. This year, he'd have to earn their applause. The crowd in right missed Ted and felt abandoned, while the fans in left were disappointed that outfielder Joe Vosmik had been traded to Cleveland. Besides, with the Sox's

The 1940 Red Sox led the league in slugging percentage, spearheaded by batsmen (left to right) Ted Williams, Jimmie Foxx, Jim Tabor, Coach Tom Daley, Joe Cronin, and Roger "Doc" Cramer. (Boston Public Library)

woeful pitching staff, visiting sluggers might just take better advantage of "Williamsburg" than Ted. The boos, however, were not yet bitter.

Although he collected two hits on opening day, Williams got off to a relatively slow start, hitting only .302 with 1 home run and 5 RBIs in April. Ted's pace picked up in May, but home runs were hard to come by. The Sox moved him up to third in the batting order, ahead of Foxx, expecting Foxx to keep "the Kid" from being pitched around. But Foxx's career had started on the decline that would lead to his release two years later. Pitchers ended up pitching around Williams to get to Foxx. And they pitched Ted differently, preferring to stay outside and chance a walk rather than give him anything to pull. Williams didn't help himself by pressing and trying to loft the ball into the bull pens. Too often, he failed.

When Williams failed at the plate the rest of his game suffered. Even though the Red Sox were in first place, Williams brooded. He was chided several times by Cronin. On May 21, as the Sox traveled from Detroit for a series with Cleveland, Cronin decided to bench Ted.

"I didn't want to do this," admitted Cronin to Harold Kaese of the Boston *Evening Transcript*. "I don't want Williams to get this kind of reputation, but there's no other way." Even some of Williams's teammates were fed up with his antics.

Joe Cronin changed his mind. Kaese, however, did not. He blasted Williams in his column, saying Ted was jealous of Foxx, felt Fenway Park hurt his performance, and thought batting ahead of Foxx would likely cost him the league RBI title. Kaese went on to rail against Williams's "extreme selfishness, egoism and lack of courage," concluding, "Whatever it is, it probably traces to his upbringing. Can you imagine a kid, a nice kid with a nimble brain not visiting his father and mother all of last winter?"

It was a cheap shot, but it drew blood. The column was controversial, and it sold papers. From that moment on, Williams was fair game in Boston's competitive newspaper wars. Writers discovered that Williams stories sold papers, particularly if they said something unkind about Ted. With seven daily newspapers, some sporting several columnists, now there was always someone harping on Williams about something. Ted exacerbated the situation by reading everything and remembering the one negative column to the exclusion of the good.

Nicknamed "The Kid" by clubhouse manager and lifelong pal Johnny Orlando, Williams was eager to prove he was no fluke. (Photograph by Leslie Jones, Boston Public Library)

Ted pitching against the pennant-bound Detroit Tigers in a lopsided 12–1 match at Fenway Park. Williams allowed one run on three hits and fanned Rudy York on an unexpected curve that caught the Tiger flatfooted. Pitcher Jim Bagby replaced Williams during Ted's one and only major league mound appearance. (The Sports Museum)

Boston fans picked up on the battle between Ted and the press and chose sides. The boos bothered Williams. The crowd, knowing they had Ted's attention, began to boo louder, longer, and more often. What happened on the field was sometimes secondary. Baseball was not the only game in Boston. The other was a test of wills between Williams, the writers, and Boston's fans.

Williams was livid at Kaese's comment about his family. As always, he tried to make amends on the field, but this time the results weren't quite so dramatic. On May 27, in Boston, Ted finally smacked a home run into the bull pen, connecting for only his third home run of the season, off the Yankees' Johnny Murphy in a 7–2 loss.

No matter what Ted did in 1940, what he said off the field overshadowed his performance. Williams couldn't seem to keep his mouth shut. Later that year, again in Cleveland, Ted told a news service reporter, "Nuts to baseball. I'd rather be a fireman." Ted's uncle was a fireman, and, for a moment, life at the firehouse might have seemed preferable to standing in the outfield being booed. The press took the report seriously, and when the Red Sox traveled to Chicago, White Sox manager Jimmy Dykes supplied his club with bells, sirens, and fire hats. The goading went on all season.

Williams felt betrayed. He didn't understand what was happening. The home runs weren't there, he wasn't getting his pitches, he was learning a new position, but he was still hitting .340 and getting booed for it. It was as if he'd fallen in love with a beautiful girl and suddenly all she cared about was whether he picked up his socks. Ted was hurt.

The explosion was inevitable. On August 12, while the Sox were in New York, Ted was still in Boston nursing a sore back. Scheduled to rejoin the team on the following day, before he left Ted sat down with veteran Boston sports columnist Austen Lake of the *Evening American*. By the time Ted stood up he'd made a bad situation worse.

"I've asked Yawkey and Cronin to trade me away from Boston," he blurted to Lake. "I don't like the town, I don't like the people, and the newspapermen have been on my back all year. Why?

"They pay you on your record. The bleachers can boo, the newspapers can sneer, but right out there in the field is where you get the dough or not, and I'm going to get mine." Ted continued his tirade and intimated he'd prefer to play in either New York or Detroit, ending the interview telling Lake, "You can print anything. That's how I feel about it. You can print the whole rotten mess just as I said it." Lake did. Boston went crazy.

Lake's scoop forced Boston's other writers to comment. The relationship between Williams and the press was never the same.

As the controversy swirled over the next several days, the mailbags at the sports desks of Boston's papers filled to overflowing. Everyone had an opinion about Ted Williams, and every word written about him generated more interest. If a writer blasted Ted, another praised him. If one called him the second coming of Christ, to another he was the devil incarnate. It didn't matter that Williams was only a pawn for circulation. Sales was everything.

Boston's newspaper scene was unique. Seven papers vied for essentially the same readership. Only the *Transcript,* which catered to the established Brahmin class, had a niche solely for itself. The remaining papers scrambled to divide the rest of the pie. In other cities most newspapers served separate and distinct constituencies. It wasn't so clear-cut in Boston. As a result coverage was narrow and parochial. Unlike their New York counterparts, for example, Boston writers couldn't afford to be stylish and austere.

This was particularly true on the sports pages, where the writing talents of the columnists combined with oversized egos to produce a keen and bitter competition. Boston's sports columnists played a private game unto themselves, a sort of competitive knee-jerking contest whereby success was judged, not on the quality of what was written, but on what degree other writers were forced to respond. Ted Williams was the most potent ammunition in this private battle.

"The Colonel," Dave Egan of the *Record,* was the acknowledged master of the game, as he skillfully played devil's advocate in advance of his colleagues. A graduate of Harvard Law School, Egan was master at controlling the focus of the contest. If the other writers took one stance, Egan took another, and that, in turn, became the reigning issue.

Bill Cunningham of the *Post,* Austen Lake of the *American,* and, later, Harold Kaese of the *Globe* were the main contestants, although there were another dozen or so lesser participants. All were immensely talented, but, by circumstance, all too often each dropped to the lowest common denominator in the battle for readers.

Williams was the perfect subject for this private war fought in public. His athletic accomplishments were immense and deserving of comment. Williams's complex, multilayered personality was ripe for analysis. And Ted found it impossible to shut up. He wasn't just the object of the battle; he played a role in it himself. He read everything written and responded, freezing out one writer and talking to the others, then reacting to some unkind remark and changing his alliances.

The writers and Williams fed on each other. Ted gave them material and they made Ted the most talked-about player of his time. In turn, Williams basked in the benefits of such attention and bashed the practitioners. They each used the other.

It didn't need to be that way, but other elements were involved. Red Sox management, like most people in Boston, were a bit mystified by Williams and awed by his talent. He was never taken under wing and shown the ropes. Neither did the Red Sox exert much pressure on the writers to back off. Each story on Williams meant one less story on the Sox. While Williams was the focus of intense scrutiny, management decisions often went unquestioned.

Ted battled enemy pitchers and Boston writers with equal ferocity in 1940. (Photograph by Leslie Jones, courtesy of the Jones family)

Sportswriter Bill Cunningham was one of the "Knights of the Keyboard" who irritated the young slugger. (Boston Public Library)

Dave Egan, a.k.a. the Colonel, would become Williams's chief nemesis, writing scathing columns about the young slugger. (Courtesy of the Boston Globe)

Williams took the heat off everyone. Besides, writers knew that to bash Tom Yawkey or one of his favorites, like Cronin, was to risk being frozen out. Ted Williams, for whatever reason, was fair game.

Just as he only heard the single boo in a stadium of cheers, so too did Williams only read the single unkind comment in an encyclopedia of support. To this day, Williams retains a large measure of bitterness about those he refers to as "the knights of the keyboard." But in analyzing what was written about him over his entire career, the coverage was far more balanced, far more kind, than Williams ever perceived. Ted Williams was written about in Boston newspapers every day for over twenty years. On any given day there was usually one story that was less than gratifying, but at the same time there were five or six that were complimentary. Harold Kaese covered the Red Sox for Williams's entire career. He wrote no less than 500 columns about Ted. Less than a dozen can be construed to be really mean-spirited or negative.

As an unintentional by-product of this battle, the writers did do Williams an enormous favor. The career of no other athlete of his time is better noted. The wealth of information accumulated about Ted Williams and available for analysis is mind-boggling. When someone today refers to Ted as "the greatest hitter who ever lived," that perception is due, in no small measure, to the writers who looked at him so closely.

Williams denied making the statements Lake attributed to him, escalating the growing animosity between the writers and himself. Williams made a vow. He couldn't stand being cheered one day and booed the next, or written about kindly one week, then slammed a few days later. People were either for him

The press and fans of baseball-mad Boston measured Williams against the highest of standards. (Photograph by Leslie Jones, Boston Public Library)

Eddie Collins once said, "That kid lives for his next time at bat." (The Sports Museum, Brown Collection)

or against him. He hated front-runners, and found friends away from baseball, where it didn't matter whether he hit or not, or what he had to say about it. He decided never to tip his cap again.

In the last six weeks of the 1940 season, Williams started to adjust. His power returned and he began to drive in runs by bunches. But it was too late to make much difference, either for Ted or the Sox. The damage was done. Nevertheless, the late-season surge continued. On the last day of the season the Sox took a doubleheader from Philadelphia, 9–4 and 4–1, to nudge into fourth place. Ted went 5–8 and picked up 5 RBIs. Williams finished with a .344 average, but with only 23 home runs and 113 RBIs. He hit only 9 home runs at Fenway Park, only 4 into the bull pens. "Williamsburg" had turned out to be a bust.

And now everyone was wondering if Ted was too. Everyone, of course, but Ted Williams.

A Storied Career

BY BILL LITTLEFIELD

Ted Williams is the stuff of stories, and in the stories you can find anything you like.

He is the monstrously arrogant young man who said that he wanted to be known as the greatest hitter who had ever lived, feuded with the newspaper writers, and spat at the crowd.

He is the gracious rookie who visited children in Boston hospitals and stayed in touch with them and their families for years.

He is the scientist who broke into component parts the act of hitting a baseball and talked about it after his retirement with such zeal that the first time Carl Yastrzemski met him, Yaz was scared to death. He spent weeks trying to stay out of Williams's way, half convinced that Ted was crazy and worried that he'd never understand what the master was talking about.

He is the pure hitter of whom Johnny Pesky once said, "Oh, hell, he used to tell me he just saw the ball and hit it."

Once, according to an account I read almost thirty years after Williams retired, he was walked with the bases loaded in the last half of the ninth inning to force in the winning run, and he responded by throwing his bat into the air because the pitcher hadn't given him anything to hit . . . a demonstration of seriousness of purpose and concentration on the task at hand so intense that the whole point of baseball—scoring more runs than the other team—was lost.

On another occasion he allegedly giggled as he ran out a pennant-winning home run. The whole Cleveland team had shifted right for him, Boudreau style, and he lofted one over the left fielder's head—he was playing the equivalent of short-stop—into no-man's-land. There is no picture of Williams giggling, but at least one person from Cleveland says it happened, and if it didn't, it should have.

And then there is the oft-told tale of the only confrontation ever between Williams, the greatest of hitters, and the legendary Steve Dalkowski, the fastest pitcher who ever lived. Dalkowski never made it out of the minor leagues, because though he averaged 13 strikeouts per nine innings, he also averaged 13 walks. His talent was so singular and so pure that it could not be disciplined to provide him a livelihood. But some impresario who understood that drama is made in moments and not careers convinced Williams and Dalkowski to face each other once on a spring training ballfield years ago, or so the tale has it. Dalkowski threw one pitch. Williams watched it unhappily, dropped his bat, and announced that it was the fastest pitch he'd ever seen and that he never wanted to see it again.

You see? Look through enough Williams stories and you will even find humility.

There are probably more stories about Ted Williams than there are about any ballplayer but Babe Ruth, and in his last at bat, Williams buried even Ruth for exit lines. Ruth would have had to quit the day he hit three home runs against the Pirates in 1935 to top the knock with which Williams punctuated his last season, the ball John Updike immortalized as "the tip of that towering construct" in Fenway Park.

You could debate forever the order of the subject and his

Only Babe Ruth could match Williams as a subject for baseball stories. (Courtesy of Brian Interland)

stories, like the sequence of the chicken and the egg. Is Ted Williams as real and present in baseball as he was thirty and forty years ago because the larger-than-life man accumulates stories the way the hull of a steamship accumulates barnacles? or because the stories pile up on each other to create the giant?

No matter. Ted Williams carries the baggage of worship, like it or not, and in his later years he's found a kind of grace with which to manage it. He plays in old-timers' games. He makes public appearances. When he showed up at a local bookstore in 1987 to sign copies of an updated reissue of *The Science of Hitting,* the crowd was so large they had to shut the doors and turn off the escalator to control it. When Williams came through a side entrance, large and rumbling, there was no cheer, just a gasp of awe. He was eleven feet tall, and when he spoke the air cracked. Grown men wept, women fainted, and books tumbled from their shelves.

Nah. It was only Ted Williams. Only the last man to bat .400. Only the fellow who announced his intention to be the greatest hitter who ever lived and then, by damn, went out and made it happen.

Bill Littlefield, a commentator for National Public Radio on "Morning Edition," is the author of a novel, Prospect. *He is an associate professor in the humanities division of Curry College.*

1941 AND .406

. . . .

On March 25, 1941, at the Sox spring training camp in Sarasota, Florida, Ted Williams held court at the afternoon training table. The Boston baseball writers, as always, hovered over his every word, knowing the next phrase out of Williams's mouth might generate enough copy for a week's worth of spring training reports. Despite Williams's problems with the press in 1940, he entered 1941 still the ever-talkative Kid, brash, unpredictable, and ebullient.

"Sure I look forward to this season," Williams pronounced. "How can they stop me?"

The writers looked at one another, silent and skeptical.

"All right," continued Williams, "I ask you, how can they stop me from hitting? They can't, that's all. They couldn't stop me my first year and they couldn't stop me my second. They won't stop me my third.

"My second year was better than my first," added the Kid. "I'll tell you why. I hit higher, .344 to .327, I struck out less, and I got more walks. I made more hits and I scored more runs. I was on base more.

Ted Williams and Joe DiMaggio at Fenway Park in 1941. Williams would later call DiMaggio the greatest player he ever saw, with DiMaggio claiming Williams as the greatest hitter he ever witnessed. (Photograph by Leslie Jones, Boston Public Library)

"I didn't hit so many home runs and I didn't knock in so many runs. So what? I was hitting third instead of fourth. I had more chances to bat in runs my first year, because Foxx batted ahead of me. And remember, I was hitting in the toughest park in the league for a left-hand hitter.

"I was the best hitter on the Red Sox last year, wasn't I? Look up the records. What's more, I got the biggest raise in baseball, except for maybe Greenberg. I guess that shows what the Red Sox thought of me. . . ."

The writers took Ted's words with a measure of disbelief. They, too, wondered if he could be stopped. But at the same time they knew his pronouncements often masked an equal measure of self-doubt and fear. For while Ted was trying to convince the writers of his talents, at the same time he was also trying to convince himself. Williams knew, and would later admit, "I'd slipped a bit in 1940."

Before the 1941 baseball season, no one, except Ted Williams himself perhaps, would have predicted the kind of season he had; one that is still spoken of in reverential terms fully fifty years later. Williams could certainly hit, but the 1940 season had raised a number of questions about his attitude and temperament; questions that in the spring of 1941 were unanswered.

While in 1940 Williams had avoided the sophomore jinx, his production dropped from 1939. His problems with the press and fans made one wonder whether he could survive the pressures of the major leagues. Joe Cronin and Jimmie Foxx were entering the twilight of their careers, and it was still an open question whether Ted, without their protection in the lineup, had the maturity to take over as team leader.

After the 1940 season Williams again went to Minnesota, fishing, hunting, and spending time with Doris. Shortly after he left Boston in October of 1940, there was talk the Kid might be traded. While the Red Sox front office wasn't actively shopping him around, they were listening.

One deal was particularly intriguing. *The Sporting News* reported that the Chicago White Sox had offered the Red Sox pitcher John Rigney, outfielder Taft Wright, and cash for Williams. Rigney was a young, talented, starting pitcher who'd won 14 games with the White Sox, while Wright had hit a robust .337 and knocked in 88 runs. For the traditionally pitching-poor Red Sox, the deal must have been tempting. Ace Lefty Grove was now 40 years old

Williams greeted by writers upon his arrival in Boston in 1941. (Courtesy of the Boston Globe)

Two .400 hitters — Ted with Red Sox coach Hugh Duffy. Duffy won a triple crown for the 1894 Boston Beaneaters of the National League, batting .438. (National Baseball Library, Cooperstown, N.Y.)

and gamely hanging on in search of win number 300. He would soon have to be replaced. Rigney might have been the answer. Besides, some thought Ted was a time bomb waiting to go off, and Wright, while no Williams, also represented no risk. The addition of Rigney and Wright might have offset the loss of Grove and Williams. If Cronin and Foxx could keep Father Time at bay for another year, the Sox might have been in position to make a run for the pennant.

The 1941 season saw Lefty Grove (right) win his 300th game with the Red Sox. He is shown in the Fenway Park clubhouse with sportswriter Joe Cashman and Williams. (Courtesy of The Brearley Collection)

While manager Cronin denied a deal was in the works, he did so with a wink and grin. The trade, however, eventually fell through. Rigney and Wright were unproven. Williams, in spite of all his troubles, was still the best young hitter in the game, his potential unlimited. The Red Sox didn't want to be accused of losing the next Babe Ruth, as they'd done with the original. Williams stayed in Boston.

The Red Sox initially offered Williams only a small raise for the 1941 season. Ted was angry and thought he was worth much more, but at age 22 he had little leverage. But as spring training approached in late February, the Sox had yet to hear from Ted. They'd telegraphed him at the only address they had, a Minneapolis hotel, but Williams had yet to respond. Ted was the club's lone holdout, and the Sox were frantic. Then Williams cabled a response.

Ted answered the query as to his whereabouts in what was becoming classic Williams style. While hunting in the great north woods, Ted told the ballclub, he'd simply lost track of the days. Finally agreeing to terms, Ted would leave immediately for Sarasota by car, which was at least a four- or five-day journey in America before the interstate. Exasperated, the Sox could do little but offer their welcome, along with an admonition to hurry along.

They needn't have worried. When Williams arrived in Florida he was in great shape. A winter in the outdoors agreed with Ted, and he proceeded to attack the baseball with his accustomed authority. He still oozed confidence and could barely be restrained from taking up permanent residency in the batting cage, but the results—line drives and long home runs—were so spectacular no one complained. Perhaps he couldn't be stopped.

Ted hustled, and showed none of the personality problems of the year before. He said he'd grown up, and everyone, his teammates, the front office, and even the writers, seemed ready to believe him.

On March 19 the Sox met minor league Newark in an exhibition game in Sarasota. Williams tripled in the first, the ball striking the fence at the 463 mark in right center. In the third, following a triple by Lou Finney, Williams smacked the ball to the gap in right. As he tried to stretch the hit into a double, Ted started to slide, then appeared to change his mind. The spikes of his right shoe caught in the soft ground and twisted his ankle grotesquely. Ted went down, as one paper described it, "like an old cow." Tagged out, Williams limped from the field.

At first the injury appeared merely to be a severe sprain, but ten days later the ankle was still swollen. X rays revealed a small bone chip on the inside of the ankle. Ted didn't need surgery, but he did need time to heal. While Williams had little trouble moving straight ahead, he couldn't stride properly at the plate.

His spring training over, Williams concentrated on getting ready for the season. Therapy for the ankle consisted of alternate baths of ice and water

Ted checking his Louisville Sluggers at the Hillerich and Bradsby headquarters. Such trips became routine for the perfectionist Williams. Above and beyond selecting the wood and supervising the turning of the bats, Williams weighed his bats before using them in a game. (The Sporting News)

heated to just below the boiling point. Ever so slowly, the ankle began to stabilize.

Williams was forced to open the 1941 season on the bench. He could now hit, but could not do the running that playing in the field required. In retrospect, the ankle was to prove a blessing in disguise. Ted detested cold weather, and the injury kept him on the bench for much of April. At the same time, Ted found Sox pitcher Joe Dobson a willing participant for batting practice. While Ted couldn't play, he could sharpen his eye.

The Sox opened the 1941 season in Boston on April 15 against the Washington Senators. In batting practice Ted smacked four balls into the right-field stands, leading infielder Jim Tabor to pronounce, "That guy could hit with one leg off." Ted still found it hard to run. Outfielder Pete Fox took over for Williams in left and batted third in Ted's spot ahead of Foxx and Cronin.

Entering the ninth inning down 6–4, Sox catcher Frankie Pytlak doubled off the wall. When Williams came out on deck to bat for pitcher Earl Johnson, the crowd was already on its feet.

Foxx and Williams played their last season together in 1941. They remained close friends until Foxx's death in 1967. (National Baseball Library, Cooperstown, N.Y.)

Washington pitcher Sid Hudson's first pitch was wild and Pytlak raced to third. Williams laced the next offering into right, scoring Pytlak while Ted struggled to first. Ted was replaced by a pinch-runner, and Dom DiMaggio's sacrifice set up an RBI single by Lou Finney. After a Pete Fox single and intentional pass to Jimmie Foxx, Joe Cronin walked to force in the winning run. Both the Red Sox and Ted Williams were batting 1.000.

Williams pinch-hit several times in the next week, collecting one hit, before first appearing in the starting lineup on April 22. Ted went 2–4 with a double in the Sox's 12–5 loss to the Senators, but failed to reach several drives in left, and it became obvious his return was premature. He sat out another four games, pinch-hitting once more, before returning to the lineup for good on April 29. His batting average was an even .400, 4–10, while the Sox were 7–4, a game behind league-leading Cleveland.

In his first game back, at Detroit's Briggs Stadium, Williams smacked his first home run of the season, and hit a rare double to left center, in a 5–3 Red Sox loss. In the field he made a magnificent shoestring catch to answer lingering doubts about the ankle. Then he slumped for the next week, despite beating out a rare infield hit, as his average dropped to .308.

Williams's slow rise back to .400 began on May 4. Lefty Grove picked up his 294th career victory in an 11–4 Sox win in St. Louis over the Browns. Williams's 2 singles were good for 2 RBIs. The next two games were rained out, but Ted took advantage of the break to take even more batting practice, convincing Sox pitching coach Frank Shellenback, Williams's old manager at San Diego, to throw for him. In the deserted St. Louis ballpark, Williams swung at hundreds of pitches.

On May 7 in Chicago, Ted erupted. In the third inning, with Boston up 1–0, Williams stepped up against White Sox pitcher John Rigney. Perhaps recalling the trade rumors of the previous fall, Williams wasted no time. He jacked a Rigney offering into the upper deck in right center, giving the Sox a 3–0 lead.

The White Sox tied the game and it went to extra innings. Rigney was still on the mound when Ted batted in the top of the eleventh. The pitcher fared no better than he had in the third. Williams's blast soared to right center, some 50 feet higher than his earlier blast, landing on the grandstand roof to give the Sox a 4–3 victory. As one paper noted, "Ted's was the stiffest and the greatest toward that sector since Babe Ruth was in his left-hand hitting prime. . . . A conservative estimate of the drive . . . was five hundred feet, which is *some* distance."

Ted followed with another multiple-hit game to bring his average to .386, before taking the collar on May 14 in a 10–7 win over the White Sox in Fenway to "slump" to .336. The Red Sox were 13–9, 3½ games behind league-leading Cleveland. The Senators' Cecil Travis led all hitters at .411. The Yankees were in fourth place at 4–14, and 1940 A.L. batting champ Joe DiMaggio, who be-gan the season hitting .528 in the first eight games, was struggling below .300.

On May 15, 1941, Ted Williams and Joe DiMaggio embarked on the great-est hitting streaks of their careers—streaks that would lead each to his finest season, and pair the two men for all time as the most representative players of their era.

Beginning in 1941 and continuing through the next decade, Williams and DiMaggio were twin stars of the highest magnitude in a galaxy that contained no others. DiMaggio, austere and remote, burned with a fine white heat. Locked in the same orbit was Williams, a smoldering, explosive red giant. Each man was best defined in the terms of the other. When asked of DiMaggio, Williams remarked, "He's the greatest ballplayer I've ever seen." When asked who was baseball's greatest hitter, DiMaggio succinctly replied, "Williams." In 1941 each man emerged as the unquestioned leader of his team: DiMaggio stepped from the shadow of Gehrig and Williams supplanted Foxx as the Red Sox's most dangerous hitter.

In 1941 the two men fired the imagination of the nation. Kids playing sandlot ball invariably chose to be either Joe or Ted. Comparisons between the two inevitably led to a series of "what if's?" What if Williams enjoyed Di-Maggio's surrounding cast? What if DiMaggio had been paired with brother Dom in the Red Sox outfield? Uncanny circumstances made such questions more compelling. Each man played in a ballpark ideally suited for the other, and each found a more favorable reception from the press in the other's home city. In 1941, at precisely the same time, each man found himself paired with the other in the beginning of a rivalry marked less by inherent combativeness than by pure differences in style. The parabola of each man's 1941 season contains the contrast: DiMaggio's long, swooping, graceful arc of a spectacu-lar 56-game achievement; Williams's the determined, tenacious plane of a season-long accomplishment. To choose either is to diminish the other. They were different but complementary. That difference contains the magnificence of each.

Each man's streak began quietly and initially went unnoticed: Williams with a single off the glove of Cleveland second baseman Ray Mack: DiMaggio with a fist hit off Chicago's Ed Smith. Williams had been smacking the ball all year, but too often in just the wrong place. He'd already lost five potential home runs to the wind, and the bad luck continued on May 17, when Ted went 3–5 against the Indians but was robbed of another when the Indians' Clarence Campbell made a magnificent catch in right center. Three games with but a single hit, plus a possible home run held up by the wind, stretched Ted's consecutive hit streak to a quiet six games. On May 21 in Fenway Park, Wil-liams started a remarkable run.

Cartoonist Willard Mullin compares the performance of Williams to that of Joe DiMaggio in the midst of his unprecedented 56-game hitting streak. In the five decades since their accomplishments, no one has hit .400, or come close to breaking DiMaggio's hitting streak. (The Sports Museum)

Ted went 4–5, his first 4-hit game of the season. He followed up the next two days with a combined 3–7, before smacking 2 hits, on May 24, including an infield hit, and scoring 3 runs in a 7–6 Sox loss to New York. That started a seven-day streak of 2 or more hits during which Ted's average rose from .374 to .430. He broke .400 on May 25, backing up Lefty Grove's 296th win with 4 hits in a Red Sox 10–3 pasting of the Yankees.

After the game, Sox manager Joe Cronin was ecstatic. "You should have seen Lefty Marius Russo bearing down on the Kid," he said. "Russo used every variation he knew in delivering the ball, and no matter what kind of pitch it was, Ted would wickedly pull it down first base and into right field." Williams's streak paid dividends in the field, too, as he made a tumbling catch of Tommy Henrich's line drive. On the 28th the A's walked Williams intentionally 3 times: Philadelphia pitchers preferred to face the aging, but still dangerous, Jimmie Foxx. After Ted went 3–4 on May 29 against Philadelphia, and the difference in the game was Williams's 7th home run, Burt Whitman of the Boston *Post* commented, "Ted the Kid—they'll be calling him King before long."

On June 1 Williams went 4–9 in a doubleheader sweep in Detroit. His streak was at 20 games, his average .430. Boston writer John Drohan sounded the first warning of what was to come. "Hughey Duffy, beware!" he wrote, in reference to the Red Sox coach's record .438 mark in 1894. DiMaggio's streak was at 18 games.

Williams couldn't be stopped. His spring training speech had been prophetic. Opponents tried some old tricks to stop him. On June 6, in Chicago, White Sox manager Jimmy Dykes pulled out the fire hats again, but they didn't distract Ted. He homered for the third time of the season off beleaguered Johnny Rigney.

Williams wasn't stopped until June 8. The 23-game streak, during which he hit a remarkable .488, was to be the longest of his career. The Sox swept Chicago, Grove gaining victory 297, but Ted, walking several times as the White Sox pitched around him, went hitless in both games. That same day, the Associated Press carried a story that gave Ted's pursuit of .400 credence. "The Kid has grown up," it said, and cited Williams's improved attitude as the reason for his success, commenting that "a lot of veteran observers rate this gangling youth a great chance of becoming the first American League hitter to hit over .400 since Harry Heilmann last turned the trick with a .403 average in 1923."

"It's a dream I've always had," said Ted, "the way I'm hitting now." When Williams hit well, he played well. When Ted wasn't hitting, he became so obsessed with his failure that the rest of his game suffered. In 1941, he hit well, and played well, all year.

Yet as the press began to take notice of Ted's quest for .400, DiMaggio's streak captured the nation's attention. Ted's quest was season-long, while

Baseball was fun when you were hitting over .400. (The Sporting News)

The 1941 All-Star game's ninth-inning, game-winning homer hit off Cub pitcher Claude Passeau at Briggs Stadium in Detroit was Williams's all-time favorite. Cartoonist Willard Mullin shows Williams being greeted by fellow All-Stars Joe DiMaggio and Joe Gordon, who were on base when Ted hit the 2–1 pitch. (The Sports Museum)

DiMaggio's was day-to-day—perfect for newspapers and newsreels. Besides, the Yankees were starting to win, and DiMaggio's hitting—which included his ongoing 24-game streak—was widely perceived to be the reason. Just as the bone chip in Ted's ankle had proven to be a bonus, so too would the press's preoccupation with DiMaggio. While they swarmed around Joe, Ted was left relatively alone.

Williams cooled from his .488 pace, but stayed hot. His average hovered around .420 and settled on that mark after he went 2–3 and keyed a three-run rally as the Sox downed St. Louis, on June 20. Williams even scored the Sox's winning run in the sixth, sparking a rhubarb as he crossed the plate standing up in a close play. The ankle bothered him and Ted was afraid to slide. X rays had been scheduled earlier in the week, but as the *Post* noted, "It's possible the Kid is a little afraid they may find some reason for asking him to stay out of the game, and, hitting the way he is in the rarified .400 circle, he just doesn't want to be told any such thing."

In fact, the ankle was bothering Williams. Yet he stayed in the lineup, playing before Babe Ruth and Ty Cobb who were both in Boston on June 24. Ted went hitless before the immortals, though he made a fine catch. The Yankees had surged into second, two games ahead of the Sox, who trailed leader Cleveland by four. There was a pennant race to worry about, after all.

Despite the sore ankle, Williams stayed above .400, but began to have trouble in the field. Playing tentatively, in a stretch of four games Ted allowed the ball to roll between his legs three times. DiMaggio broke George Sisler's modern hitting-streak record of 41 games on June 29, then tied Willie Keeler's all-time 44-game mark against the Sox in a doubleheader in New York on July 1. Williams went 2–6 but the Sox dropped both games to the Yankees. The Yanks were now in first place, while Boston had dropped 7 games back, the pennant race all but over for the Red Sox. Williams's average slipped to .401 on July 2, but in the three games before the All-Star break he went 7–15 with 6 RBIs to pull up to .405. For the first time it was noted in the press that Williams, as a favor for teammate Dom DiMaggio, was keeping track of Joe's streak through the Red Sox left-field scoreboard.

At the break Williams had 16 home runs and 62 RBIs to go along with his .405 average—some 30 points ahead of Cleveland's Jeff Heath. The triple crown seemed within his grasp, although both DiMaggio and Charley Keller of the Yankees led Ted in RBIs and DiMaggio led in home runs. But if Ted's first half season performance was still seen as a footnote to DiMaggio's record-breaking streak, the All-Star game would serve notice that the second half belonged to Ted.

Disappointed in his performance in the 1940 contest, Williams was pleased that the game was in Detroit, one of his favorite parks and perfect for a left-handed pull hitter. A.L. manager Del Baker installed Williams in the cleanup spot, directly behind DiMaggio.

The American League broke a scoreless tie in the fourth. Cecil Travis doubled. DiMaggio moved him to third with a fly ball. Facing Cincinnati's Paul Derringer, Williams lashed the ball to right. The Pirates' Bob Elliott froze, then started in before realizing the ball was over his head. Travis scored and Williams pulled into second with a double. After the N.L. tied the game with a single run in the sixth, the A.L. took the lead again in the bottom half of the inning. DiMaggio walked, and Williams sent him to second with a long fly. DiMaggio scored on Lou Boudreau's single.

In the seventh the N.L. tallied twice. Enos Slaughter singled to left, but Williams muffed the ball and Slaughter went to second. Shortstop Arky Vaughan then slammed a home run to right. Vaughan came up again with one man on in the eighth and duplicated the feat, giving the National League a commanding 5–2 lead.

DiMaggio led off the eighth with a double. Facing the Cubs' Claude Passeau, Williams took a called strike three: his opportunity for heroics had seemingly passed. But Dom DiMaggio followed Ted with a single to make the score 5–3. The N.L. failed to score in the top half of the ninth.

With one out, the Indians' Ken Keltner reached first on an infield hit. The Yankees' Joe Gordon singled, then Travis walked. DiMaggio came to the plate with the bases loaded. The crowd was on its feet, as everything seemed to point to DiMaggio's at bat.

Joe disappointed, hitting an apparent double-play ball to short, but Cecil Travis barreled into second baseman Billy Herman, allowing DiMaggio to beat the relay to first. Keltner scored, making it 5–4.

Up stepped Williams. He had played this scenario through his mind a million times while playing "Big League" at North Park in San Diego. Perhaps it seemed as if his entire baseball career had pointed to this one moment. Although the Giants' Carl Hubbell was warming up in the bull pen, N.L. manager Bill McKechnie, remembering Passeau's success the inning before, elected to stick with the Cub hurler.

Joe DiMaggio scored just ahead of Williams on the latter's game-winning, ninth-inning, three-run homer at the All-Star game held at Detroit's Briggs Stadium. (Wide World Photos)

Williams took the first pitch low, for a ball. After fouling off the second pitch Williams later said he admonished himself to be quicker. The next pitch was letter high and in. Williams was quick.

The ball shot on a high arc just inside the right-field line, soaring against a stiff crosswind and clattering off the third deck; a magnificent, awe-inspiring shot that gave the A.L. a 7–5 victory.

Williams half ran and half jumped around the bases, waving his arms and grinning from ear to ear. As he later wrote, "I was just so happy I couldn't stop laughing." His teammates swarmed him at home plate and Ted led the charge to the locker room. Manager Del Baker kissed him, then did it again for the benefit of the press.

Williams sat in front of his locker, accepted congratulations, and talked, to everyone, to no one, just exuberantly talked. He was happier than at any other moment in his life.

"I had a funny feeling after I struck out in the eighth," he said, "that I was going to get up there at least one more time and hit one. I get funny hunches that way. I never say anything about them, for as sure as I do, they don't come true. I figured I was going to get up there again. I was sure of it as anything and when that one came up fast and about elbow high, I said to myself, 'This is it.'

"I know one thing. The happiest woman in America right now is my mother."

And the happiest son, without doubt, was Ted Williams.

Joe Cronin kept milling around the clubhouse, saying over and over, "He was great, wasn't he?" and Williams's teammates echoed those sentiments with praise of their own. In the National League clubhouse, however, it was a different story. Same sentiment, but in a different mood. Manager Bill Mc-Kechnie summed up the feeling for everyone. "He's just not human."

The Red Sox opened the season's second half in Detroit, where Grove failed in a bid for win 300 as the Sox lost 2–0, Williams going hitless and his average dropping to .398. Williams left the lineup the next day.

Ted hurt himself taking a lead off first. Detroit catcher Birdie Tebbets fired a pick-off throw behind him to first baseman Rudy York. Williams hurried back safely, but jammed his sore right ankle against the base. Ted stayed in the game, but after batting in the sixth, was forced to leave.

Williams didn't return to the lineup until July 22, although he pinch-hit four times, even delivering a three-run homer, while the ankle healed. His average dropped to .393.

When Ted returned, manager Joe Cronin decided to shuffle his batting order. Williams moved from third to fourth, flip-flopping with Cronin, while Foxx still batted fifth. The move was to have a lasting impact on the remainder of Williams's season.

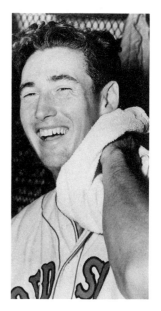

"I laughed out loud. I've never been so happy. It was a wonderful, wonderful day for me." —Ted Williams, July 8, 1941 (National Baseball Library, Cooperstown, N.Y.)

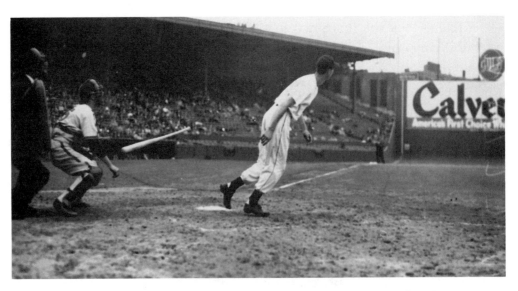

Williams batting against the first shift ever devised to stop him, against the White Sox on July 23, 1941. Here he foils White Sox manager Jimmy Dykes's best laid plans by doubling to left in the seventh inning. The shift was abandoned until 1946, when Cleveland player/ manager Lou Boudreau utilized it to greater effect. (Courtesy of The Brearley Collection)

In his first game back versus Chicago at Fenway Park, Williams's 18th home run keyed a 6–2 victory, as Ted again connected off Johnny Rigney. The White Sox were desperate to stop Williams. On July 23, they unveiled a shift.

A full five years before Cleveland manager Lou Boudreau would receive credit for devising a similar maneuver, White Sox manager Jimmy Dykes tried out his version. Only used with the bases empty, Dykes's shift entailed moving the shortstop to the right of second in short field, moving the third baseman into the vacant hole at shortstop, and swinging the entire outfield toward right, so that the left fielder stood just to the left of center, and the right fielder hugged the line. The logic of the shift was to stack the field with players where Williams generally hit. If Ted hit to left, he'd lose power, and a single to left was better than a double or home run to right.

It didn't work. In the seventh Williams doubled to the left-field corner, sending the entire shift into reverse. The Sox won, 10–4. Dykes abandoned the strategy.

Williams went on a tear; his average went back over .400 on July 25 as Ted went 2–3 to support Lefty Grove's 10–6 win over Cleveland, his 300th, and last, major league victory. During an off day on July 28, Williams flew to New York for a photo session with *Life* magazine. DiMaggio's streak was snapped on July 17 at 56 games, and now Williams's pursuit of .400 took center stage.

In late July and early August Ted put on a power show. On August 3 a headline read "WILLIAMS HELD TO ONE SINGLE." On the 4th he had his first hitless day, apart from pinch-hitting appearances, since July 11, but walked three times. Teams began to discover they could pitch around Ted. Foxx simply wasn't hitting as he used to, and with Cronin batting third, they could afford

Ted the Kid, Boston's Hero

The Boston Globe*'s Gene Mack captures the essence of Williams's All-Star heroics. (The Sports Museum)*

to put Williams on with a walk. They tried everything to stop Ted, including cheating.

On August 15, with Williams coming to bat in the eighth inning against the Senators, it began to rain. Washington stalled and the game was halted. The Senators, not wishing to face Williams, neglected to cover the field. After the game was called because of the wet field, the Red Sox filed a protest. It was upheld a month later.

On August 19 and 20, Williams went wild. On the 19th, as the Sox split a doubleheader in St. Louis, Williams crashed 3 home runs, all onto the roof of the right-field pavilion in the St. Louis ballpark. The next day, although the

The 1941 Yankee outfield of (left to right) Tommy Henrich, Charley Keller, and Joe DiMaggio pose with Williams at Fenway Park. (Photograph by Leslie Jones, Boston Public Library)

Red Sox dropped both games, Williams hit 2 more homers. For the four games he was 8-14 with 5 home runs and 8 RBIs, walking 4 times. On the 21st, in Chicago, Ted went 2–3 to lift his average to .414, his highest since June 21.

Williams now set his sights not only on .400 but the triple crown as well. On September 1, in a doubleheader at Fenway Park against Washington, Williams homered 3 times, giving him six in five games, and taking the league leadership from New York's Charlie Keller, at 34. The Sox won both, 13–9 and 10–2. Ted also walked 4 times, bringing his total for the year to 127.

On the following off day, Williams took a well-needed rest on the Cape, trying out a new rifle and revolver. He told a reporter that the walks frustrated him, but "give me full credit for the times I score, after being walked, because, after all, you got to get those runs, and enough of them, if you're going to win that ball game."

Williams did receive credit. The Boston press and fans stood foursquare behind him. The troubles that marred 1940 had disappeared. Bill Cunningham wrote in the *Herald,* "Theodore Samuel Williams is already an automatic choice for the supreme accolade of the year, the 'Most Valuable Player' award. Whether he gets it is something again, because Joe DiMaggio . . . led his Yankees from the ruck to the runaway leadership of the American League. . . .

"The boy [Ted] has arrived. He's practically all anybody's talking about in a baseball way. . . . The personal side of the young man has been largely unrecorded this year, for everything has been calm, clear and under control . . . the Kid is in first. Let's hope he stays there."

He did, although over the season's last month Williams walked so often his home run output dropped. The Yankees clinched on September 3, and in New York, on September 7, Williams received a fine ovation when he came to bat for the 400th time, enough to qualify for the batting title.

Never was the pitcher's fear of Williams more pronounced than on September 12 and 13 in St. Louis. While Ted went a combined 0–4, he also walked 5 times. Williams made a different kind of news the next day. Playing in front of the Sox's largest home crowd of the season during a doubleheader sweep of Chicago, Ted struck out for the first time since August 25. On the 15th, he pummeled his 6th home run—and 35th of the year—off the infamous John Rigney.

For the next week Ted clung to the .400 mark. While he was still being pitched around, he received help from other quarters. On the 23rd he went 1–3, his only hit a routine fly dropped by the Senators' Roger Cramer. The papers called it "tainted." Ted started to press, and in a doubleheader on the 24th, managed only one hit in seven attempts. The single a very close call, only Ted's third infield hit of the year, brought 7,500 fans to their feet. They let umpire Bill Grieve know what they thought of his call. The fans wanted Ted to hit .400, but they wanted it the right way. His average dropped to .401.

Before entering Philadelphia for the final three games of the season, the Sox enjoyed two off days. Williams used the time to take massive amounts of extra batting practice. Frank Shellenback, Tom Daly, and Tommy Cary all took turns on the mound. Joe Cronin talked of benching Williams if it looked as if his average would drop below .400.

It did the next day, and it was front page news in Boston. Against knuckleballer Roger Wolff, Ted went 1–4. For the first time since July 25 his average dropped below .400, to .39955. The doubleheader on September 28, the last day of the season, was his last chance.

There was talk, again, that Williams might sit out the two games to protect his average, officially .400 if rounded off according to custom. Cronin suggested it to Ted, but Williams wanted no part of the plan. There were too many reasons to play.

Ted's quest for .400 had received so much attention that anything less than a "pure" .400 wouldn't have been accepted by either Ted or the public. Had Williams sat out, this book wouldn't have been written; people don't commemorate .39955. Williams's dubious .400 would have carried a sizable asterisk. Besides, in the last week, two of his hits had been gifts of the umpire and scorekeeper. Given the scrutiny that surrounded Williams, the two hits would certainly have been credited with allowing Ted to reach .400.

There were two more reasons for Ted to play the doubleheader. He led the league in average and home runs, but trailed DiMaggio by only a few RBIs. With a good day, he could conceivably snatch the triple crown. Also, Lefty

Ted kisses the bat he used to go 6 for 8 against the Philadelphia Athletics on the final day of the 1941 season, finishing the year with a batting average of .406. Prior to the doubleheader with the Red Sox, A's manager Connie Mack warned his pitchers that anyone suspected of aiding Williams with soft pitches would be banned from baseball for life.
(Courtesy of Brian Interland)

Grove was pitching in search of win 301. He had been pitiful since picking up win 300 on July 25, and Williams, a big Grove fan wanted to send Lefty off to retirement with a victory. In truth, there was never any serious discussion, until well afterward, that Williams would sit out either game in the twin bill.

Ted hardly slept that night. He and Johnny Orlando walked the streets of Philadelphia. Orlando steeled himself against the cold by dropping into the occasional neighborhood tavern.

It was not going to be easy. The Athletics were playing out the string, and manager Connie Mack chose a couple of kid pitchers to start. What always mattered most to Ted about pitchers was whether he had seen them pitch before.

A crowd of 10,268 fans turned out in Philadelphia to watch Ted try to make history. When Williams approached the plate for the first time, Philadelphia catcher Frankie Hayes pulled his mask over his face and spoke to Williams, "Mr. Mack told us if we let up on you he'll run us out of baseball. I wish you all the luck in the world but we're not giving you anything." A's pitchers, however, had been instructed to throw strikes and give Ted a chance. Umpire Bill McGowan echoed the sentiment, telling Williams, "To hit .400 a batter has got to be loose."

Ted came to the plate leading off the second inning against Dick Fowler. With the count 2–0, he hit a hard ground ball to the right of first baseman Bob Johnson for a single. His average nudged above .400. He hadn't been stopped all year and he wasn't now. The pressure was easing up.

It lifted completely in the fifth. Ted smashed another Fowler delivery some 440 feet, well over the right-field wall and on to 20th Street for a home run. In the sixth Williams duplicated his second-inning single and followed with a line-drive single to right in the seventh. Ted reached base on an error in the ninth to finish the day 4–5 with 2 RBIs. The Sox won 12–11 and Williams was safely over .400. He set his sights on DiMaggio and the triple crown.

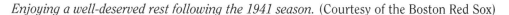

Enjoying a well-deserved rest following the 1941 season. (Courtesy of the Boston Red Sox)

Going for win 301, Grove was knocked out in the first inning. While the Sox went down 7–1, Ted singled in the first and made myth in the fourth. To top off his spectacular day, Williams hit a vicious line drive to right center. High up on the wall was a large loudspeaker. The ball crashed into, and through, the speaker before falling back into play. It was like something in *The Natural.* Williams pulled up with a double. In the most resounding fashion he'd silenced all critics.

After flying out to left in his last at bat, Ted ended the day at .4057, rounded to .406, a combined 6–8. He still missed the RBI title by 5, trailing DiMaggio 125 to 120, but led the league with 37 home runs.

The numbers speak for themselves. Despite walking 145 times, Williams was held hitless only 22 games. The 23-game streak was the longest of his career, and he slugged over .700 both at Fenway and on the road. At Fenway Park his average was a gaudy .428. His best month, May, he hit .458. His worst, April, he still hit .389. His longest hitless streak was seven at bats. His slumps for the year were better than most players' hot streaks. Nevertheless, DiMaggio was named league MVP.

Entering the 1941 season, Williams had asked whether he could be stopped. His performance appears to answer that question. Entering his prime, it seemed as if '41 might be just the beginning. Ted had improved each season, and in private said he might be able to hit .450. How, indeed, could Ted Williams be stopped?

On December 7, 1941, the Japanese bombed Pearl Harbor.

ACHIEVING THE IMPOSSIBLE DREAM: TED WILLIAMS AND .406

BY STEPHEN JAY GOULD

I will reach my fiftieth birthday at the end of the 1991 baseball season. I find it hard to view this half-century milestone, a sure sign of entry into life's second and ultimately declining half, as a source of joy; nor was 1941, ending with Pearl Harbor, the best of years. Still, I must also consider the blessings of my gestating days, particularly the two great events of the 1941 season: Joe DiMaggio's 56 game hitting streak, and Ted Williams's batting average of .406. Of these two milestones, Ted's .406 intrigues me more powerfully than any other figure in the history of baseball. DiMaggio's 56 is just an island of uniqueness*; Ted's .406, on the other hand, is a puzzle representing the most intriguing and important general pattern in the history of baseball numbers.

Hitting .400 was a commonplace in the early days of baseball—a routine matter in the nineteenth-century, and also achieved in nine of the first thirty years in our century. Then came the drought. Bill Terry hit .401 in 1930, and no one hit .400 again during that decade.

Then Ted Williams batted .406 in 1941; no player has achieved this lofty level since. And, as I said in my opening line, Ted did it fifty years ago, as I was gestating and tasting the first fruits of extrauterine life—and I'm not getting any younger. How could something once so common become so rare (even impossible, according to Wade Boggs, baseball's greatest current hitter)? And how extraordinary was Ted Williams's .406 year, an event so isolated from all other occurrences (eleven years after Bill Terry, followed by fifty subsequent years with no repeat)?

I believe that both questions can be answered with reasonable confidence, and that the answers reveal the truly amazing and extraordinary ability of the greatest hitter I ever saw. (By the way, to make a necessary admission, I grew up in New York and am—dare I say it—a Yankee fan. Joe DiMaggio was my childhood god, and is still my adult idol. Ted Williams was a revered enemy. So I speak with abstract appreciation, not with a fan's blind devotion.)

The disappearance of .400

hitting is the most widely discussed and misunderstood phenomenon in the history of baseball. Conventional answers take two different forms. The first, that players tried harder with greater devotion in the good old days, is romantic twaddle and misplaced nostalgia. Modern artists of hitting—the Boggses, Carews, Bretts, and Gwynns—play with as much intensity as the great .400 hitters of our past—the Cobbs, Hornsbys, and Sislers. The second category demands more respect, but is, I believe, equally wrong. This second style contends that something about the game has become more difficult for hitters, and that the great ones therefore can't achieve the levels of their predecessors. Proposed factors include too many night games, too gruelling schedules, and such innovations in pitching as the invention of the slider and the development of relief pitching as a specialty.

I am confident that these conventional answers are wrong because, in my mind, the disappearance of .400 hitting reflects one cardinal phenomenon that

*Gould, S. J. "The Streak of Streaks." *The New York Review of Books* (1988), vol. 2, no. 2: 10–16.

neither addresses—the near certainty that average play in major league baseball has become substantially better through time. I know that this sounds paradoxical. After all, the disappearance of .400 hitting has removed a previous, common standard of excellence. So doesn't this have to mean that something has gotten worse—either the quality of play (first conventional answer) or the pressures on players (second conventional answer)?

I have set out my case in two long articles*, but let me present a summary here. (If I am right, then Ted's .406 in 1941 is more than just a great achievement; it is fabulously and uniquely awesome.) By all social and demographic criteria, players should be better now. Training has become an industry and obsession, an upscale profession filled with engineers of body and equipment, and a separate branch of medicine for the ills of excess zeal. Few men now make it to the bigs because they tossed a ball against a barn door during their youth; and athletes take care of themselves during the off-season, with rigorous programs of weights and calisthenics, rather than an occasional game of golf and too much beer and chicken on the rotary club circuit. We now provide access to men of all colors and social backgrounds, thus correcting the greatest shame of baseball's

early years. Moreover, the pool of potential recruits has increased five-fold in one hundred years by simple growth of the American population.

This unavoidable expectation of improvement can be readily affirmed in any sport with absolute standards—particularly measurement against a clock. Spiridon Loues won the 1896 Olympic marathon in one minute under three hours; modern champions have shaved nearly an hour off that mark. All fans of my generation remember the "impossible" four-minute mile, a barrier that scarcely exists today. If all sports show this pattern, how can baseball be uniquely different, experiencing a decline of greatness?

In baseball, the pattern must be sought in other criteria, because our favorite sport uses relative, not absolute, standards. A batting average is a relationship between hitters and pitchers, not an absolute figure like running a four-minute mile. Thus, batting averages might remain stable through time (I

will show in a moment that they have in a crucial sense), but this stability might reflect a continuing balance as both hitting and pitching improves.

In fact, mean batting averages for ordinary players have remained remarkably stable—at about .260 (see Table 1)— throughout the history of baseball (except for a temporary rise in the 1920s and 1930s, and we will come to this important point in Ted's story later). Thus, hitting and pitching have stayed in balance as both improved through the history of twentieth-century baseball. An inevitable result of this improvement must be the decline and disappearance of .400 hitting for the following reason.

Physiology and mechanics put limits on human achievement (those running times will not decline forever, and the rate of decline has slowed considerably in most sports). A very few men must always possess a happy combination of natural gifts and obsessive zeal that place them near this unchang-

Table 1. League Averages for Our Century

	American League	National League
1901–1910	.251	.253
1911–1920	.259	.257
1921–1930	.286	.288
1931–1940	.279	.272
1941–1950	.260	.260
1951–1960	.257	.260
1961–1970	.245	.253
1971–1980	.258	.256

*Gould, S. J. "Losing the Edge: The Extinction of the .400 Hitter." *Vanity Fair*, March 1983, 120, 264–278; and "Entropic Homogeneity Isn't Why No One Hits .400 Any More." *Discover*, August 1986, 60–66.

ing limit—Cobb then, Williams later, Boggs now. In the 1910s, these gifts translated to batting over .400 for Cobb because he stood so far above ordinary play, expressed as .260 hitting. But play today, though still expressed as .260 hitting (the conserved balance of batting and pitching), has greatly improved, and ordinary players stand much closer to the limiting wall of human possibility. The best can no longer rank so high above the ordinary, because the average player has moved so much closer to the wall, while the best have no place to go—so the distance between the best and the ordinary must shrink, and this shrinkage entails the disappearance of .400 hitting. Boggs (though as good as Cobb) hits closer to the unvarying league average of .260 because the diminished space between ordinary and best brings the batting average of the best down to .350 or so.

If my theory is correct—that the disappearance of .400 hitting records the improvement of general play—then one test obviously suggests itself. The distance in batting average between ordinary and best (also ordinary and worst) should diminish constantly with time. Table 2 (based on the five best and five worst hitters among regular players for each season) shows a regular, symmetrical decrease of variation in the league average during the history of baseball. This shrinkage of variation reflects the increasing excellence of performance: ordinary players are moving toward the limiting wall and decreasing their distance from the best, while the worst are dropping out because ordinary play has so improved that teams need no longer hire in the category of "good field, no hit."

In this context, Ted Williams had no business, *absolutely no business*, hitting well above .400 in 1941. The phenomenon of .400 hitting had already become extinct! Ted's .406 is a much loftier achievement than Rogers Hornsby's all-time twentieth-century high of .424 in 1924, for Hornsby achieved his mark when .400 hitting remained in vogue, and during a decade (see Table 1) when averages had risen above the .260 norm, thus boosting everyone. Let us, then, consider the two reasons for crediting Ted's .406 as the greatest achievement in twentieth-century hitting.

First, following the general argument outlined previously, 1941 came far too late in the history of shrinking variation for anyone to hit .400. Consider Table 2, and note that the decline in difference between the five top hitters and the league average has occurred in three stages, with little variation in each stage. Nineteenth-century values ranged from 89–95 points, 1900–1930 figures de-

Table 2. Patterns of Change in the Difference Between Highest and Lowest Averages and the General League Average Through Time

	Difference between five highest and league average	Difference between five lowest and league average
1876–1880	95	71
1881–1890	89	62
1891–1900	91	54
1901–1910	80	45
1911–1920	83	39
1921–1930	81	45
1931–1940	70	44
1941–1950	69	35
1951–1960	67	36
1961–1970	70	36
1971–1980	68	45

clined to 80–83; all subsequent decades have averaged from 67–70 points—with very little variation. Now all .400 averages, except Williams in 1941, come from seasons during the first two plateaus, when the best stood far above the average. Only Williams achieved .400 during our modern era of stabilization and reduction of variation. Moreover, he didn't reach his mark at the beginning of the modern era, when some volatility still remained, but well into the period of stability, during the second of the current plateau.

Second, a particular reason: I stated that hitting and pitching have remained in balance during the history of baseball, with league averages varying little from .260. But this generality has suffered several exceptions, most of short duration as the moguls of baseball change the rules to bring the conventional balance back (introducing the foul strike rule in 1901 to bring averages down; lowering the mound and reducing the strike zone to bring averages up after

the drought of 1968 when Yaz led the American League with .301, and Gibson achieved his phenomenal ERA of 1.12).

But this tendency to quick equilibration has one important exception. After the Black Sox scandal of 1919, and following Babe Ruth's mayhem on the ball—a style of hitting adored by fans at a time when the game's future looked bleak—hitting got ahead of pitching, and the moguls, noting public approbation, for once made no adjustments. Debate continues as to whether or not a "lively ball" was introduced in 1920; I will bypass this old argument here and merely record that, for 20 years, hitting achieved the upper hand. Decadal averages for full-time players were .286 and .279 in the American League, and .288 and .272 in the National League, for the 1920s and 1930s. The average, everyday player hit over .300 in the National League in 1930! But decadal averages have ranged between .245 and .260 for all other twentieth-century years—see Table 1.

If anyone were to hit .400

near the end of an era that permitted such achievement, it should have happened during the 1930s when league averages remained elevated (Table 1) and the distance between average and best also stood high on the second plateau (Table 2). But, after Bill Terry in 1930, no one did—for the whole decade. Consider Table 3, and note the steady decline of league leading averages from the 1920s to the 1940s and, more importantly, the difference between these averages and the single best figure for each decade. Now we can sense the phenomenal character of Williams's record. Williams's feat aside, maximal difference between average and best is 34 points (Hornsby at .424 vs. .390 for the 1920s in the N.L., and Terry at .401 vs. .367 for the 1930s). But Williams, at .406 vs. an average of .349, stood 57 points above the mean achievement of the best during his decade.

Will it ever be done again? Some have come close—Carew at .388 in 1977, Brett at .390 in 1980, and most amazingly,

Table 3. History of League Leading Averages, 1920–1950

	American League		National League	
	Average for yearly best	Difference between average and best single value	Average for yearly best	Difference between average and best single value
1920s	.392	28 (Sisler, .420, 1922)	.390	34 (Hornsby, .424, 1924)
1930s	.370	20 (Simmons, .390, 1931)	.367	34 (Terry, .401, 1930)
1940s	.349	57 (Williams, .406, 1941)	.354	22 (Musial, .376, 1948)

"KID 400" . . . . By Gene Mack

HE DOESN'T NEED A CLIFF IN LEFT FIELD —NOT WITH THAT REACH !

TED WILLIAMS

A HOMER BY KELLER IN THE FOURTH ?

BETWEEN INNINGS THE SCOREBOARD BOY TELLS HIM THE LATEST NEWS ON RIVAL SLUGGERS

LIKE GLENN CUNNINGHAM, BOBS HIS HEAD WHILE RUNNING

GENE MACK

THE WILDEST PITCHERS HOLD NO TERRORS FOR TED

BUT— HE'S REALLY AFRAID CATCHERS WILL HIT HIM WHEN RETURNING THE BALL

(The Sporting News)

Williams himself at .388 in 1957, the season of his 39th birthday! (Williams got 163 hits in 420 at bats that season; five more hits would have given him an even .400.) Let us also not forget the lost opportunity of Ted's 4.7 seasons missed for military duty in two wars. In his book *What If*, Ralph Winnie calculates that Williams would have gotten 4,043 hits, including 711 homers, if he had played a full career without interruptions. Some day someone will hit .400 again (Boggs actually did during a 162-game stretch from June 1985 to June 1986). But .400 hitting is now a once-per-century impossible dream—and the greatest hitter of our century is the only man who has succeeded in the 61 seasons between Bill Terry and now.

Numbers prove points, but can become distressingly impersonal. I can spout the figures on Williams (and have throughout this article). But I revere Williams more from the memories of an awe-struck youth,

than for the calculations of my adulthood. I remember a man of burning pride and intensity, of obsessive commitment to be the best hitter of all time. I remember the "Williams shift" used again this greatest of pull hitters—three infielders between first and second, and a virtually unguarded left side. Williams could easily have pushed the ball into this empty territory, but pride would not permit such an expedient, and he always found a hole in his favored zone. Nothing could stop the greatest of all hitters in his prime. And let us not forget the finest and oldest story of the .406 season—Williams's guts and integrity in playing a doubleheader on the last day, when he could have sat out and preserved his average at an even .400, but chose to play, jeopardized his chance at this species of immortality, and raised his mark to .406 instead.

Excellence is the scarcest and most precious of all human commodities—an attribute almost rarer than .400 hitting in

an age of passivity and mediocrity. Academics like myself often make the mistake of praising intellectual excellence as an outcome of struggle, but viewing superlative athletic performance as a lucky gift of inherited brawn. But all great achievement requires zealous commitment and obsessive striving (combined, of course, with fortunate gifts of mental and physical constitution). Williams's .406 is a beacon in the history of excellence, a lesson to all who value the best in human possibility. Williams's .406 is as thrilling as a great novel, as inspiring as a wonderful symphony.

Stephen Jay Gould has taught geology, biology, and the history of science at Harvard for the past twenty-three years. He has been a baseball fan since 1948, when he first saw his beloved Yankees play the Red Sox and Ted Williams.

WORLD WAR II
AND A PENNANT

. . . .

Ted Williams was eating breakfast in the kitchen of a Princeton, Minnesota, hotel when he heard about the bombing of Pearl Harbor over the radio. Initially, Ted wasn't worried. As he put it, "All I was interested in was playing ball, hitting the baseball, being able to hunt, making some money." Ted now considered Princeton home. In November he had registered with the local draft board in Princeton and been designated 3A, listing his mother, May Williams, as his dependent. He'd been sending her money for years, but with his parents now divorced and his brother Danny in and out of scrapes with the law, May depended entirely upon Ted, even if she ended up giving most of the money away.

Pearl Harbor changed everything. In an off-season interview with Cleveland Amory, Ted talked of his dreams. "I want to be an immortal," confessed Ted. World War II put a definite crimp in any long-range plans. Draft boards became stricter in their interpretation of the law and more sensitive to public criticism. Without warning, on January 3, 1942, Ted was notified he had been reclassified to 1A. He could be called into the service at any time.

Practice, practice, practice. . . . Fenway Park clubhouse, circa 1942. Williams was quickly becoming the idol of countless Boston bobby-soxers. (Courtesy of The Brearley Collection)

The idea of military service didn't bother Ted, but at the time he felt he was entitled to the deferment. He secured an attorney and appealed the decision. On January 28 he was turned down.

Williams had enjoyed three spectacular seasons in the big leagues, but the big money, both in salary and endorsements, was just starting to come his way. In 1941 he'd started to plan for his future, taking out several life insurance policies, and needed another year in the big leagues to pay them off.

Ted's attorney filed for another appeal, this time with the Presidential draft board. It may have been a good decision for Ted Williams, United States citizen, but it was a terrible decision for Ted Williams, celebrity ballplayer. Williams won the appeal and in late February was again designated 3A.

The goodwill that had come his way following the 1941 season began to erode. Some members of the press charged that he was a slacker who benefited from special treatment. All of a sudden Williams was in the center of yet another controversy.

The Red Sox didn't help. They'd given Ted no advice for counsel during the appeal process, and now, with the appeal won, the Sox feared the public relations fallout of the decision. They tried to convince Ted not to come to spring training. This made everything worse.

Williams was not without his defenders. Dave Egan was particularly staunch in his support of Ted's right to deferment. Most other Boston writers didn't choose sides on the issue but cautioned, as Harold Kaese did, that "if he clears the challenge of public opinion, that .406 batting average will seem putty by comparison."

The bulk of the criticism came from sportswriters outside New England. Williams remained unaffected. He felt his classification was legitimate and he had no reason to apologize to anyone. He signed a new contract for $30,000 and went to Sarasota.

While Williams's mail ran about 50–50 over the question of his deferment, relatively little criticism came from members of the military. Servicemen attending spring training games in Florida cheered Williams as they did every other ballplayer.

On opening day at Fenway Park, Williams quieted most of his critics. Before a crowd of just over 11,000, including 1,200 servicemen admitted free, Ted started 1942 as he finished 1941. In the first inning, with two men on base, Williams homered into the bleachers in right. He followed with a 2-run single and the Red Sox defeated Philadelphia 8–3. As the *Post* noted, "His batting average at the conclusion of the game was .750." Another Williams watch was on.

As the Red Sox visited other league cities, Williams was greeted with dreadful criticism in the press and an outpouring of support from fans. He was hitting well and by the time the Sox returned to Boston from Cleveland in late May, Williams had won the battle of public opinion.

Williams receives The Sporting News *1941 Major League Player of the Year plaque from (left to right) J. G. Taylor Spink, Asst. Lt. Commander Randolph Philbrook, Lt. R. P. Fuller, and Jack Malaney, at Fenway Park in 1942.* (Courtesy of The Brearley Collection)

So he decided to enlist.

Williams had been toying with the idea since the spring. Like his request for a vacation with San Diego several years before, the question of the deferment had become a matter of principle. When it became obvious that the war was not coming to a quick conclusion, and the Navy was able to guarantee he wouldn't be called up before the season's end, Williams, with his mother's financial security assured, enlisted in the Navy Air Corps. Ted found the idea of flying irresistible. Like catching the most fish or hitting the longest home run, flying appealed to his need to seek out challenges. During the remainder of the 1942 season he studied hard to qualify for flight school.

While Williams hit the flight manuals by night, by day he battered American League pitching. The Red Sox enjoyed no similar success. The Yankees jumped out to a big lead and the Sox watched helplessly from a distant second for most of the year. Midway through the season Williams again found himself the object of criticism. Angered by jeering Boston fans, Ted first tried to strike out on purpose, then attempted to line a few foul balls off his hecklers' skulls, and then, after accidentally slicing a hit off the wall, dogged it around the bases. Cronin fined him $250.

Ted didn't hit .400 in 1942, but with Foxx in full decline and Cronin in semiretirement, Williams had no protection in the Red Sox lineup. He compensated with improved power. Johnny Pesky and Dom DiMaggio had good years and provided Ted with plenty of opportunities for RBIs, and Ted responded. At the year's end he won the triple crown with 36 home runs, 137 RBIs, and a .356 average. No hitter in either league matched any of those figures. Any other player but Ted would have been a shoo-in for the league MVP award.

Williams's medical examination for enlistment in the Naval Air Corps, 1942. His eyesight was determined to be the best of any air cadet tested. (Photograph by Leslie Jones, Boston Public Library)

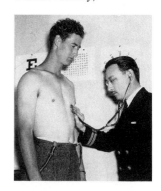

Leaving the Naval Air Corps Enlistment Center at 150 Causeway Street, Boston. (Courtesy of The Brearley Collection)

Ted Williams was never just any other player. He was special, and people expected more, perhaps more than they had any right to. Despite Williams's 1942 performance, the Yanks completely outclassed the Red Sox. Yankee second baseman Joe Gordon won the MVP award despite hitting only .322 with 18 home runs and 103 RBIs. Ted, like the Red Sox, finished second, collecting 249 points to Gordon's 270.

In mid-November Williams reported, one day late, for ground school in Amherst, Massachusetts, after taking a cab all the way from Boston. His group of thirty Naval Aviation Cadets included teammate Johnny Pesky, and fellow major leaguers Buddy Gremp, Joe Coleman, and Johnny Sain.

The cadets received no special treatment, although the press was allowed some liberty to report on their progress. The Navy was keenly aware of the ballplayers' publicity value.

Williams did well in the Navy. His physical condition, hand–eye coordination, vision, and intelligence combined to make him an excellent pilot. Ted was able to apply the same concentration that made him successful in the batter's box to his work in the cockpit.

Williams's three years in the Navy were uneventful. Ground school was followed by preflight training in Chapel Hill, North Carolina. From there he went to Kokomo, Indiana, for basic flight training, then on to Pensacola, Florida, for advanced training. The Navy regimen agreed with Ted. Never physically imposing, Williams bulked up and increased his stamina while in the service. His body hardened and he became more focused. Ted was "the Kid" no more.

Ted's 1942 contract for $30,000 assured his mother (right) of the financial security he wanted her to have, should he be called into active service. (The Sporting News)

Opening Day, 1943, at Fenway Park. Top row (left to right): Williams and John Sain. Bottom row (left to right): Johnny Pesky, Lt. Commander E. S. Brewer, Buddy Gremp, and Joe Coleman. (Courtesy of The Brearley Collection)

Trained to fly both the F4U and PNJ, Williams easily earned his officer's commission. He then applied to instructor's school, reasoning that additional flying would better prepare him for combat. He also married.

He first met Doris Soule in Minnesota in 1938, where her father was a fishing guide. In 1941 she moved to Boston to be closer to Ted, and worked as a hotel cashier and beauty salon hostess. The couple wanted to marry earlier, but Navy regulations prohibited trainees from marrying. After Ted completed training in Pensacola, on May 4, 1944, Doris Soule became Mrs. Ted Williams.

Naval Air Cadets Williams and Pesky in uniform at Fenway Park, Opening Day, 1943. (Photograph by Leslie Jones, Boston Public Library)

Ted grew to love flying almost as much as hitting. (The Bettmann Archive)

Ted married Doris Soule on May 4, 1944. Doris was the first of Williams's three wives. Ted met Doris in Minneapolis while playing for the Millers. (Courtesy of the Boston Globe)

Ted Williams lighting one up for Babe Ruth prior to a Braves Field charity exhibition game in 1943. (The Sports Museum)

Ted Williams, Rabbit Maranville, and Babe Ruth at the Braves Field clubhouse, 1943, gathering prior to a charity exhibition game. (Courtesy of Brian Interland)

The two shared a love of the outdoors and swing music, although Doris admitted that, "I'm not crazy about baseball." She was particularly unenthused with the effect it had on Ted, for during baseball season he thought of little else. The young couple enjoyed their life in Florida. Ted was a handsome young pilot, Doris a devoted Navy wife. For company the couple kept a German shepherd, aptly named "Slugger."

While in Florida Ted fell in love with fishing the warm Atlantic waters. He'd gone deep-sea fishing before for barracuda and tuna, but in Florida he was introduced to more competitive sportfishing. Once Ted took a nibble he was hooked. Much like hitting or flying, sportfishing appealed to his competitive nature. Ted promised himself that when he returned to baseball, he'd head south early each spring just for the fishing.

He was transferred once more, to Jacksonville, for operational training. That meant only one thing—combat. Fortunately, the war was winding down. Williams was in San Francisco on his way to the Pacific on V-J Day, though it wasn't until he was in Hawaii that his orders were finally cancelled. For Ted, one war, anyway, was over.

Reunited after the war (left to right), Williams, Doerr, and Dom DiMaggio formed the nucleus of the 1946 pennant winners. (Photograph by Leslie Jones, Boston Public Library)

Had Williams not enlisted in 1942, there's no telling what he may have done from 1943 through 1945. With major league rosters depleted due to the war, teams scrambled to fill squads. Borderline major leaguers suddenly became stars, minor leaguers found themselves with a place in the big leagues, while aging veterans were suddenly rejuvenated by the dropoff in talent. Williams, at age 24, was at his peak, coming off a triple crown year, one year removed from .406. Against weakened competition it is not outlandish to think he may have hit .400 again, clubbed 60 home runs, or had 150 plus RBIs. The Red Sox might even have snuck in a pennant, as the hapless St. Louis Browns did in 1944. Even if Williams had performed at anything approaching the level of the years just before, and just after the war, he would have set career marks that would be extraordinary.

At spring training in 1946 Ted quickly dispelled any thoughts that his time in the military had cost him his swing. On March 3 he knocked in 7 runs while going 3–3 with 2 home runs versus the Braves.

Ted excelled and so too did the 1946 Red Sox. Williams, Pesky, Doerr, Dom DiMaggio, and pitchers Tex Hughson, Joe Dobson, and Mickey Harris all returned from the war with their skills intact. Slugger Rudy York was acquired from Detroit to complement Williams. Pitcher Boo Ferris improved on his 21 rookie wins in 1944, and the Red Sox suddenly found themselves with their best team in twenty-five years. The Yankees were in transition and Detroit couldn't score enough runs to support a fine pitching staff. The Red Sox ran away with the pennant.

Except for a few days in April, the Red Sox led all year. Entering June the squad boasted a stellar 32–9 record, leading the Yankees by 5½ games. They proceeded to finish off a 12-game winning streak, and never led by less than 10 games after mid-July.

Williams did his share. Although in April he hit .346 with only 1 home run and 10 RBIs, he surged in May and June as the Red Sox took control, belting 19 home runs and driving in 53 base runners. Ted also provided one remarkable moment.

On June 9, 1946, the Red Sox played Detroit in a doubleheader at Fenway Park. In the first inning of game two, with Catfish Metkovich on first, Ted came to bat against pitcher Freddy Hutchinson. Ted swung and the ball soared long and deep to right field. Sitting near the aisle in the 33rd row of the bleachers, Joe Boucher, a construction engineer from Albany, New York, squinted into the bright afternoon sun. As the crowd rose to its feet Boucher looked toward the plate but was blinded by the glare. All of a sudden Boucher's world turned dark. Williams's ball hit him squarely on the head and bounded away. Momentarily stunned, Boucher removed his straw hat and discovered that Williams's blast had cut a neat hole into his bowler. After being checked by doctors he commented, "I didn't even get the ball. After it hit my head I was no longer interested." The ball traveled some 430 feet before being stopped by Boucher.

Williams easily made the All-Star team and looked forward to his first appearance in the classic since 1942. Boston hosted the contest, and Williams was excited by the prospect of playing before the home crowd.

Fenway Park was filled to overflowing. In a 12–0 pasting of the National League, Williams responded with perhaps his best day in baseball. It was certainly his most memorable.

In the first inning, Williams walked before Charlie Keller of New York homered to give the American League the only runs it would need. Leading off the fourth against the Dodgers' Kirby Higbe, Ted drove a curveball into the center-field bleachers for a home run. In the fifth and seventh Ted singled. The American League led, 8–0.

Rip Sewell of the Pirates opened on the mound for the Nationals in the eighth. Sewell's repertoire of pitches included what he called the "eephus" pitch, a blooper ball that floated to the plate in an arc some thirty to forty feet from the ground. Sewell developed the eephus to frustrate overeager sluggers, and the pitch had been successful. Batters were forced to provide all their own power. Only the Cardinals' Stan Musial had ever managed an extra base hit off the pitch.

Williams spoke with Sewell before the game. Ted asked him to demonstrate the pitch and watched incredulously as the ball floated in a long, slow arc. "Would you throw one of those in a ballgame like this?" queried Ted. "Yes, but only one," answered Sewell. In the eighth, with the game all but over, the fun-loving pitcher decided to experiment.

New York's Snuffy Stirnweiss singled, then pitcher Jack Kramer doubled off the wall, neither hit off the eephus. With two out Sewell faced the Browns'

While on deck in the eighth inning of the 1946 All-Star game, Ted has visions of Rip Sewell's eephus pitch. His home run off Sewell's trick pitch landed in the right field bullpen and capped a 12–0 American League victory. (Photograph by Laban Whitaker, courtesy of the Whitaker family)

Clowning at the All-Star game with former Red Sox coach and self-proclaimed "Clown Prince of Baseball," Al Schact. (Photograph by Leslie Jones, courtesy of the Jones family)

Vern Stephens. But Sewell wanted to try the eephus on Williams. He decided to walk Stephens intentionally.

He threw an eephus wide for a ball, and the crowd roared its approval. He lofted another pitch but it came to earth too near the plate. Stephens reached out and poked it into shallow right, crossing up the defense for a double.

Up came Ted. As Sewell said later, "I wanted Williams up there. What I intended to do was walk Stephens to fill the bases and give the customers a real thrill in case Williams smacked one. I thought I'd throw a couple to see what he could do with it." In all the best ways, the All-Star game suddenly had more in common with the playground. It was time for fun. Ted was right at home.

Williams sliced Sewell's first eephus high and foul to left. Then Sewell snuck a fastball in for a strike before lofting another eephus wide. Then he tried the pitch again.

As the ball floated down, Williams shuffled forward in the batter's box and swung from his heels. The ball duplicated the arc of the pitch but on a larger, grander scale, soaring over the fence and into the bull pen in right field for a home run. The crowd went wild.

After the game a grinning Williams told the press, "I want to tell you that I've never swung on a pitch as hard as I swung on that one. Say, my wife thinks I'm a pretty good hitter, what do you guys think?"

The press agreed with Doris Williams. For the day Ted was 4–4, with two home runs, 4 runs scored and 5 RBIs. Jack Malaney of the *Post* led his game report with "The greatest hitter in baseball completely dominated the show yesterday afternoon as the 13th playing of the All-Star game took place at Fenway Park. . . . Teddy had the most perfect day he has ever had," ending the story, "It was Williams's day. He was great before the game. He was greater after it." The feeling was unanimous.

Five days later, on July 14, Williams provided further evidence for any remaining disbelievers. In a doubleheader sweep of Cleveland, Ted forced a change in the way baseball was played. With the Red Sox down 5–0 in game one, Ted came to bat with the bases loaded and 2 out. He hit Steve Gromek's second pitch into the first row of the right-field bleachers. Leading off the fifth, he smacked Don Black's first toss into the runway behind the Red Sox bull pen to pull the Sox to within 2, 8–6. In the seventh he singled. The Sox trailed 10–8 when Williams came up in the eighth with two men on. After watching 2 balls, he hit his third home run of the day down the right field line off Jonas Berry. His 8 RBIs almost beat Cleveland single-handedly.

The Boudreau shift, as employed on July 14, 1946. The shift bedeviled the stubborn Williams, who insisted on hitting to right field. Contrary to the information on the photograph, Williams grounded out to Boudreau in his first at bat against the shift. (National Baseball Library, Cooperstown, N.Y.)

Between games the unexpected happened. First, Ted allegedly cut out of the ballpark and ate a bowl of ice cream in a shop on Landsdowne Street, leaving other customers in a state of shock. Then Cleveland manager Lou Boudreau, stunned by Williams's game-one performance, scrambled to come up with a strategy that would keep Ted cool at the plate. He found one.

After Williams doubled in his first at bat in game two, Boudreau put his plan into motion. When Ted came up in the third he called for what he termed the "C formation."

All four infielders swung to the right side of the infield. The center fielder shifted to right center and the right fielder hugged the line. Alone on the left side of the diamond, in short left, was left fielder George Case. Williams grounded out to Boudreau.

Within weeks most Sox opponents installed similar shifts, and they would be used, on and off, for the next decade. The logic behind Boudreau's strategy was twofold.

By stacking the defense and busting the ball inside on Williams, the shift made it difficult for Ted to pull the ball safely. He could still hit home runs, but other hits were difficult; there were simply too many men covering the right side. And if Williams went the opposite way, he would do so without his accustomed power. For the opposition, a single was better than a home run.

But the major effect of the shift was psychological. It gave Williams something else to think about, and challenged his ego. Boudreau gambled that Williams would refuse to either bunt or change his swing and hit to left, but instead would stubbornly try to beat the shift and pull the ball without his accustomed success. For a time, Boudreau was right.

Initially, the shift did bother Williams. He kept trying to pull the ball and it did affect his average. His 1946 average before the shift was .354, afterward .327. He didn't often try to bunt, and correctly so; that wasn't what he was being paid to do. But over the next several seasons Williams did change, all the while insisting he hadn't, until the shift actually worked to his advantage long before teams stopped using it.

Williams had always hit to left on occasion and he continued to do so. The adjustment wasn't severe. And he learned to do so with power, as Harold Kaese's analysis of Williams's hits and home runs by field bears out. All of Williams's home runs to left field were after the shift was installed in 1946. While Williams's power output did drop slightly, it is impossible to determine whether the shift was responsible.

Besides, the shift could only be employed when no one was on base, for maybe 150 or so at bats per season, and Ted still drew walks like no other hitter in the game. At most, the shift cost Ted only 10 to 15 hits a season.

A week later, on July 22, against St. Louis, Williams hit for the cycle. The Red Sox continued to cruise. The pennant became an afterthought.

The former high school pitcher stays limber pitching batting practice. (Photograph by Leslie Jones, Boston Public Library)

With the race all but decided, Williams again became the target of criticism. The press started taking occasional swipes at his attitude, claiming he was aloof, self-centered, and remote from his teammates. On occasion they'd quote other Red Sox players, always anonymously, saying the club really didn't need Williams to win.

It is more difficult to write about a winning team. The writers' gripes were as much a case of boredom and jealousy as anything else.

In August, Williams authored a ghostwritten column for the *Globe* entitled "Talking It Over with Ted." Some writers resented this entry into their arena. If they or anyone else felt Ted was aloof and self-centered, it was a problem of perception. He'd always gravitated toward relationships with people outside baseball, and mistrusted those who came only to praise him, even to the point of being much more accessible after a bad day than a good one. He didn't drink, like many of his teammates, and was more content squirreled away in his hotel room or at his new home in Newton than prowling the streets. An off-season fisherman, Ted kept to a fisherman's schedule, into bed early and up at dawn. He roomed alone and liked it that way. The discipline and distance in his life allowed him to devote all his energies to hitting. He didn't care what others thought.

On the verge of clinching the pennant, the Sox went into a tailspin, dropping six in a row, all the while keeping champagne on ice. On September 13, Friday the 13th, they finally clinched against the Indians in Cleveland. Williams was the reason.

In the first inning Ted came to bat with none on and 2 out. Against a shift employed by Detroit a week before, Ted had tried to bunt. Boudreau had heard and adjusted Cleveland's shift, pulling left fielder Pat Seery in to the edge of the infield grass.

The pitch was outside and Williams went with it, driving the ball on a soft line over Seery's head. While Seery raced after the ball, Ted toured the bases. He was halfway to third before Seery gathered the ball in near the left-field fence. Williams rounded third and kept going, sliding across the plate 10 feet ahead of the relay. It was Ted's first, and only, inside-the-park home run in the major leagues, and also his first big league home run to left field. Boudreau, the Indians, and the shift were thwarted. Tex Hughson spun a 3-hitter and the Red Sox, for the first time since 1918, were American League champions.

But the clincher on Friday the 13th was like a black cat that crossed the Red Sox's path to the world championship. Success and failure have always been perilously close to the same thing for the Red Sox, opposite sides of the same coin. While up to that point everything had gone well for the club, much of what came after didn't.

The Sox finished at 104–50, 12 games ahead of Detroit. In the National League, St. Louis and Brooklyn tied with identical 96–58 marks. A best-of-

three play-off would determine the winner. The Red Sox, looking at a potential five-day layoff, were forced to improvise.

Instead of playing intrasquad games or having extended workouts, the Sox recruited a group of American League All-Stars for a series of exhibition games. The Sox felt such a series would help keep their competitive edge, and besides, with Williams making noises that he was going to be asking for more than $80,000 in 1947, the Sox hoped to squeeze out a couple of extra dates in the schedule. Every penny could help. It seemed like a good idea.

The Sox went after the best players in the league. Joe DiMaggio and Luke Appling agreed to play, as did pitchers like Ed Lopat and Hal Newhouser.

The game was played on October 1. Tex Hughson and Joe Dobson were scheduled to split mound duty for the Sox, while the Senators' left-hander Mickey Haefner and Stubby Overmire twirled for the stars.

Only 1,996 fans made their way into Fenway Park to witness the tune-up. Most Sox fans were more interested in the outcome of the St. Louis–Brooklyn series than the exhibition.

The Sox scored twice in the second. Williams walked and Doerr doubled off Haefner. After a York walk, Higgins grounded to Cecil Travis at third, who stepped on the bag to force Doerr but then threw wildly to first, York scoring behind Williams to give the Sox a 2–0 lead. The score held entering the fifth.

Dom DiMaggio led off with a single. In one of the game's oddities, Joe DiMaggio, playing center for the stars, wore a Red Sox uniform, his Yankee pinstripes misplaced.

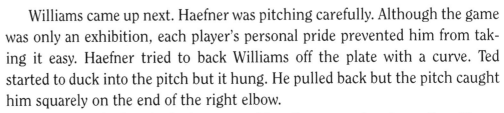

Rudy York, Tex Hughson, and Bobby Doerr (left to right) join Ted to celebrate the clinching of the American League pennant in Cleveland on Friday, September 13, 1946. The game was won by a 1–0 score by benefit of Williams's only career inside-the-park home run. (The Sports Museum)

The Red Sox had several days to work out before the start of the 1946 World Series, because the Cardinals and Dodgers had a best-of-three-game pennant playoff. (Photograph by Leslie Jones, Boston Public Library)

Williams came up next. Haefner was pitching carefully. Although the game was only an exhibition, each player's personal pride prevented him from taking it easy. Haefner tried to back Williams off the plate with a curve. Ted started to duck into the pitch but it hung. He pulled back but the pitch caught him squarely on the end of the right elbow.

Ted was rushed to the locker room. The elbow was already swollen. X rays showed no fracture, and Red Sox Doctor Ralph McCarthy released the following statement, "A bad bruise, but no fracture. It will be sore tomorrow, but Ted will not be able to play for three or four days." Thus forewarned, neither team took any chances the remainder of the game and the Sox took an empty victory, 2–0. The Cards beat Brooklyn 4–2, and everyone now hoped the playoff would go all three games.

It didn't. On October 3 the Cardinals beat the Dodgers 8–4 to win the pennant. With the series now scheduled to start in St. Louis on October 6, the Sox should have been mentally preparing for game one.

St. Louis was the last thing on everyone's mind. As if Williams's injury wasn't already enough to disrupt everyone's concentration, there was another distraction. A New York paper stated that Williams was going to be traded.

In Boston the story knocked everything else off the front page, every thought of the Cardinals out of the Red Sox's collective consciousness, and every measure of concentration from the mind of Ted Williams. Being hurt was bad enough. He already knew he'd have to play the Series without having swung a bat in almost a week. Now he'd have to play not knowing who he going to play for next year. It was crazy.

The papers reported that Yawkey was balking at the salary he knew he'd have to pay Ted in 1947, and the Yankees were dangling Joe DiMaggio, Bill Johnson, and Aaron Robinson for Williams. Detroit was allegedly offering Hal Newhouser and Dick Wakefield, while Cleveland was interested in an even exchange of Ted for Bob Feller.

After being hit on the elbow by Mickey Haefner in a pre-series exhibition game, swinging a bat became painful for Williams and had a dramatic effect on his series performance. (Photograph by Leslie Jones, Boston Public Library)

While the Sox had every right to try to trade Williams, they had no business trying to do so on the eve of their first World Series in twenty-eight years. A simple denial from either Cronin or Yawkey would have solved everything.

Inexplicably, neither man would deny the report. Each refused to be quoted in any fashion. On the eve of the Series the trade story dominated all pregame speculation.

"The strangest World Series in the history of baseball," is what Gerry Hern of the *Post* termed it before game one. "No Sox player doubts the blow-off is coming on Ted Williams. And Williams knows it. . . . The timing couldn't have been worse for the Bostonians and better for St. Louis. . . . A great hitter under pressure, Williams tonight faces the most difficult test he has ever known."

Ted was kept completely in the dark. One day before the Series, Williams was reduced to asking writers what they thought. "What do you think?" he asked, "Is the story true? Are they really gonna sell me?" Williams took batting practice for the first time on October 5. Although he knocked two batting practice pitches for home runs, he reported the arm was still sore and he had trouble straightening it out.

Had the Red Sox tried to subvert their own chances in the Series they could not have done better. With Williams at his peak, on the eve of the most important games of his life, the sensitive slugger was physically and mentally handicapped.

Nevertheless, the Red Sox managed to win game one. Down 2–1 entering the ninth, and only one strike away from defeat, the Sox's Tom McBride singled in pinch runner Don Gutteridge to tie the score. In the tenth Rudy York homered to give the Sox the win. Williams faced left-hander Howie Pollet five times, managing a single and two walks. The Cards employed their own version of Boudreau's shift, but still pitched carefully to Ted. In the tenth Williams extended Pollet before fouling out, and some gave Ted credit for tiring the pitcher before York's home run.

In game two, Cardinal pitching remained sharp. Harry "the Cat" Brecheen held the Sox to only 4 hits. Williams took the collar; his best effort was a sixth-inning line drive that failed to make it through the St. Louis infield.

Before game three, Ted announced he hoped to stay in Boston. "Why should I leave?" he asked rhetorically. "I've played my whole career in Boston. I've never played anywhere else in the majors. . . . They say I don't like the fans. That's not true. . . . Sometimes I try too hard . . . and the boos get a little louder." If Ted hoped his announcement would placate Cronin and Yawkey and lead them to quell his fears, he was mistaken. The Red Sox hierarchy remained quiet.

Game three was in Boston. Boo Ferris pitched magnificently and shut down the Cardinals, 4–0. Rudy York again delivered the big hit, a first-inning home run after Pesky's first Series hit and an intentional walk to Ted. But Williams gathered his share of headlines. In the third inning he bunted for a single.

That hit has often been cited as a symbol of Williams's frustration with Cardinal pitching, but the interpretation is incorrect. Apart from York, none of the Sox were hitting, and when Ted came to the plate with 2 outs the bases were empty. The way York was hitting it made sense for Ted to bunt. On his way to first, Williams was even reported to be laughing. Although York failed to deliver, the bunt had the desired effect. When Ted came to bat in the eighth, the Cardinals abandoned the shift. Ted lined out hard to right.

Game four was all St. Louis. The Cards scored 3 times in the second before Williams ever came to the plate. The score was 6–0 in the fourth when Ted singled in his second at bat, eventually scoring the Sox's first run. The Cardinals went on to win, 12–3.

Ted started things off for the Red Sox in game five. In the first, after Gutteridge and Pesky singled, Williams lined a hit to right, knocking in his first run of the Series to give the Sox a 1–0 advantage. It was only the third time

Harry Brecheen shut down the Red Sox while his Cardinal mates clinched the seventh and deciding game of the 1946 World Series at St. Louis. (The Sports Museum)

The eyes of America were fixed on Ted during the 1946 World Series. (Courtesy of The Brearley Collection)

in the Series Ted had been allowed to hit with men on. On every other occasion, he'd walked. Joe Dobson scattered 4 hits and the Sox won, 6–3, to take a 3–2 advantage.

The two teams returned to St. Louis. In game six Ted had an opportunity to break the contest open. In the first, with 1 out and 2 on, he faced Brecheen. The Cat refused to give him anything to hit and Ted walked. York followed by hitting into a double-play. The Cards scored 3 times in the third to take the lead and score the only runs they needed. Ted could only manage a ninth-inning single before York bounced into a game-ending double-play. St. Louis won, 4–1.

None of the Sox were hitting. In an attempt to lift their spirits, Cronin gave trainer Win Green a drum and had him lead a Red Sox parade as they marched from the team bus to Sportsman's Park for game seven. Cronin gave Williams a toy fishing pole, apparently trying to lighten Ted's mood. If Cronin thought it would help, the pole was a strange choice. Williams had been fishing for hits the whole Series while the Sox had been casting his name about in trade talks. Ted didn't need to be reminded about either.

In the litany of Red Sox disappointments, game seven ranks as one of the saddest. The Cardinals won, 4–3, when Enos Slaughter scored from first on a ninth-inning double as Pesky was slow throwing home. Williams had his best game of the Series but got absolutely nothing to show for it. Twice he flied deep to the outfield, only to be robbed by Cardinal fielders. In the sixth and eighth he left men stranded as he flied out and popped up.

After the game Williams was disconsolate. He waited until the clubhouse cleared before breaking down and crying. He was the last to remove his uniform, the last to dress and leave the ballpark. As he walked to the bus he was surrounded by Cardinal fans who chided him with calls of "Where's Williams? Where's superman?" When Williams boarded the train he broke down again, only to look out the window and see it full of the laughing faces of Cardinal fans. He was crushed.

The 1946 World Series would prove to be the last for both Williams and National League counterpart Musial. (The Sporting News)

Williams didn't alibi. He never used either the sore elbow or the trade talk as excuses for his performance. The defeat had not been his fault. None of the Red Sox had hit. Williams had few chances to make a difference in any of the Red Sox defeats. In the four Cardinal wins, had Williams homered each time he made an out with men on base, it would have made a difference in only game seven. Eight times during the Series, Williams led off the inning. In 30 appearances, Ted batted with the bases empty 18 times. While he stranded 14 base runners, in the Sox's 4 losses Williams came to the plate with a total of only 6 men on base. He finished with 5 hits, all singles, in 25 at bats, 5 walks, 2 runs scored, and 1 run batted in.

On October 18 the Sox returned to Boston. Owner Tom Yawkey distributed nearly $100,000 in bonuses and told Williams the Red Sox had no plans to trade him. Yawkey would have done well to have kept his money and made the decision not to trade Ted two weeks earlier. Williams gave the money to Johnny Orlando.

In November, Williams won the Most Valuable Player award, gathering 224 points, including 9 first-place votes. In his first active season since 1941, Ted finished the year at .342, with 38 home runs and 123 RBIs.

For Ted Williams, 1946 was a season of personal accomplishment and team failure. In the seasons to follow, this was to become a far-too-familiar refrain.

THAT SWING

BY DONALD HALL

"I t don't mean a thing if it ain't got that swing . . ." When Duke Ellington first recorded the tune in 1932, Ted Williams was fourteen, seven years away from Fenway Park. Granted that the lyrics do not refer to hitting a baseball: As the song alludes to its own art— also compact of grace, fluid energy, and completion—it grants us comparison or analogy. Duke Ellington's swing, like Ted Williams's, is a product of genius, labor, power, and wit; yet to the observer, both feel as natural as leaves to trees. Ted Williams studied hitting with the concentration and diligence that composers and piano players bring to their art. In the history of baseball, no other player's swing is so handsome, so lucid, or so well-disguised as a product of natural abundance.

Back before television, we studied that swing mostly in still photographs. We heard Williams's work described on radio; we saw him occasionally on newsreels; on memorable occasions, some of us watched him lord over the batter's box at

WILLIAMS OF RED SOX IS BEST HITTER

The most sensationally consistent hitter in big league baseball is a gangling, 22-year-old outfielder named Ted Williams of the Red Sox. With most of the season behind him, Williams' hefty .400 plus average is almost certain insurance that he will ease into the American League batting title.

Williams is a great hitter for three reasons: eyes, wrists and forearms. He has what ballplayers call ''camera eyes,'' which allow him to focus on a pitched ball as it zooms down its 60-ft. path from the pitcher's hand, accurately judge its intended path across the plate, and reach for it. He even claims he can see the ball and bat meet. The rest of his formula is never to stop swinging. On and off the field he constantly wields a bat to keep the spring in his powerful wrists. Even when he is in the outfield he sometimes keeps waving his arms in a batting arc. And, more than most other great batters, he keeps his body out of his swing and puts all his drive into his forearms.

Here are high-speed pictures taken by Gjon Mili which show the great co-ordination of these factors, the split-second release of power which enables Ted to hit safely four out of every ten times he comes to bat.

REPETITIVE-FLASH PICTURE SHOWS TED REACHING FOR A HIGH ONE, HITTING IT

Life magazine captured the swing of a twenty-two-year-old Williams in July 1941.

Fenway Park. Mostly, when my memory plays images of that incomparable swing, I catch him in stillness, wound on the invisible axis of his balance, turned on himself like a barber's pole in its shapely curving. As the mind's carousel switches from one still to another, the gallery of spirals becomes a helix doubled and tripled by repetition. If we flip these pictures fast enough, they become one sleek, mighty ripple through an unlucky pitcher's pitch—starting from the attent-sleek cat-coil of waiting, releasing in a surge of pivoting hips to extend powerful arms, concluding with the satisfying recoil of the follow-through. Even if we dwell on the photographer's still moment, motion remains implicit in every millimeter of arrest, always turning on itself, powerfully contained within its cylinder.

For any scholar of the bat, be he Wade Boggs or an aging writer remembering decades past, there is one fundamental text. The obsessive composition called *The Science of Hitting* bears the names of Ted Williams and John Underwood—and bares the sullen exact demanding soul of the man who created that swing and carried it with him (remaking, improving) from California to Boston. His sentences are grumpy and demanding, with an affectation of sober investigation. Pedagogue, he publishes his scholarship by reminiscence of research, of practice, of daily revision as he seeks that swing from youth through middle age: "My feeling was if I stayed more vertical, thereby increasing the loop in the swing, I could get the ball in the air better." The two nouns tuck into each other by a preposition. Watch Ted Williams at the plate and see *the loop in the swing*.

He has the old fellow's distaste for many successors, and he is right—we are always right—when he mutters about hitters downstroking. He makes the observation—with Heraclitus, Longinus, and Freud—that we progress (in our thought, in our art, in our lives) by the reconciliation of opposites, dialectics or irony here applied to hitting a baseball: "It's a pendulum action. A metronome—move and countermove . . . you throw a ball that way, you swing a golf club that way, you cast a fishing rod that way." Always thesis and antithesis roll into synthesis. You hit that way, as you write a poem or drive a car or run a business: *move and countermove*. You also play a piano that way, you compose music that way. . . .

Duke Ellington began to study the piano at the age of seven. He worked through classical composers but increasingly admired ragtime, turned professional at seventeen, and a year later devoted himself to jazz. By love's labor he developed that swing for which we know him.

Donald Hall has been a Red Sox fan since 1940. He is the author of Fathers Playing Catch with Sons, Dock Ellis in the Country of Baseball, *and* Old and New Poems.

NEAR PENNANTS AND OTHER POST-WAR HEROICS

．．．．．．．．．．．．．

In the spring of 1947 the Sox looked forward to a rematch with the Cardinals. After a March exhibition against the Sox, Cardinal manager Eddie Dyer quipped, "I thought I'd save the shift for a more important occasion. It may come in handy later on." Cardinal pitchers continued to follow their World Series pattern and busted Williams in on the hands, forcing him to pull. Ted's reaction was predictable. "I'll tell you one thing," he said. "That is not the way to pitch me. *You'll see.*" Williams was right, as he was later to prove. Dyer was wrong. He wouldn't need the shift because neither the Cardinals nor the Red Sox would be making an October trip to the World Series.

The 1947 Red Sox appeared to have all the makings of a dynasty. The nucleus of the club—Doerr, Pesky, DiMaggio, and Williams—were all in the prime of their careers, while the pitching staff, paced by Tex Hughson and Boo Ferris, seemed capable of improving on their stellar performance in 1946. For once, so it seemed, the Red Sox could simply overwhelm the American League with talent. All that was left for manager Joe Cronin was to turn the machine on and turn it off 154 games later.

On deck at Fenway, 1947.
(Courtesy of The Brearley
Collection)

The Red Sox blew a gasket in April and the smooth machine of 1946 never got started in 1947. Ferris, Hughson, and Mickey Harris, who'd combined for 62 wins in 1946, all suffered from arm miseries and racked up only 35 wins in 1947. Joe Dobson, Denny Galehouse, and Earl Johnson couldn't make up the difference.

As happened so many other years, the Yankees leapt out front and forced the Sox to play catch up. Most of the club seemed stuck in the same slump they had fallen into during the Series the year before. Only Johnny Pesky and Williams started the season with any fire, but even those flames appeared on the verge of flickering out.

A week in May typified the season. Knotted in a six-game pack at the top of the American League, an early season series with the Yankees offered the Red Sox an opportunity to set the tone for the remainder of the season. It did, in all the wrong ways.

On May 10, in front of a near capacity crowd at Fenway Park, the Yankees battered Dobson for 7 runs in the first two innings. In the second, the Sox rallied for 3 runs. With 2 out and the bases loaded, Williams struck out. In the sixth Ted came to the plate with 2 on and 2 out, but struck out again. If Williams didn't come through, the Sox had no chance. It made his failures loom even larger than his successes. The boo birds let Williams have it. The Sox lost, 9–6.

Three days later Williams, and the Red Sox, showed another side. On May 13, Joe Dobson's wife, a nurse in a Malden hospital, asked Ted to visit 11-year-old Glenny Brann, who'd had both legs amputated in a railroad accident.

Opening Day, Fenway, 1947. Williams has claimed that hitting a baseball is the single most difficult act in sports, and no one swung a bat more powerfully or gracefully than the Red Sox left fielder. (Courtesy of The Brearley Collection)

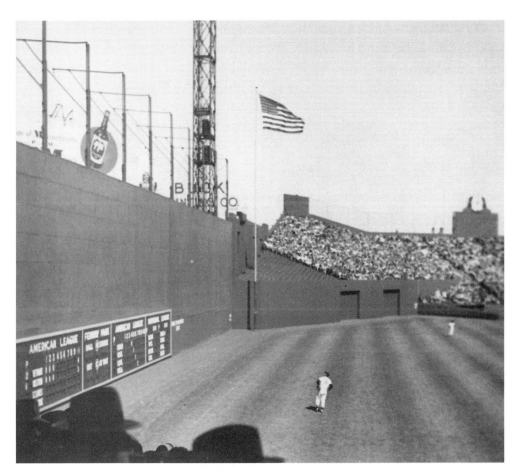

Left field at Fenway, with newly placed light towers, in the late forties. The first night game at Fenway took place on June 13, 1947, before a full house of 35,410. The Red Sox beat Chicago 5–3. (Courtesy of The Brearley Collection)

Williams readily agreed. He often made such visits. In this regard Ted was no one but May Williams's son. Ted rarely said no to charities, particularly if he could ensure that his contribution, either of time or money, was kept anonymous. More than one Williams acquaintance, including the hated writers, found hospital and other bills mysteriously paid.

This time the press did learn of Williams's visit. In Ruthian fashion Ted promised to hit a home run. He'd successfully answered the same request for another youngster in spring training. In the seventh inning, Williams smashed a solo home run into the center-field bleachers, keying a 5-run rally to give the Sox a 10–4 lead over Chicago. In the eighth he hit another home run, this time into the screen in left. The Sox won, 19–6, and for a little boy in a Malden hospital a terrible tragedy became a little more bearable.

The second home run was Ted's first ever over the "green monster" in left. He was adjusting and hitting to left with power. Three days later he doubled off the scoreboard. All pitchers could do was pitch carefully and hope Ted walked. By mid-May Williams had already walked over 30 times.

The walks were beginning to get monotonous. Fans in Boston and in other cities around the league wanted two things from Williams—the right to see him hit and the right to give him the raspberry when he failed. By the All-Star break it was a matter of leaguewide concern. Walking Williams was costing clubs at the gate. In an unprecedented maneuver, American League owners met and allegedly made a pact to let Williams swing more often.

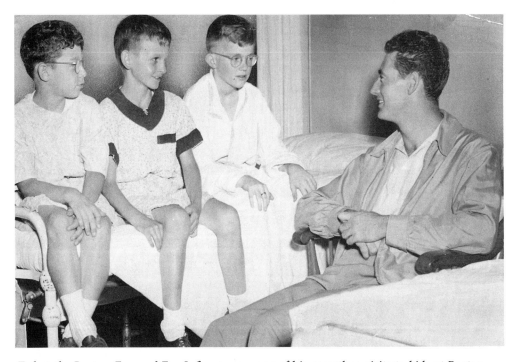

Ted at the Boston Eye and Ear Infirmary on one of his countless visits to kids at Boston hospitals. Williams also spent many hours visiting disabled war veterans at area hospitals with his only stipulation being that no publicity be given his visits. Williams's altruism was much like that of his mother, who devoted her life to service in the Salvation Army.
(Courtesy of the Boston Globe)

To a generation of youngsters he was simply "Teddy Ballgame." (Courtesy of the Boston Red Sox)

Ted went 2–4 in the All-Star contest at Wrigley Field, including a double. In the sixth the spurious wisdom of ever pitching to Williams was demonstrated. His sixth-inning single sent Luke Appling to third. Appling then scored on Joe DiMaggio's double-play ball for the American League's first run in a 2–1 win. Even Ted's singles hurt.

There was little one man could do to check the Sox 1947 slide, even if that man was Ted Williams. In July the Yankees reeled off 19 straight wins to lock up the race. Williams did see more pitches in July and did what he could with them, hitting .348 for the month with 10 home runs and 29 RBIs, but it wasn't enough. In September, with the pennant decided, Williams confided to a friend that the only thing keeping him going was his desire to win the MVP award. The award, felt Williams, would confirm his place as the game's dominant hitter and prove he had beaten the shift. "I want this more than anything in the world," he said.

He appeared up to the cause. At the season's end Ted won his second triple crown, finishing with 32 homers, 114 RBIs, and a .343 average. He walked an astounding 161 times.

The Yankees won the pennant and Joe DiMaggio was named MVP. While Ted didn't begrudge DiMaggio, the pattern of voting angered Williams. DiMaggio collected 202 points to Williams's 201. DiMaggio earned 8 first-place votes to only 3 for Ted, but Williams collected 10 second-place votes. The difference between the men, however, was a tenth-place vote. Twenty-three writers listed Ted on their ballot. The 24th, thought by Williams to be Mel Webb of the *Globe,* felt Ted was undeserving of a place anywhere on the ballot.

*A perch fit for the 1947
triple crown winner —
a gift from Gardner,
Massachusetts, the chair
capital of America.*
(National Baseball
Library, Cooperstown,
N.Y.)

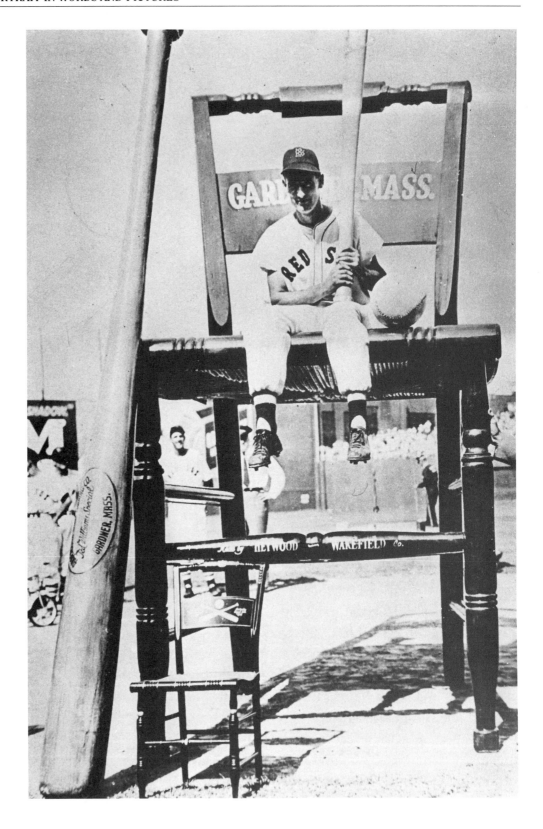

The incident embittered Williams and solidified his feelings of contempt
for writers. Not even an apologia issued by the *Globe*'s Harold Kaese made any
difference. "What would Williams have had to do," wrote Kaese, "to be voted
most valuable player? Stolen 75 bases? Or have told the baseball writers what
great fellows they were?"

It was not a Boston writer who left Williams off the ballot, a fact reported at the time and ignored ever since. Mel Webb didn't even have a vote in 1947. Boston was represented in American League balloting by Jack Malaney of the *Post,* Joe Cashman of the *Record,* and Burt Whitman of the *Herald.* All three enjoyed a good relationship with Ted. Malaney was later hired by the Red Sox as publicity director. Cashman was a Williams favorite, as was Whitman. When Whitman died in 1952, Williams reportedly broke into tears.

The Red Sox lost a pennant to the Yankees, and Williams lost yet another MVP award to Joe DiMaggio. (Courtesy of The Brearley Collection)

According to Harold Kaese, all three gave Williams a first-place vote, the only three he received. The 24th ballot came from a midwestern writer.

Even Joe DiMaggio himself, whose .315 average, 20 home runs, and 97 RBIs led the Yankees in those categories, was listed on only 21 ballots. MVP voting was becoming increasingly suspicious. In 1949 a minor betting scandal involving a pool among the writers was discovered, leading to procedural changes to ensure the integrity of the ballot. It came too late for Ted in 1947.

Williams retreated to the solace of fishing in Florida. The Sox bolstered their lineup with a gigantic trade, sending ten players and $150,000 to the Browns for pitchers Ellis Kinder and Jack Kramer, and infielders Billy Hitchcock and Vern Stephens. The trade was one of the best the Red Sox ever made, as Kramer and Kinder shored up the pitching while Stephens, a quintessential right-handed Fenway Park slugger, protected Williams in the Sox lineup. The Sox made Joe Cronin general manager and lured ex-Yankee manager Joe McCarthy out of retirement. Many thought the opinionated McCarthy was being brought in specifically to discipline Williams and salivated at the potential fireworks.

In the meantime, Ted Williams prepared for fatherhood. Doris was due February 11. But the winter of 1948 was bitterly cold in Boston and Williams couldn't stand being cooped up. He went fishing in Florida, planning to return to Boston on February 3, in plenty of time for the birth. This seemed reasonable enough to Ted.

Mother Nature is not so predictable. Doris delivered a 5-pound, 6-ounce girl, Barbara Joyce, on January 28, 1948.

"Everyone knows where Moses was when the lights went out," wrote Kaese in a column the next day. "And apparently everybody knows where Ted Williams was when his baby was born here yesterday. He was fishing." The column went on to give a relatively evenhanded appraisal of Ted's absence, quizzing fans and even the author's aunt for her opinion on the subject. One young father commented, "After he walks the floor with his baby and gets up in the middle of the night he'll wish he was fishing in Argentina."

The story incensed Williams. He felt it maliciously intruded on his private life. He may have been partially correct, for the writers were miffed that Ted had decided not to attend the annual writers dinner. When the *Globe* called Williams in Florida about the birth of his daughter, he told them in no uncertain terms his opinion on the subject.

Ted views his five-day-old daughter Barbara Joyce on February 2, 1948. (Courtesy of the Boston Globe)

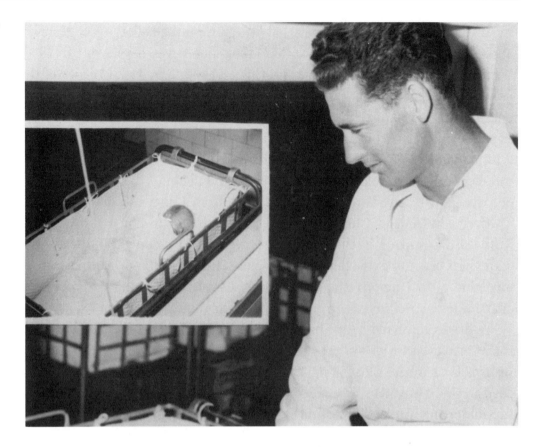

An innocuous, watered-down version of the conversation appeared in the paper. For internal distribution an anonymous *Globe* staffer set the actual conversation to type. This far more unflattering version was never printed. While Ted blasted away at the press they still protected him, practicing the same delicate dance they did for Williams's entire career. Even Dave Egan got into the act. "This, my dear friends," he wrote, "is what is known as yellow journalism at its very dirtiest. It is an invasion of the domestic life of Ted Williams, his wife, and his child. . . . I am no friend of Williams, I am simply a reporter . . . I'll belt him and flay him when he fails to pursue a ball that has burst through his legs . . . but I shall lay it down as a cardinal principle that his relations with his mother, his wife, and his baby are not the concerns of sportswriters."

Doris Williams dismissed the controversy with a single comment, diplomatically responding to a reporter's question with, "She's got Ted's eyes and my mouth." Williams returned from Florida, hung around a few days, said all the right things, and then headed south. Spring training was about to start, and it was still cold in Boston.

For the Red Sox, it would stay cold well into spring, despite the fact Mc-Carthy showed up at spring training sans tie. The new manager made it clear to everyone he intended to get along with Williams. For the first of four consecutive seasons the Sox were *The Sporting News*'s preseason pick for the American League pennant. The Red Sox, however, started the season in reverse, with a mad dash to the cellar, dropping 6 of 9 in April and then winning only 11 of 28 in May to end the month 14–23, 11½ games behind first-place Philadelphia.

Only Ted Williams performed up to expectations. Wrote Harold Kaese in his late May assessment of the team, "The Red Sox, except for Williams, have not been hitting. The Red Sox, except for Williams, have not been fielding." It was true. Only Ted's .374 batting average, 11 home runs, and 42 RBIs by Memorial Day kept the Red Sox out of a cemetery decorated with flags.

Williams's hot hitting continued in June. Joe McCarthy finally got the pitching sorted out and everybody else started to hit. Williams went off the chart, hitting .460 for the month. The Sox entered July only 6 games out. Ted was hitting .407.

On July 10, battling for first place with the Yankees, Indians, and A's, Williams suffered what could have been a season-ending blow. While on a train during a road trip, Williams and outfielder Sam Mele started fooling around, cuffing each other like boxers. After landing a number of harmless blows, the two separated. Minutes later another player came to Mele and asked incredulously, "What'd you do to Williams?" Mele didn't know what he was talking about, but Williams was lying in his berth, scarcely able to move.

An errant punch had separated Ted's ribs. He'd be out of the lineup for two weeks. The Sox responded, losing only 3 times during his absence and pulling into first place by the end of the month. In August Philadelphia fell back and the Red Sox, Yankees, and Indians traded places at the top, only 2 or 3 games separating the three clubs.

With 7 games left, all three clubs had identical 91–56 records. The crosstown Braves clinched the National League title, and Boston braced for its first-ever streetcar series.

Williams's off-season agenda even included a driving contest with Babe Didrikson Zaharias in Florida. Ted still shoots in the low eighties at age seventy-two. (Courtesy of the Boston Red Sox)

Slugging shortstop Junior Stephens, at left and shown with Williams, Pesky, and Dom DiMaggio, proved a key addition to the 1948 Red Sox. (Photograph by Leslie Jones, courtesy of the Jones family)

Williams and Tom Yawkey had high hopes for the 1948 season. In five decades of ownership, Yawkey never celebrated a world championship. (National Baseball Library, Cooperstown, N.Y.)

Williams with (left to right) Wally Muses, Sam Mele, and Dom DiMaggio in 1948. (Photograph by Leslie Jones, Boston Public Library)

Then the Yanks and Sox slumped. With 3 games left, both the Yankees and Sox trailed Cleveland by 2. Then the Indians stumbled against Detroit while the Sox knocked out New York. On the season's last day, October 3, while the Indians hosted Detroit, the Sox squared off against New York, needing a win and a Cleveland loss to force a play-off with the Indians.

New York jumped to a 2–0 lead. But in the second inning fans began yelling reports of the Cleveland game down to the field. Detroit had erupted for 4 third-inning runs to take the lead.

The Sox responded. In the bottom of the third, Dom DiMaggio singled. Williams, whose home run the day before had beat the Yankees, doubled to left. The onslaught continued until five Boston base runners crossed the plate.

The Yankees didn't quit. Joe DiMaggio keyed a 2-run Yankee fourth before the Sox put the game away with 4 runs in the sixth, eventually winning, 10–5. Cleveland lost 7–1, tying Boston for the pennant. While his teammates whooped with joy, Williams was reported to be absolutely silent, staring deeply into his locker after the game, not allowing his concentration to lapse. In the final two games against New York, Ted reached base 8 out of 10 times. There would be a play-off the next day, October 4, in Fenway Park.

Ted and Dom DiMaggio (seen here with Dom's brother Joe) were key contributors to the season-ending victories over the Yankees that forced the first pennant playoff game—against Cleveland at Fenway Park on October 4, 1948—in American League history. (Courtesy of The Brearley Collection)

That the Sox made it this far was due to Williams. He kept them alive in April and May, carried them in June and July, and finally got everyone moving in August and September. Williams seemed to be peaking at the precise time when he was needed most. "The story of the Boston Red Sox miracle drive toward the American League pennant," wrote Lawton Carver of INS, "is the story of a club that couldn't be whipped because Ted Williams is a genuine pro. . . . The fellow once was only great. Now even Bostonians, who delighted in riding him, admit he's terrific." There was one more game for Ted to prove Carver correct.

For reasons that made no sense then and no sense now, Sox manager Joe McCarthy chose Denny Galehouse to pitch the pivotal contest, despite the fact Galehouse had warmed up a full six innings the day before. The Red Sox never had a chance.

With 2 out in the Cleveland first, Boudreau homered over the wall to give Cleveland a 1–0 lead. In the Sox half of the inning, DiMaggio grounded out, then Pesky doubled off pitcher Gene Bearden. Bearden, rookie of the year in 1948, had pitched a shutout only two days before. The knuckleballer had handcuffed the Sox three times in 1948 and he was up to the task. Williams grounded out to short, then Stephens singled in Pesky to knot the score.

Ted popped out in the third with the score still 1–1. In the fourth the Sox came undone. Boudreau and Gordon singled. Keltner cracked a home run, and before you could say "Denny Galehouse," the game, and the Red Sox pitcher, was gone. Williams reached base on an error in the sixth and singled to left against a shiftless Indian defense in the eighth. The Sox lost, 8–3.

Once again, when the rest of the Red Sox left the clubhouse to head home, the last thing they saw was Ted Williams, still in uniform, as if he were already waiting for next year.

Ted finished with a .369 batting average to lead the league, the second best of his career, but slumped to 25 home runs and 127 RBIs, although he led the league in doubles. In spite of the fact Ted still paced the league in slugging percentage, some harped on his reduction in power and said he'd changed his swing to beat the shift. Harold Kaese claimed Williams made at least 75 hits to left in 1948 and went so far as to say, "The Cleveland Indians won the pennant on July 14, 1946," the day Boudreau first installed the shift. To no one's surprise, Lou Boudreau was elected 1948 American League MVP with 324 votes. Ted finished third with 171.

For the Red Sox, the 1949 season was nearly a carbon copy of 1948. They had the same slow beginning, same midseason comeback, same bitter disappointment at the end. So, too, with Ted Williams. Again he led the team in the early going, keeping the Sox within reach of the Yankees, until Boston took off in August and September. One of the curiosities of these years is that in the press, Williams, while the acknowledged team leader, nearly fades from view. When Williams was great and the Red Sox weren't, he got his due, both good and bad. When the Sox and Ted were great, other players received the attention, and sometimes credit, quite out of proportion to what they deserved. In 1949, Williams shared the limelight.

Although his average hovered around .300, Ted crashed 11 May home runs as the Red Sox struggled to stay above .500. Joe DiMaggio was out with bone spurs in his heel and the Yankees couldn't take advantage. While the Sox slumped, Williams provided everyone with something to talk about.

On May 24 in Boston the Red Sox played Detroit. In the first, Ted homered into the left-field net for the fourth time of his career to give the Sox a 1–0 lead. In the fifth he doubled to left and scored, and in the seventh lashed a hit

How to keep a splinter splendid, Fenway Park, 1949. (Courtesy of The Brearley Collection)

"Mr. Williams's neighborhood," the old Green Monster complete with National League scores. The old tin left field wall was removed following the 1975 season and was replaced with a fiberglass version, and a scoreboard that shows only American League scores. (Courtesy of The Brearley Collection)

to right, which he stretched into another double. With the Sox leading, 6–4, Ted came up again. On the mound was the Tigers' Dizzy Trout. With 2 strikes and Williams looking for a screwball, Trout crossed him up with a fastball down the middle for strike 3. Ted looked the ball into the catcher's mitt, stepped away from the plate, and heaved his bat into the air.

It soared, nearly straight up, amazingly high, before tumbling to the ground. One tongue-in-cheek observer noted the bat flew "high as the Custom House," then Boston's tallest building, while more sober observers estimated its path as even with the grandstand roof. Fortunately for Ted, none of the three umpires saw the toss. Tiger manager Red Rolfe argued long and loud to have Williams similarly thrown, but Ted remained in the game, the Sox winning in 10, 8–7, to move into third place.

The Red Sox slumped in early June before bouncing back to win 10 of 11. Then the Yankees came to town.

Returning to the lineup after the heel injury, Joe DiMaggio was magnificent. In his first game back he crashed a 2-run homer. The next day he hit a 3-run blast, and duplicated the feat in the third game. The Sox lost all three and looked to be out of the race.

They were not. The sweep woke the club up, and as the weather warmed in late summer, so did the Red Sox. By August they'd pulled back to within 6 games of the Yankees. Now it was the Red Sox's turn. The Yanks came into Boston on August 8 hoping to bury the Sox. Ted lashed out 7 hits in the 3 games and Boston took 2 of 3. By September the Sox trailed by 2. Ted already had 38 home runs.

The Red Sox surge continued. In August and September they were 43 and 13. Entering the season's last 2 games in New York, Boston led New York by 1.

The Yankees chose to make October 1 Joe DiMaggio Day, and it would be Joe DiMaggio Day in more ways than one.

The Red Sox scored first, Dom DiMaggio and Williams singling in the first and DiMaggio scoring on Junior Stephens's liner to left. In the third, Yankee pitcher Allie Reynolds walked the bases loaded, including Williams. Doerr singled and relief pitcher Joe Page walked 2 more to give the Sox a 4–0 lead.

It didn't hold. Joe DiMaggio keyed two rallies and the Yankees tied. In the eighth Johnny Lindell homered off Dobson and the Sox lost, 5–4. Just as it had been the year before, the season was now down to one game.

The result was no better in 1949 than in 1948. The Yankees scored 1 in the first but Ellis Kinder shut them down after that. Meanwhile the Sox couldn't touch Vic Raschi. In the eighth McCarthy pinch-hit for Kinder. Parnell relieved. Henrich immediately hit a home run. Bauer singled, then Williams juggled Johnson's hit, allowing Bauer to reach third. Hughson relieved and walked a man before giving up a bases-loaded bloop double to Jerry Coleman. The Yankees led, 5–0.

Williams came to bat with 1 out in the ninth. Even with a 5-run lead, the Yankees gave Williams nothing to hit. Again the bat was taken out of his hands. Williams walked. Boston managed to score 3 runs but the rally died. The Red Sox finished in second place again. As had happened in the 1946 World Series, in the 1948 play-off, in the two games against the Yankees, Williams didn't have an opportunity to change anything. Williams finished the year with a league-leading 43 home runs and 159 RBI, both career highs. He narrowly missed a record third triple crown, as Detroit's George Kell edged him out for the batting title by .0002.

After the game the Red Sox clubhouse was morose. Players sniped at one another, frustrated at having come so close to a pennant only to fall short again. One Red Sox player blasted Williams for his eighth-inning error. Williams later described the five-hour trip back to Boston as "like a damn funeral train." Ted immediately left town for Minnesota to go hunting and fishing.

Williams didn't return to Boston until February to appear at the annual Sportmen's Show at Mechanics Building. He earned $5,000 for his week-long

Ted at the throttle of the Merchants Limited heading to Yankee Stadium, September, 1949. With two games to play and a one-game lead, the Red Sox suffered two crushing defeats to the Yankees and lost another pennant on the last day of the season. (Photograph by Leslie Jones, courtesy of the Jones family)

The 1949 pennant was another one that "got away"—Ted with Eddie Collins and Joe Cronin. (Courtesy of the Boston Globe)

Ted Williams entertained crowds at the annual Sportsmen's Show at Boston's Mechanics Building as he cast his fly rod with Chief Needabah, a standby at these shows. (Photograph by Leslie Jones, courtesy of the Jones family)

The 1949 American League MVP as depicted by Gene Mack of the Boston Globe. (The Sports Museum)

Williams with 1950 American League batting champ Billy Goodman. (Photograph by Leslie Jones, courtesy of the Jones family)

appearance. Although Ted's baseball salary was now some $75,000 plus, he was just beginning to make serious forays into other areas. His business manager, Fred Corcoran, had always steered Williams toward the easy endorsement (Ted's Root Beer, Quaker Oats, Chesterfields), but Ted had refused offers such as book and movie deals. The outdoor show, however, appealed to him. Ted enjoyed appearing before the crowds in a different light, giving casting demonstrations and talking about fishing.

Fishing was becoming more important. In the off-season Ted purchased his first home, in Miami, closer to his favorite fishing grounds. Williams was spending more and more time in the Florida Keys, and liking it better. Losing pennants on the last day of the season wasn't fun.

The 1950 season was no improvement. The Red Sox opened in Fenway against the Yankees on April 19. The *Post*'s Jack Malaney captured the pattern of the day—and the preceding several seasons—when he wrote, "The Red Sox went from the heights of sublimity to the lowest depths of ridicule," all in nine innings.

The Red Sox jumped out to a quick 9–0 lead, Williams contributing 2 hits and 2 RBIs. It was only opening day, but Boston finally looked like the team writers picked for first every spring. Doing this to the Yankees seemed particularly telling.

In the sixth inning, the Yankees erupted for nine runs to tie and went on to win, 15–10. On the heels of their losses in New York the previous October, the Red Sox defeat was a bad omen.

As if the loss to New York weren't enough to set the writers after the ballclub, Sox players, by unanimous vote, had decided to ban reporters from

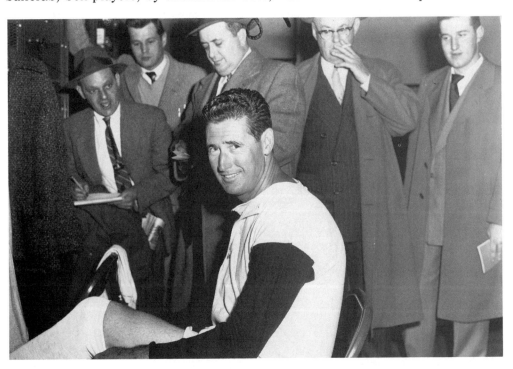

In 1950, Sox players voted unanimously to ban writers from the clubhouse both before games and for thirty minutes after games. (Photograph by Leslie Jones, Boston Public Library)

the clubhouse before games and for thirty minutes afterward. The ban, allegedly Williams's idea, strained an already uncomfortable relationship between the team and the press. By the time the writers got into the clubhouse after opening day, only six ballplayers remained.

The Red Sox got off to their usual slow start, but for once no one team jumped out too far in the lead. On May 11, Detroit entered Fenway Park tied with the Red Sox for first place, percentage points ahead of New York and Washington. A doubleheader sweep might have set the tone for the season. It didn't.

Detroit swept. The Tigers blasted the Sox in game one, 13–4. In the sixth Ted dropped an easy fly ball and the boos began in earnest. As described in the *Globe,* when Williams left the field, "he raised two fingers skyward to let those fans who booed him know how he felt about them." In the eighth the boos turned to cheers after Williams hit a grand slam to account for all the Red Sox scoring. But Williams hated such fickle behavior. Cheer him or boo him, but never do both. He loathed the word *front-runner.*

Entering the eighth inning of game two, the Sox led 2–0. Detroit loaded the bases and with 2 out, Vic Wertz singled to left. The ball skipped past Williams for his second error of the day and 3 runs scored.

The crowd of over 27,000 fans booed unmercifully. As Williams ran off the field at the end of the inning, be repeated his first game exhibition in universal sign language, gesturing three times to three different areas of the ballpark. It was as if both Williams and the Red Sox fans had suddenly decided, en masse, to vent their pent-up frustrations of the past several seasons. Perhaps they were more alike than either cared to admit.

After the game, which the Sox lost, 5–3, to drop from first to fourth place, it was clear something had to be done. The writers were poised to blast away at Williams. Egan wrote, "Even in its crummiest days . . . [baseball] never wallowed lower in the muck than it did on a softly wonderful day in beautiful Fenway Park."

The Sox asked Williams to apologize. Ted was as upset as anyone. He disliked these emotional outbursts and afterward would be overwhelmed with shame, but at times he just couldn't control himself. After meeting with club officials, Ted agreed to apologize.

The club issued a terse statement that read, "After a talk with Mr. Yawkey, Ted Williams has requested that this announcement be made to the fans. Ted is sorry for his impulsive action on the field yesterday and wishes to apologize to any and all whom he may have offended."

Ted later told the press he felt ill the entire game and was worried Doris might have to undergo some surgery. While the apology smoothed things over with the fans, relations between Ted and the writers went from a permanent chill into a deep freeze.

Ted making a point with the writers. At various times in his career, Williams was himself a writer working for the Boston Globe *and* Life. (Courtesy of Brian Interland)

On Memorial Day the Sox dropped a doubleheader to New York. Williams was hitting only .286, his lowest mark since 1939, at that point in the season. He was down and he was fair game. New York's sporting press blasted away at both the Red Sox and Williams. New York scribe Jimmy Cannon wrote that Ted was asking the Red Sox for a trade. Williams was incredulous and denied making any such statement. While controversy again swirled all around him, he silenced it the only way he knew, with his bat.

On June 2, one day after Cannon's story broke, Williams wowed the Indians by belting 4 of the first 5 batting-practice pitches into the stands. Then he keyed an 11–5 Sox win with his twelfth home run of the season.

While Williams went on a minitear, the Sox continued to falter. Manager Joe McCarthy seemed disinterested, and after the Sox dropped 11 of 13, he resigned on June 23. McCarthy was replaced by Steve O'Neill.

Eight games out of first at the All-Star game, the Sox hoped for a second-half turnaround. They needed a few breaks. They got an unexpected one.

Williams started in left field for the American League in the classic on July 11 in Chicago's Comiskey Park. In the first inning the Pirates' Ralph Kiner drove the ball to deep left center. Williams tore after the ball, chased it down, then crashed into the fence, stiff-arming the wall with his glove hand.

The bones of his lower and upper arm took the force of the blow, smashing into each other, breaking seven bone chips from the left elbow, the largest the size of a dime. Williams stayed in the game, even knocking in a run with an

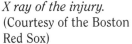

X ray of the injury. (Courtesy of the Boston Red Sox)

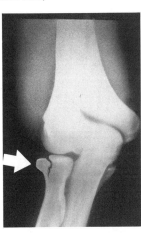

The catch off Ralph Kiner in the 1950 All-Star game that broke Williams's elbow. (Wide World Photos)

eighth-inning single, before taking himself out. The National League won in fourteen innings, 4–3. Ted went back to Boston holding his arm in his lap like a loaf of bread.

X rays uncovered the break and on July 13 Williams's elbow was operated on by Dr. Joseph Shortell in Cambridge's Sancta Maria Hospital. While the surgery was successful, Williams's season was all but over.

Billy Goodman replaced Ted in the Red Sox lineup, and the club responded with its best sustained stretch of baseball since Babe Ruth was best known as a left-handed pitcher. Starting on August 15 the Sox won 11 in a row and 16 of 17 to get back in the race. In anonymous reports Boston players confidently predicted, "We can win it without Williams."

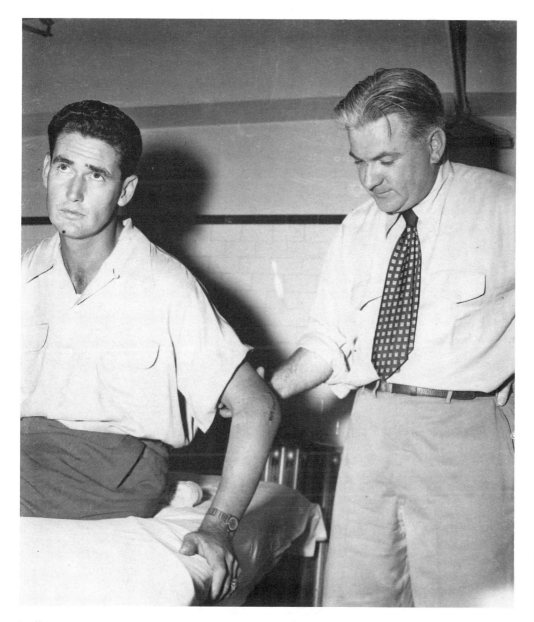

Dr. McCarthy with the bone chips. (Courtesy of The Brearley Collection)

Williams with the team physician, Dr. McCarthy, following surgery by Dr. Joseph Shortell to remove bone chips from the injured elbow. (Courtesy of The Brearley Collection)

Ted returned to the lineup on September 15. The elbow was sore but the Sox were in the race. The club pulled to within 1½ games of first on September 19 before collapsing, losing 4 in a row. Williams played well but the club finished third, 4 games behind New York.

At the end of the season speculation about Williams raged. In the second half the Sox had played better without him, and that seemed to give credence to those who felt Williams's clubhouse presence was disruptive. The trade rumors began again, and many felt Ted would begin the 1951 season in Detroit. He had hit only .317 in 1950, but in only 89 games Ted had hit 28 home runs and knocked in 97.

He spent the winter fishing and tutoring at a Florida baseball school. In February Ted returned to Boston for another appearance at the Sportsmen's Show. Coming off the injury, Ted announced that he'd set his own pace in the spring of 1951. Otherwise Williams kept silent, wisely deciding that it was better to keep quiet than to open his mouth and give controversy a chance to get started.

Former world heavyweight boxing champ Jack Sharkey was a frequent guest with Ted at the Sportsmen's Show held at the now demolished Mechanics Building in Boston's Back Bay. (Courtesy of The Brearley Collection)

Controversy happened anyway. Manager Steve O'Neill, ultraconfident of his own ability following the Sox second-half performance, was not convinced of Ted's value to the club. He faced Williams down over his appearance in road exhibition games. Ted agreed to appear whenever asked. In response, Dizzy Trout of the Tigers awarded Ted a tongue-in-cheek varsity "B." Williams took the gift in stride, and even briefly wore it on field.

Once the season started the old pattern returned. The Sox got off to a decent start but seemed stuck in third place no matter how well they played. Coming off the elbow injury, Ted Williams was beginning to look his age.

No longer the "Splendid Splinter" or "the Kid," Williams was 32 years old and returning from a severe injury. The elbow had healed, but still bothered Ted. He found it hard to straighten, and the muscles remained atrophied. In mid-May his average was below .250.

Yet Williams was still the most feared hitter in the game. On May 15, White Sox manager Paul Richards gained notoriety when he utilized a forgotten strategy in an effort to stop Ted. Trailing Chicago 7–6 in the ninth, Williams led off. Richards moved right-handed pitcher Harry Dorish to third base and brought in lefty Billy Pierce to face Ted, who had already doubled and homered. Ted popped out, Pierce left the game, and Dorish resumed his mound duties. Chicago won, 9–7.

Ted's average reached a nadir on May 20 at .226. People were whispering that Williams was finished, and the Sox were starting to regret their decision to keep him after 1950. As he had done so many times before, Williams used the low point as motivation to explode. On May 21 Ted smacked 3 hits to left, including a home run and a double, as the Sox whipped Detroit, 9–7. Said Tiger pitcher Dizzy Trout, "Williams doesn't look any different to me, slump or no slump."

On Memorial Day, Ted keyed a sweep of the Yankees before 35,824 fans at Fenway Park. He even scored from second base on a bunt. Hitting to all fields, during the last ten games in May, Ted went 26–53, including 4 home runs, with 9 doubles, knocking in 22 runners and walking 13 times. The Sox won 10 in a row and Ted raised his average to .321, leading the league with 12 home runs and 41 RBIs.

By mid-July the Red Sox were in first and Ted was again being talked of as an MVP candidate. For the first time since 1948, Williams was being roundly praised for his hustling and fielding. Finally, it seemed, the Sox might come out on top.

It was too little, too late. The emerging dynasty of 1946 was approaching retirement. Walt Dropo, who'd won the rookie of the year award in 1950, finished 1951 in the minor leagues. Bobby Doerr hurt his back, and hardly played the second half, and retired. Only Mel Parnell and Ellis Kinder saved the pitching staff from complete embarrassment. In September the Sox collapsed and the Yankees roared to yet another pennant. Boston finished third,

Williams worked long hours to shake the effects of elbow surgery. (Photograph by Leslie Jones, courtesy of the Jones family)

Sharing a joke with the 1950 Rookie of the Year, Red Sox first baseman Walter Dropo. Dropo, a former football star at the University of Connecticut, hit 34 homers while driving in 144 runs. (Photograph by Leslie Jones, Boston Public Library)

11 games behind. Williams ended the season in a slump, finishing with a disappointing .318 average and only 30 home runs with 126 RBIs.

During the World Series the Red Sox actively encouraged speculation that Williams would be traded, before finally concluding that whoever they received in return might not be able to draw a soul into Fenway Park, no matter how well the Sox did. When MVP voting was announced in November, Williams finished a disappointing 13th.

Steve O'Neill was fired and replaced by Lou Boudreau, who was brought in to initiate a youth movement. Boudreau started it sooner than expected.

In early January, Williams was called back into the service. Since returning from the Navy, Ted remained a member of the Marine reserves, never thinking this left him vulnerable to recall. As the Korean War escalated, the Marines called over a thousand veteran pilots back into action.

As he had eventually done in World War II, Ted went quietly, later writing, "In my heart I was bitter about it, but I made up my mind I wasn't going to bellyache." Privately, he questioned America's role in Korea, and wondered why reserves were being called back for war duty while professional soldiers remained behind. He half-expected someone, somewhere, to step in on his behalf and question the military wisdom of the recall, but the thought processes of America's military hierarchy have never been easily discerned.

Ted went to spring training anyway. There was a chance his left elbow might not meet the Marines' stringent requirements and he'd be refused readmittance on physical grounds. When Williams reported for his physical, it was clear the Marines had decided he was going back, no matter what. The elbow was X-rayed and while Williams waited for a report, a Marine doctor came out, looked at the elbow and stated, "It's all right." The X rays were never even looked at.

Lou Boudreau joined the Red Sox as player/ manager for the 1951 season. (Photograph by Leslie Jones, Boston Public Library)

Ted was ordered to report in May. He opened the season in a Red Sox uniform and played a handful of games. Everyone thought this was the end for Ted Williams. He'd played fourteen seasons, including his time in World War II, and was 33 years old. Even if he came back from Korea unscathed, there seemed little chance of Ted's regaining his position as baseball's most dangerous hitter, and no one thought Ted would play if he felt his skills had declined. On April 30, 1952, the Sox staged the Ted Williams Day.

Fenway Park has never seen such an emotional ceremony before or since April 30, 1952, when Williams was bid farewell by the Detroit Tigers, 25,000 fans, and his teammates, prior to re-entry into the service. The entire crowd joined hands and sang "Auld Lang Syne" in a moving pre-game ceremony. Notice that the line of players is shaped like a wing as it stretches from dugout to dugout. (Courtesy of the Boston Globe)

Joining hands with Private Fred Wolfe, a wounded veteran of the Korean War. Williams was a frequent visitor at Boston's Jamaica Plain Veterans Administration Hospital, where he loved to talk baseball with the patients. (Courtesy of the Boston Globe)

In ceremonies before the game both Red Sox and Tiger squads linked hands with Ted and Private Fred Wolfe, a wheelchair-bound soldier injured in Korea. Ted was presented with a new Cadillac, a replica of a Revere Bowl, and other gifts, including a wish book bearing the signature of 400,000 fans. Newspapers cited Ted's career highlights and most writers extended their best wishes, burying the hatchet in their running battle with Williams, although Dave Egan wondered, "What are we giving *him* a day for?"

In a brief speech before the game, Williams was gracious and humble. "This is a day I'll always remember," he said, "and I want to thank you fans, in particular, from the bottom of my heart." Standing next to the injured soldier, surrounded by his teammates, he looked the part of a Hollywood hero. Before the ceremony ended, Ted turned to each section of the park and waved, but did not tip, his cap. The crowd of 24,764 stood and cheered.

During the game Williams gave them reason to continue cheering. With the score tied 3–3 in the bottom of the seventh, Dom DiMaggio singled. Piersall flied out, setting the stage for Ted. On the mound was Dizzy Trout, one of Ted's closest friends in baseball. Trout threw Williams a curve, low and inside. Ted swung.

The ball soared to right field, landing in the grandstand next to the runway, eight rows deep, Williams's 324th career home run. The entire Red Sox squad emerged from the dugout and met Williams at home plate. The lead held and the Sox won, 5–3. For all anyone knew, Ted Williams had hit a home run in his last big league at bat. After the game Ted held a party at the Kenmore Hotel, inviting his friends—the bellhops, cops, cabbies, and batboys—as well as his teammates.

Harold Kaese wrote a tribute to Ted the following day. "With Williams," he wrote, "a 34-ounce bat isn't a billet of wood. It is the scepter of a king, the wand of a musician.

"Williams could commit no offense on the playing field he couldn't easily obliterate with his bat. . . . Williams has lived by the bat as others have lived by the sword, by the pen, by the good word, and the good deed. He has shown us how much power there is, indeed in a powerful bat."

"This is a day I'll always remember, and I want to thank you fans, in particular, from the bottom of my heart." (Courtesy of The Brearley Collection)

Ted with the Cadillac he received on Ted Williams Day. (Courtesy of The Brearley Collection)

Bidding farewell to Boston on the way to Pennsylvania, and Marine duty. (Courtesy of The Brearley Collection)

A few days before, Williams provided George Carens of the *Herald Traveler* with his own career summation. "If you ask me to sing a swan song," said Ted, "I'd say the happy memories never will disappear, whatever the future holds. I've never tried to hurt anyone, never criticized any player, and tried to help young players. It would be nice to wake up some morning and find that the whole world is at peace, but in the meantime, the deadline is getting closer, and I'll be ready to go."

At midnight, May 1, Ted Williams, slugger supreme, reported to Willow Grove, Pennsylvania, as Ted Williams, Marine captain. The baseball wars were over. Another was just beginning.

YES, HE WAS THE BEST

BY GEORGE V. HIGGINS

There is a problem these days in accounting for the casual manner in which we New Englanders, now become quite long of tooth, nonchalanted our access to nineteen years of what to date at least has been the most consistently superb performance of the sport of baseball that America has ever seen. Ted Williams played in more than 1,100 Boston Red Sox home games between 1939 and the end of 1960, but for one reason or another we did not fill cozy Fenway to its pigeon-ridden rafters for every single one.

Supposing that some several thousand Austrians between 1756 and 1791 for some reasons of their own that seemed sufficient at the time must have omitted to attend even one public concert by Wolfgang Amadeus Mozart, or that a hundred fifty years before Englishmen in like numbers with no taste for theater somehow never bothered to enjoy what William Shakespeare wrote, somehow does not explain fully how we could have been so dense. Buffeted we certainly were by mean media barrages disrespectful of his deeds (as he sadly was himself), but that's no real excuse: right before our very eyes Ted

Williams surpassed every standard that intrusive world events—two wars that robbed him of five years in his very prime—permitted him to challenge.

In his nineteen years here, Ted Williams by Pete Palmer and

John Thorn's painstaking calculations (in *The Hidden Game of Baseball*) brought to the Red Sox some 97 victories that they would not have tallied without his sterling play. Babe Ruth in three more years than Williams was allowed to play made win-

Williams on deck for one of his 3,887 Fenway Park at bats. (Courtesy of The Brearley Collection)

ners of his teams in 117 outings that they would otherwise have lost. Thorn and Palmer think those war years took away from Williams and the Red Sox victories that would have left him with a total of 133, and made him indisputably successful in his effort to achieve what he identified as his sole ambition: to prove he was the greatest hitter who ever lived.

Well, he was, and he did it. Time in its habitual cruelty occasionally lets up a bit and forgives us all our lapses, and as Ted Williams and the rest of us have become three decades older, it's rewarding to us spectators to see the now-elder statesman of the batted ball savoring at least somewhat the approbation and gratitude he neither got nor enjoyed fully while he was engaged in doing what he did so well. I realize many baseball fathers have nudged their kids and pointed when some hero of other days, from another team, appeared in public view, and assured those children, unimpressed, that Mantle, Joe D., Sandy Koufax, Stan Musial, or Hank Aaron was the greatest ballplayer who ever took the field. Well, we older parties in New England have done that in our turn, but we have an advantage over all who have made competing claims: when we say that of Number 9, we are speaking God's own truth.

We may have missed a thousand or more games that he played in his routine splendor, but the ones we saw were enough to assure us to this day that he was the very best. So, how many homers did Mozart hit in his career, anyway, and while you're at it, if you know, what was Shakespeare's lifetime average?

George V. Higgins has written twenty-two books, including the recent Victories *and* Progress of the Seasons, *his best-seller on life as a Red Sox fan. Higgins is currently a professor in the creative writing department at Boston University.*

SIX

FROM KOREA TO .388

• • • • • • • • • • • •

I f Williams's tour of duty in World War II was marked by training and inactivity, it served him well during his second tour. Ted's second military stint meant one thing: combat.

Williams signed up for jet training, learned to fly the F-9 Pantherjet, attended ground school in North Carolina, and went through cold-weather training in the Sierra Mountains. Only ten months after returning to active duty, on February 4, 1953, Williams arrived in Korea as a member of the First Marine Air Wing.

Ted hated Korea. Never a fan of cold weather, the constant cold and dampness kept him under the weather. No sooner would Ted shake a cold than he would come down with another. The Marines lived in near primitive conditions, and neither Williams nor any of his fellow pilots enjoyed the creature comforts.

With only two combat missions under his belt, Ted Williams nearly became a casualty.

Flying with the 33rd Marine Air Group, Williams was one of 200 flyers in a huge air mission aimed at Kyomipo, fifteen miles south of the North Korea

Recalled to the Marines, May, 1952. (The Sporting News)

Captain Ted Williams sits in the cockpit of an F-9F Panther jet at Cherry Point, North Carolina, while training for combat duty in Korea. (Courtesy of the San Diego Hall of Champions)

capital of Pyongyang. Coming in low over his target, a troop encampment, Williams lost sight of the plane in front of him.

He dropped down to regain visual contact, but went too low. North Korean soldiers in the encampment blasted Williams with small arms fire. He completed his run over the target and tried to pull up. Every warning light in the cockpit was lit and the plane was vibrating. The stick started to shake and Williams knew he'd sprung a leak in the hydraulic system.

The landing gear came down and the plane was hard to control. Williams got the gear up and started climbing. He knew he was in trouble and got on the radio, but the radio went dead. Another pilot pulled close and tried to signal Ted to bail out, but Williams didn't know his plane was on fire.

He increased altitude and turned the jet toward the nearest American base. Nearly all his instruments were out. The airspeed indicator read zero. The wing flaps were frozen and Ted was unable to lower the landing gear. Every message given by the plane told Williams to eject.

He continued to climb, still not knowing the plane was on fire, but took the precaution of climbing to higher elevation anyway. A companion aircraft, piloted by Lieutenant Larry Hawkins, led Williams back to the field and radioed ahead that he was in trouble.

Williams again considered bailing out but resisted the idea. He was afraid if he ejected his kneecaps would crash against the cockpit.

With the field in sight, Ted turned to land when an explosion rocked the craft. A wheel door had blown off. Smoke was pouring from the brake ports. Down below, the residents of a small Korean village on the outskirts of the field scattered. Williams's plane was a mass of fire and smoke.

Unable to check his air speed and almost powerless to do anything about it, Williams approached the ground at 225 miles per hour, almost twice the recommended speed. He dropped the emergency wheel latch and only one wheel dropped into position. He hit the strip level, but with no way to slow the plane. Soon the plane settled on its belly, sparks, fire, and smoke trailing after it, as Williams held on, hoping it would stop.

The F-9 screamed down the field out of control for more than a mile, shedding strips of metal and on the verge of exploding. Twice the plane nearly barreled into fire trucks waiting for the inevitable blowup. Finally, at the very edge of the field, the plane groaned to a stop.

Williams popped the canopy. With the exception of the cockpit the entire plane was aflame. He dove headfirst to the tarmac, where he was grabbed by two Marine flight crewmen and hustled away. Angry, both at himself and the close call, Ted took off his helmet and threw it on the ground. When he returned to look at the plane, it was a blackened hulk, completely destroyed. He had avoided death by the narrowest margin.

The next day Williams was back in the sky. Two months later, on April 28, Ted had another close call.

Following thirty-nine missions, and his famed crash landing, Williams was awarded an Air Medal and two Gold Stars before receiving a discharge for health reasons. (The Sporting News)

This time he was on a Marine raid of Chinnampo on Korea's west coast. Heavy winds forced the mission closer to the ground than usual and Williams's plane was hit by antiaircraft fire. Fuel reserves in the wing didn't ignite and Williams made it back safely.. He was lucky.

The weather caused Ted more trouble than the North Koreans. He developed pneumonia and spent several weeks on a hospital ship. No sooner did he return to active duty than he became ill again. The remainder of Williams's tour of duty was a yo-yo: fly a few missions, get sick, fly a few missions, get sick again.

In June of 1953, the Marines decided Ted Williams had enough. Military doctors discovered an inner ear problem that made it impossible for him to remain a pilot. Ted was scheduled to be sent to Hawaii for treatment. But before leaving Korea, Ted had a few things to get off his chest.

While Williams was the consummate soldier, following orders without complaint, he was still the same Ted Williams who had no compulsion against speaking his mind. Before leaving Korea he told reporters that, "The United States of America ought to be ashamed of itself the way this thing [the war] is going on out here.

"Do you think we ought to be in Korea?" asked Ted. "Do you think we are trying? We've sat on the 38th parallel for a year and a half and more. Guys are getting killed every day in the line. Do you think we're trying? Don't believe it, buddy, that we're trying."

He went on to characterize the war as a "forgotten war—to all but the wives and mothers and maybe the girls of guys over here." The speech was not popular, but Williams cared little about popularity. He knew how he felt. When Williams got to Hawaii he found out how the Marines felt. The ear problems left Ted hard of hearing and he was mustered out of the service. The Marines took advantage of the PR possibilities, holding a full-scale press conference upon his return to California.

While in Korea, Williams flew 39 missions. He later downplayed his record, writing: "I was no hero. There were maybe seventy-five pilots in our two squadrons and 99 percent of them did a better job than I did." But Ted Williams's record is nothing to make light of. He served, and did so with distinction, when others might have resisted the recall in the first place. Given his private feelings about the war, Williams's record is all the more remarkable. As he said when recalled, he didn't "bellyache." He did his duty.

Ted officially left the Marines in July. He hadn't given playing baseball much thought. He was 34, tired, and sick. He must have wondered if he could come back at anything approaching his accustomed level of performance. Besides, the 1953 Red Sox weren't going anywhere. Ted wanted to go fishing.

He received a call from Baseball Commissioner Ford Frick asking if he'd throw out the ball for the All-Star game in Cincinnati. Williams agreed, still

The real John Wayne. (National Baseball Library, Cooperstown, N.Y.)

Signing a contract for the remainder of the 1953 season on July 29, with Joe Cronin and Tom Yawkey at Yawkey's Fenway Park office. (Photograph by Laban Whitaker, courtesy of the Whitaker family)

unsure about returning to the game. His business manager, Fred Corcoran, had invested in a fishing tackle business with Sam Snead, the golfer, and Ted found the prospect of fishing for a living tempting.

The reception he received in Cincinnati made him reconsider. The fans went wild, and even the players pleaded with Ted to return. DiMaggio had long since retired, and Williams was the biggest star in the game. His return would help everyone.

Ted needed the money. Two years at a serviceman's salary had cut into savings, even with the investments. Corcoran advised Ted to return to baseball, at least for a few years, and make some money.

He still might not have returned to baseball if not for his wife Doris. The marriage suffered while Ted was away. He simply hadn't been around, and that took its toll. Baseball looked more inviting every day.

On July 29, 1953, Williams returned to Boston and signed a contract for the remainder of the season. He said it felt good to get out in the sun and swing the bat again, even if his hands blistered and bled under the effort. For Ted, it was good to play ball. It told him who he was.

Williams returned to action, unannounced, before a crowd of just over 6,000 fans at Fenway Park, on August 6, pinch-hitting for Tom Umphlett against the Browns' Marlin Stuart. He popped up.

Ted continued to pinch-hit occasionally while working his way into shape. When he finally returned to the lineup for good, it was as if he never left. For the remainder of the season Ted went on the longest sustained power streak of his career. Quipped one writer, "Williams has set spring training back ten years."

Ted finished the year with a .407 average in only 91 at bats. Thirteen of his 37 hits were home runs, good enough for second on the club and accounting for most of his 34 RBIs. His slugging percentage was a remarkable .901.

The Red Sox were not so spectacular, finishing fourth, 16 games behind New York. The pitching, for once, did the job, but without Williams, the Red Sox simply lacked punch. For much of the rest of the decade the Red Sox story would be much the same. The club would perform at or near .500 and never, with one notable exception, be in the race. For most of the fifties there was only one team that mattered—the Yankees. Everybody else played for second.

Ted returned to fishing with a vengeance in the off-season. Things still weren't going well at home. In December he entered the International Sailfish Tournament in West Palm Beach and took top honors.

Williams was no Sunday fisherman. He practiced the art just as he had practiced baseball; tying his own flies, studying scientific literature about the habits of various fish, and picking the best fishing brains for insight into the

Leo Egan, of WBZ radio, interviews the returning hero. (Courtesy of the Boston Globe)

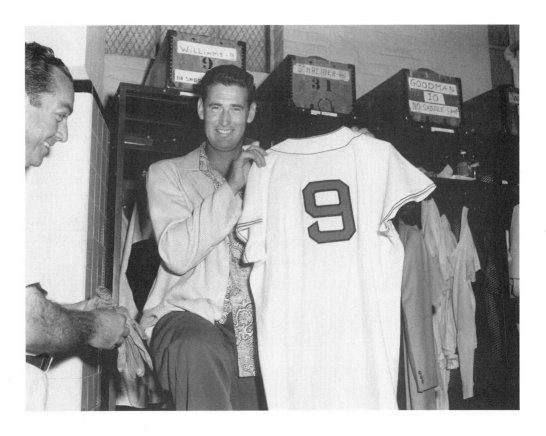

Number 9 is back! Ted, with Johnny Orlando, at his Fenway Park locker. Orlando was one of Ted's best friends, and the man who assigned number 9 to Williams in 1939. (Photograph by Laban Whitaker, courtesy of the Whitaker family)

August 6, 1953–Getting in some batting practice prior to his first game since returning. Initially he saw duty as a pinch hitter. (Photograph by Laban Whitaker, courtesy of the Whitaker family)

craft. He was determined to be the best. Ted was already a master caster and his accumulated knowledge impressed everyone, even professional fishing guides. More and more, Ted gravitated toward the world of fishing, making friends with other fishermen, and leaving baseball alone from October to March.

On January 22, 1954, Doris Williams filed for divorce, citing a six-year "course of conduct" that had made her life "an intolerable burden." Two weeks later reports surfaced linking Williams to another woman, but he denied marriage reports. After the initial charges, neither Williams nor Doris made further comment, but left the matter to attorneys.

Williams was getting older. He now weighed 215 and the once thin body had thickened. Ted wasn't fat, but he'd filled out. He reported to spring training in Sarasota on March 1, determined to get in shape and leave his personal problems behind. Fifteen minutes later spring training ended for Ted Williams. Moments after taking the field, he raced after a line drive by Hoot Evers, stumbled as the ball fell short, and rolled onto his shoulder.

Ted felt and heard something snap. "I've broke it," he called to teammate Jim Piersall. His collarbone had snapped in two.

Williams returned to Boston and underwent surgery. His collarbone was reinforced with a permanent, four-inch, stainless steel pin. Ted's season wasn't over, but the forced inactivity frustrated him.

For years publishers had been after Ted to author his life story, but Williams always refused. With nothing else to do, and for $25,000, he agreed to

author a series for the *Saturday Evening Post,* to be ghostwritten by Joe Reichler and Joe Trimble. The decision wasn't surprising. Many ballplayers had coauthored similar stories. But Ted's subject matter shocked everyone. The story appeared in April and was entitled "This Is My Last Year." Ted Williams was planning to retire.

The story served several purposes. By working with Reichler, a New York writer, Ted delivered a none-too-subtle slight to the contingent of Boston writers he hated. They'd pursued him for similar stories for years. By giving the story to a member of the enemy camp, Williams scored a point. He was also worried about the divorce.

As the proceedings continued, it became clear that Doris was not going to let Ted walk away without getting what she felt she deserved financially. Williams didn't share her perspective, but if he retired, Doris couldn't count on his baseball income in any settlement.

Fifteen minutes into the first day of spring training in 1954, Williams broke his collarbone. (Courtesy of the Boston Globe)

Red Sox trainer Jack Fadden tends to the sutures of Ted's collarbone surgery. Williams returned to action ahead of schedule on May 16 in Detroit, where he went 8 for 9 in a doubleheader, hitting 2 home runs and driving in 7 runs in a legendary performance.
(Photograph by Leslie Jones, Boston Public Library)

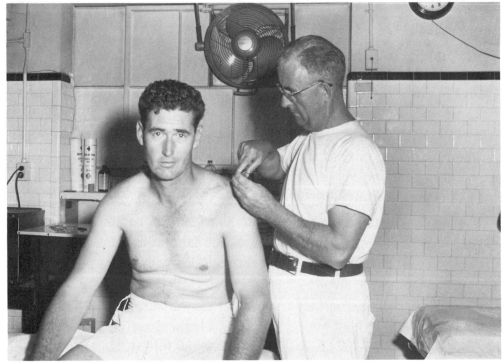

There were other factors. The Sox had changed and all his friends—Doerr, DiMaggio, and Pesky—were gone. Boudreau was playing kids, and Ted hardly knew who they were. The war had sapped Williams of energy. He wasn't sure he still cared to deal with the pressure, from writers or anyone else, for very much longer.

Reaction in Boston was predictable. The writers blasted away at Williams, abandoning any remnant of goodwill they had felt toward him since his return from Korea. They saw the story as Ted's way of saying, "Nothing has changed."

The writers agreed, and let Ted know it. Bill Cunningham wrote that Williams "says it all when he says that 'I haven't changed.' He came into baseball a sour mixed-up kid wearing chips for epaulettes . . . [and] despite fame, fortune, and the impact of two wars, that's what he still is sixteen years later." Dave Egan echoed Cunningham's charges, writing, "The Red Sox would be well-served by Williams if he should make his retirement retroactive. . . . One like him is enough."

In what appeared to Ted to be his last major league at bat, he homered off Washington pitcher Constantine Kerizazkos. (Courtesy of the Boston Red Sox)

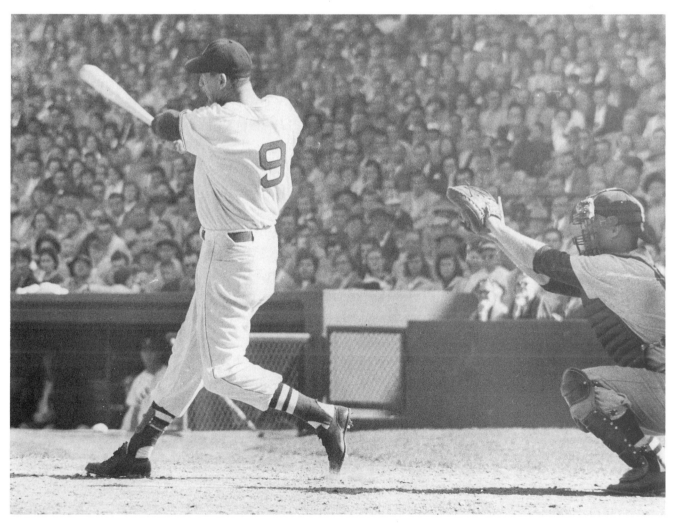

Most fans responded with cynical disbelief, as did the Red Sox. They all expected Ted to change his mind.

Williams returned to the lineup and went 8–9 in a doubleheader against Detroit. It made little difference. The Red Sox were terrible.

By the end of June the club was in last place. Cleveland was having a superb season, eventually winning 111 games and finishing 43 games ahead of the Red Sox, who struggled to finish in sixth place at 69–85. All the while Ted Williams insisted his retirement was real.

On September 26 he played what should have been his last ballgame, in front of only 14,175 people, on a damp, cold day at Fenway Park. For any other player of his stature, in any other season, the event would have been surrounded with appropriate pomp, but few took Williams at his word. Only the *Globe* bothered running anything like a tribute.

The crowd reacted quietly most of the game, finally stirring in the seventh when Williams raced down a drive by Washington's Pete Runnels and made a fine catch. Realizing that perhaps Ted really *was* retiring, they began to cheer.

Ted led off the Boston seventh against Washington pitcher Constantine Keriazakos. Williams swung at the first pitch and the ball sailed to right, landing in the fifth row of the grandstand. In what appeared to be his final major league at bat, Williams homered.

The crowd rose as one and cheered as Williams raced, head down, around the bases for the 366th time in his career. But Keriazakos was no All-Star, and the Sox battered him for 4 more runs.

Ted came up again in the eighth, this time facing a pitcher with the unlikely name of Bunky Stewart. Stewart induced Ted to pop up. Williams took his position in left to open the ninth, then was replaced by Karl Olson. The crowd cheered and Ted ran into the dugout, his head down and his cap on. Williams finished the year with a .345 average and 136 walks in only 117 games. Due to his low number of at bats, Ted failed to qualify for the batting title, but he came so close the rule was later changed.

After the game Williams reiterated his plan to retire. "I've decided that's it," he told the writers, adding, "There was only one of you I really hated." Then he left for Maine. Baseball season was over. Fishing season was already under way.

In the spring of 1955 Williams was in Florida, but only because of the bonefish and tarpon. In the off-season the Red Sox replaced Boudreau with Mike "Pinky" Higgins and prepared to play their first season without Williams.

In left field they installed Faye Throneberry, brother of the infamous "Marvelous" Marv Throneberry of the 1962 New York Mets. With nothing to lose Higgins initiated wholesale changes in the Red Sox lineup, particularly the pitching staff, where only four of ten hurlers had previously completed a full big league season.

During his "retirement," Ted caught rays instead of fly balls during spring training of 1955.
(Courtesy of the Boston Globe)

All spring the Sox and baseball writers kept a watch out for Williams, expecting him to show up and start playing, as he had so many years before. But Williams stayed away, out of the spotlight, all the while insisting his retirement was for real.

The Red Sox opened the season in Baltimore on April 12 without Williams, and managed to go 8–8 during April. But in May, Faye Throneberry began to hit more like his brother Marv and the Sox went into a tailspin. Worse yet, over the first month of the season, attendance at Fenway Park was down some 70,000. The Sox were desperate for Williams.

If Ted wanted to return, he was running out of time. On May 12 rosters had to be cut to 25 active players. If Williams remained inactive, the Sox had no choice but to place him on the voluntarily retired list. Then he would be ineligible to return for another 60 days.

The break came just in time. On May 9 Williams's divorce decree became final. The Sox were tipped off and put him on the roster, taking him off the restricted list. All that was stopping Ted from returning was the financial settlement of the divorce.

On May 11 in Miami, Circuit Court Judge George E. Holt awarded the ex-Mrs. Williams $50,000, the house in Miami worth $42,000, $9,000 in attorney fees, and $100 per month child support for Barbara Joyce. The settlement cost Ted well over $100,000.

Ted returns to Boston after several months of "retirement." (Courtesy of The Brearley Collection)

Tom Yawkey welcomes Williams back to Boston on May 13, where he signed a contract for $98,000. Attendance at Fenway had dropped dramatically in the slugger's absence. (Photograph by Leslie Jones, courtesy of the Jones family)

Now larger, and no longer a splendid splinter, Williams had to work especially hard to stay in shape. Here he's shown jogging in Fenway Park with John Pohlmeyer, a club employee. (Courtesy of the Boston Globe)

Williams didn't have that kind of money. His years in the service had cost him, and while he was comfortable, he was by no means ready to retire. He was also beginning to wonder about his place in baseball history. While his career marks were admirable, his time in the service had cost his cumulative totals. In the record books, Ted was still a sizable notch below his boyhood heros. He was not yet an immortal. On May 13, Ted returned to Boston and signed a contract for $98,000. He started working out immediately.

Freed from the responsibility of marriage, Williams was able to concentrate on the two things he loved best, almost to the exclusion of everything else, baseball and fishing. At his age, preparing for baseball season required more and more effort. He spent the rest of his Boston baseball career sequestered in a private suite at the Somerset Hotel, not allowing himself to be distracted. In the off-season, it was all fishing. Ted purchased a cottage in Islamorada in the Florida Keys, near his favorite fishing spots. Later, he purchased a similar camp in New Brunswick, on the Miramichi River.

But for now it was all baseball. Williams made his first appearance in uniform on May 23, before a Fenway Park crowd of 23,323 in an exhibition against the Giants. Too anxious in his first at bat, Ted popped up a 3–0 pitch. In his next at bat, he came back all the way, smacking a delivery from pitcher Paul Giel 385 feet into the bleachers in right. For a change, the Sox won, 4–3.

Williams wasn't yet satisfied with his condition and waited several more days before officially returning to action on May 28 against Washington. He didn't take long to get going, throwing a runner out at second on the game's

*Williams, a big boxing
fan, shows Willie Pep
how he hits 'em.*
(Courtesy of The Brearley
Collection)

first play and singling in the first inning of a 5–3 Red Sox loss. The following
night Williams doubled and tripled, leading the Sox to a 12–7 win. All of a
sudden, the silent Red Sox bats started booming. Ted was back and he brought
everyone else with him.

Williams's importance in the Sox's youthful lineup cannot be overexag-
gerated. Ted was constantly on base, by hit or walk, and suddenly hitters Norm
Zauchin, Jackie Jensen, and Jimmy Piersall were being pitched to instead of
around. Williams always got along well with younger players, and took time
to offer encouragement. Batting in the presence of the game's greatest hitter,
the other players tried harder and produced better results.

The Sox took off, playing the best baseball in the major leagues, winning
44 of their next 60 ballgames. In June Ted contracted pneumonia and missed
two weeks, but the Sox continued to win. At the break they'd pulled within 7
games of New York. By mid-August the Yankees' lead was down to 1½ games.
For the next three weeks the Sox stalked the Yankees, unable to overtake the
team from the Bronx but gamely hanging on.

Too many good pitching performances in April and May had been wasted.
The staff broke down and the Red Sox fell back, finishing the year in fourth
place at 84–70, 12 games behind the Yankees. Nevertheless the club improved
on their 1954 record by a full 16 games.

The 1955 Red Sox featured the outfield trio of (left to right) Williams, Piersall, and Jensen. Note the black armbands in memory of Harry Agganis, who died in June of that season. Many have compared this outfield trio to the great unit of Tris Speaker, Harry Hooper, and Duffy Lewis from the Red Sox glory years of 1912–1916. (Photograph by Leslie Jones, Boston Public Library)

At age thirty-seven, Ted batted .356 with 28 homers in 98 games and had much to smile about. (Photograph by Laban Whitaker, courtesy of the Whitaker family)

Forty-one games without Ted Williams was 41 games too many. With Williams's bat in the lineup all season, the Sox might have won the pennant. Williams finished with 28 home runs and a .356 average in only 98 games. His slugging percentage of .703 was his best since 1941. He was 37 years old and getting better.

The year passed quietly for Ted. Fans and writers alike seemed to take a different, more appreciative attitude toward him. Yet if Williams thought that his days of controversy had passed, the 1956 season was to be a rude reawakening.

The Sox let Ted set his own pace in the spring of 1956, satisfied if Ted was able to appear in 100 games or so. The club was a year older, and, everyone thought, a year better.

They were certainly a year older, but were no longer the hustling, overachieving ballclub of 1955. Higgins didn't show much patience with the young club and they never got in gear, getting off to their accustomed slow start and staying around .500 most of the year as the Yankees raced home. The excitement was left to Ted.

Williams got back in the headlines in March. Dodger pitcher Johnny Podres, fresh off two World Series wins, had just been reclassified from 4F to 1A and made eligible for the draft. Reminded of his own situation in World War II, Williams blasted what he called "gutless politicians, gutless draft boards, and gutless sportswriters," for taking advantage of Podres's sudden notoriety. "Podres is paying the penalty for being a star," said Williams. Ted was criticized for the blast, but its major effect was in ticking off the writers.

Williams started slowly in 1956, battling an April instep injury, and hitting only .256 at the end of May with no home runs. People started whispering, and writers started printing out loud, that Ted was over the hill. As usual, Williams responded in his own inimitable fashion.

Ted made headlines at spring training with his remarks about the military reclassification of Johnny Podres. Because of his military service, and enormous celebrity, he was asked to comment about his controversial remarks. (Courtesy of The Brearley Collection)

Spitting toward the press box, July 18, 1956, at Fenway Park. (The Sporting News)

Homer number 400, July 18, 1956, hit on the same night as the infamous spitting incident.
(Courtesy of The Brearley Collection)

He started hitting in mid-June and zeroed in on 400 career home runs. He hit number 400 in the second game of a doubleheader against Kansas City on July 18, knocking the ball six rows deep into the right-field grandstand to give the Sox a 1–0 victory. Ted didn't let the momentous occasion slip by. As he crossed home plate, he turned his head toward the press box and spat with schoolboy wrath, letting the writers know exactly what he thought.

They didn't take the bait, although the *Herald* did publish a picture of Ted in mid-expectoration on page one. The occasion of Ted's 400th home run was no time to battle with the hitting star. Neither was Joe Cronin Night three days later, when Ted repeated the performance. It was as if Williams was intentionally goading the writers, but first in deference to Ted, and then Cronin, they let it pass. Their revenge would come later.

On August 7 the Red Sox played host to New York; 36,530 fans filled Fenway Park, the largest crowd since World War II. For ten innings Sox pitcher Williard Nixon battled the Yankees' Don Larsen, and neither team was able to push a run across the plate. In the top of the eleventh inning, Mickey Mantle lifted a high fly ball toward Ted in left. Williams camped under the ball, then watched it bounce from his glove to the ground. Mantle got to second and the crowd started to boo.

Yogi Berra was up next. Nixon was tiring and Berra looped a line drive to left center. Williams raced back, reached the wall, and snagged the drive, preserving the scoreless tie.

Ted trotted to the dugout to an earsplitting ovation that wrankled him. He couldn't stand to be booed one moment and cheered the next. To Ted, the crowd's reaction smacked of front-running, and he hated front-runners.

A few steps from the dugout Williams stopped, puckered his lips, and spat toward the crowd along first base. Then he turned toward third and did it again before storming into the dugout, head down. The crowd hooted and booed, confirming Ted's assessment of the depth of their convictions.

There was still a ballgame to be played. Nixon led off for the Sox and reached on an error. Billy Goodman put down a bunt toward first. Moose Skowron fielded it and threw to second to get the lead runner, but the throw sailed wide. Everyone was safe. Billy Klaus stretched the count to 3–1, then walked to load the bases.

Up came Ted. The Yankees pulled Larsen and brought in left-hander Tommy Byrne. Again the crowd booed. It was time for Ted to explode.

Byrne pitched carefully and ran the count to three balls. The next pitch was off the plate and Williams walked. Nixon chugged home with the game winner and the crowd went wild.

That was too much for Ted. He tossed his bat some thirty or forty feet in the air and stomped to first. He'd wanted to hit, to swing and silence the crowd, to show them the error of their ways. Instead he walked. He was mad. He was frustrated. He was angry with himself and everyone else.

A fan ran onto the field to congratulate Ted, but was intercepted by umpire Ed Rommel, probably saving the man from either a good thrashing or an unwanted shower.

Reaction was swift and immediate.

In New York Tom Yawkey was listening to the game on radio and heard Mel Allen describe the incident. Boston announcer Curt Gowdy was looking the other way so Boston listeners learned about the incident in the papers the next day. Yawkey called Cronin and demanded something be done. They'd warned Ted on Joe Cronin Day that such behavior had to stop. They decided to fine Ted $5,000, the largest fine in baseball since the Yankees slapped Babe Ruth with a $5,000 fee after breaking curfew in 1925.

Dubbed "the Great Expectoration," the incident was reported in Boston newspapers with unbridled zeal. The *Record* ran a photo of Ted in mid-spit on page one. It was the biggest story in Boston since the Brink's robbery and the local press played it for full impact.

Harold Kaese called for Williams to retire, writing, "Ted Williams should do himself a favor. He should quit baseball before baseball quits him. He is getting too old for the game — old physically and mentally. His body is wearing out and so, apparently, is his nervous system. He never could take it well. Now he is near the point where he can't take it at all.

Despite his on-field antics, Ted was still a hero to the kids of New England. (Photograph by Leslie Jones, Boston Public Library)

Family night, 1956—Ted displays his sense of humor following his hitting a homer against Baltimore. His closed-mouth "speak no evil" pantomime was reported in every paper in New England, and helped him recapture the affection of the fans. (Courtesy of The Brearley Collection)

Dave Egan, referring to Williams as "T. Wms. Esq.," was equally direct. "A kid with a small *k* would be spanked and sent to his room for doing the same thing that this man of almost forty has done consistently, and this seems to indicate the man is sick . . . it will be a good day for the Red Sox when he retires and stays retired." Even ex-Baseball Commissioner Happy Chandler got into the act, saying Williams had a "persecution complex."

Ted was unrepentant, telling reporters, "I'd spit again at the same people who booed me today. I wouldn't be at the ballpark tomorrow if I could stand a fine of $5,000 a day. Get those quotes right. This is probably my last year." The apology was left to Cronin to issue. "I've talked with Ted," he said, "and the minute he had done it he was doggone sorry." No one believed a word Cronin said.

The next day 33,338 fans turned up for Family Night, wondering if Ted was going to do anything appropriate for family viewing. During warmups and the game's first few innings the crowd cheered him politely, wondering what he'd do. Then the remarkable happened.

With the game tied at 2–2, Williams came to the plate against Baltimore pitcher Connie Johnson. Johnson threw, Williams swung, and a towering fly ball sailed over the fence in right for a home run.

The crowd roared as Williams circled the bases, then quieted. He crossed home plate and slowed as he approached the dugout, just as he had done before turning to the stands and spitting the night before. Thirty thousand pairs of eyes stared at Ted intently, waiting to see if he'd do it again.

With the consummate skill of a trained mime, Williams stretched out his arm, and in a grand gesture, clamped his hand over his mouth. Polite cheers turned into raucous laughter. Thirty thousand people smiled. In the dugout, it was all Williams could do to contain a grin of his own.

In one fell swoop Williams regained the fans he'd alienated the night before. Over the next few days they came to his defense in a growing crescendo. Even though they had helped instigate his outburst, they seemed to understand his behavior. Everyone, at one time or another, has wanted to thumb his or her nose at the world. Williams did it, said he meant it, and in a moment of pure comedy, forgave everybody. Everybody, of course, except the writers.

While they continued to pound away at Ted by typewriter, Williams now seemed immune to their attacks. Public opinion rested squarely on his side. From that moment on, the cheers inevitably drowned out the occasional boo. Williams was now a treasure, no longer an object of misguided ridicule. It was as if two lovers, after a long estrangement, decided to go on a second, extended honeymoon. Suddenly, almost everybody in Boston loved Ted Williams.

The writers turned defensive. They justifiably felt they'd helped his career with their unending attention, but were unwilling to admit they occasionally went overboard, grinding their sometimes private axes in print before thousands. But ever so slowly, they too would begin to look at Williams in a different light.

The remainder of the season passed quietly. Williams gave Mantle a race for the batting crown, but the Yankee slugger hit .354. Ted finished at .345. The Sox finished fourth.

Williams resumed his fall and winter ritual of fishing. Despite the early difficulties, 1956 had been a satisfying year. In his year-end sports review, Harold Kaese, who only four months before had called for Williams's retirement, ate crow. Williams, he wrote, "fought the Battle of the Draft Boards, the Battle of the Instep, the Battle of the Pttt, and the Battle of the Batting Average, winning all but the last."

When Williams arrived at spring training in March of 1957, it was as if someone had turned back the clock. The Kid was back. Not that Williams looked as he had some fifteen or twenty years before, but for the first time in recent memory, Ted was again the irrepressible character he had been his first few seasons with the Sox. Indeed, the 1957 season was to play out in rough imitation of 1941.

On his first swing at the first pitch he saw with his first day of camp, Ted shattered his bat. If that were an omen, it meant that batting marks were going to be broken by Ted all season. He took his time getting in shape, not appearing in an exhibition until March 17, when he doubled his first time up.

Ted with Mickey Mantle, 1956 American League MVP and triple crown winner. As DiMaggio's successor, the young Yankee center fielder was invariably compared with Williams. (Courtesy of The Brearley Collection)

Being interviewed by a young Howard Cosell at Sarasota. (National Baseball Library, Cooperstown, N.Y.)

A week later the Sox traveled to California to play three exhibitions in San Francisco before traveling to San Diego.

Ted hadn't been home in years. His mother, May, was supposed to attend a game. Unbelievably, she had yet to see Ted play in the major leagues. Unfortunately, May became sick and missed the game. Except for the rare television appearance, May Williams never saw her son play for the Red Sox.

Heading back east, on March 31, the Sox flight was delayed in New Orleans. While waiting in the airport lounge, Williams had an informal chat with Crozier Duplantier, sports editor of the *New Orleans States,* and writer Hy Hurwitz of the *Globe.* Williams should have known there was no such thing as an informal chat with a sportswriter. The next day Ted's conversation was big news all across the country.

Ted and Duplantier had talked about the service, and Ted was asked about Korea. Williams launched into a rambling diatribe about his recall. "I wouldn't have resented it," he told Crozier, "if they'd recalled everyone in the same position as myself, but they didn't. They picked on me because I was a ballplayer and widely known." Ted blamed "gutless politicians" for his fate and said he had "no use" for the Marine Corps.

When other writers collared Williams after the story broke, he didn't back down but added to his list of grievances, tossing gasoline on the growing controversy. The Red Sox hurriedly issued a mimeographed apology, but when Williams met the press again he reiterated his earlier remarks and blasted the government for harassing boxer Joe Louis over back taxes.

It took ex-President Harry Truman and a telegraph to the Marines from Ted to end the controversy. Truman said Williams's statements didn't bother him, and, "he's a great ballplayer. I like to watch him." In a wire to General George Pate, Williams said, "My four years in the corps are the proudest of my life. . . . I will always be a Marine at heart." To close the door on the incident, Ted did the sensible thing: he shut up.

For the rest of the season Ted was a virtual clam. It kept away distractions and he again staked claim to the title of baseball's greatest hitter.

In the season opener against Baltimore, Williams collected two singles, the thirteenth consecutive season Ted had opened the season with a hit. He remained hot, starting the year with a batting streak of eight games and a .455 average. In May he was slowed by a cold, but snapped back with a remarkable performance.

On May 8 in Chicago's Comiskey Park, Williams homered in the first and duplicated the feat in the third, for his fifth straight hit and eleventh consecutive time reaching base. The streak ended with a flyout, but in the eighth Ted cracked another home run, his third of the day, lifting his average to .443.

A mini-controversy erupted in late May but only demonstrated how the tide had turned in Ted's favor. Before a game at Fenway, Williams sat in the Red Sox bull pen with a shotgun and did his part to drive the Fenway Park

Williams, manager Pinky Higgins, and teammate Mickey Vernon discuss hitting in Sarasota, 1957. (Courtesy of the Boston Red Sox)

pigeon to extinction, shooting thirty to forty of the birds. Owner Tom Yawkey often did the same thing. But Williams was Williams, and someone reported the incident to the Massachusetts Society for the Prevention of Cruelty to Animals.

In earlier seasons, the incident would have sparked an analytical frenzy over Ted's character, personal habits, and mental condition. This time the Red Sox apologized and the incident faded. Ted was just being Ted, and for once no one blamed him.

His batting pace slowed in June and his average dropped below .400. On June 13, Williams became so disgusted with his performance in batting practice that he launched his bat into the sky. It came back to earth apparently reenergized. Facing eventual Hall-of-Famers Early Wynn and Bob Lemon, Ted went out and cracked 3 home runs, good for 5 RBIs and leading the Red Sox to a 9–3 win.

He slumped again, managing just 2 hits in his next 18 times at bat, reinforcing a season-long pattern of minitears followed by minislumps. By the All-Star break his average stood at .340, complemented by a remarkable 22 home runs.

Ted came out of the All-Star game, where he went hitless in 3 at bats, absolutely blistering. On July 23 he started a 17-game hitting streak, the second longest of his career, during which he hit .533, and his average rose toward .400. There was now serious speculation that Ted might cross the magic line again.

But on September 2, Williams was forced from the lineup with a severe chest cold. Confined to bed for over a week, he returned to pinch-hit on September 16, smacking a 2-run homer off the Athletics' Tom Morgan to tie the score in an eventual 9–8 Red Sox win. Two days later, he pinch-hit again and hit another home run, this time off the Yankees' Whitey Ford. On September 21 he returned to the starting lineup and cracked a second-inning grand slam against the Yankees. Ted walked in his next three appearances, as he did in his first at bat against Tom Sturdivant the next day. Then he hit *another* home run, his fourth in a row, spread across a week. Cracked Williams after the game, "I feel horrible, but every time I take a swing the ball goes out of the park."

It was almost impossible to get Ted out. Not until September 24 against Washington, when he grounded out in his first appearance, did anyone retire Ted, as he set a record by reaching base safely 16 consecutive times.

Williams ended the year with a flourish, winning the batting title with a .388 average. In the month of September, he went 12–19, a .632 average, and hit 5 home runs. In his last 31 plate appearances, Williams reached base 25 times.

At age 40, he became the oldest batting champion. His .388 was the highest average in the major leagues since his own .401 in 1941, as was his slugging percentage of .731. His 38 home runs were his most since 1949. Had Ted been able to leg out 5 more hits, he'd have hit .400.

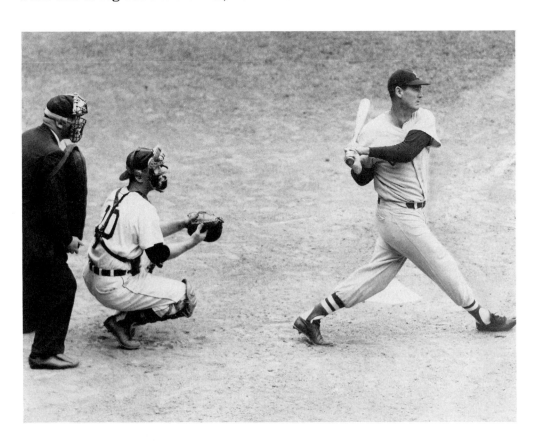

At age forty, Williams still had a .388 swing. In many ways, this was his greatest season, as his experience as a hitter more than made up for his diminished physical skills. (Courtesy of the Boston Red Sox)

Holding his silver bat signifying his 1958 batting championship. (Courtesy of the Boston Red Sox)

Nevertheless, Mickey Mantle was named American League MVP, beating Ted by thirty votes, 233 to 203. Ted finished second. The Yankees won the pennant, Red Sox finished third. The Kid went fishing.

Some things never change.

AN ARTIST IN WOOD

BY MARTIN F. NOLAN

He once said that "Baseball is one of the arts." If so, he was an artist whose achievements include memories as vivid and compelling as moonlight by Monet or a heroic marble by Michelangelo.

The monuments to and by Ted Williams could fill a museum. The dominant theme, a free-standing sculpture, would be three giant numbers—.406. This should be Everest-sized, because for six decades many have tried to conquer it. A showcase for the .344 lifetime average would be nice, plus the five other batting titles, including one he won at age 40, plus the four home run crowns and the four RBI titles.

Here in our minimalist pavilion is something most Williams-esque, the eight times he led the American League in walks. The achievement was controversial among many, from umpires to pitchers to the tradesmen Williams scornfully called "the Knights of the Keyboard." To a perfectionist like Williams, a walk was "a helluva play. It gets a runner to first base." The fabled Williams eyesight was a boon to his hitting and a bane to

pitchers. He struck out 10 percent of the time as opposed to Babe Ruth's 16 percent. Throughout the 1940s and 1950s, American League umpires created an ethereal strike zone: if Mr. Williams did not swing at it, it must have been a ball.

To a newspaper reporter, a base on balls is the essence of dullness. By extension, a batter who collects many of them, even though he be talented, must be dull, too, and probably not a good team player. Thus was another canard spread by the detractors of Ted Williams, that wretched band who eventually taught me a lesson about life and the work I was to follow.

In this dispute, my early hero-worship of Williams was justified. He knew more about baseball than his critics did. Of all the things that hero-worship taught me, nothing was more important than the lesson: don't believe everything you read in the newspapers.

As urchins from Roxbury, we would hike to the ballpark in our Bowery Boy getups. As fractious as Leo Gorcey or Huntz Hall ever were, we would

argue over the merits of various players. About Ted Williams, we never argued, except as to the proper punishment for the tabloid columnists who vilified our hero.

With intense savagery, my 9-year-old fingers would clip the offending column and paste it in the scrapbook, there to be embellished by graffiti. "Liar!" was my most eloquent or at least most frequent commentary on the commentators. In Boston, where newspaper wars made truth the first casualty, the things they wrote were patently untrue (except for the 1946 World Series, where Ted went 5 for 25 and was outhit by the St. Louis Cardinal catcher, Joe Garagiola.)

This introduction to this seamy side of newspapers was valuable to me later, after I had made newspapers my field of work. The lesson was: cowardice was unprofessional. If you tag a guy in print, fairness dictates that you show up the next day to hear his side of it. In several decades of reporting politicians, I tried to follow this code. Some of the Williams-baiters lobbed their shots from the safety of the

Portrait of the artist as a young hitter. (Photograph by Leslie Jones, courtesy of the Jones family)

press box, but shunned the locker room.

Staunch admiration of Ted Williams did not, alas, teach me the value of good deeds as news. That Ted Williams visited children in hospitals was meritorious but not newsworthy. Years later, I heard Roger Angell instruct Mike Barnicle on how to judge the character of ball-players: "They are what they do." We should judge them on how they play the game and not expect sainthood. Broken water coolers and other results of Ted's tantrums became part of the overall picture. He was a perfectionist and his anger, while regrettable, was at himself for violating his own high standards.

We excused his spitting at taunting fans in the left-field stands, even giving the finger (or, as cartoonist Bob Coyne delicately described it, "a French salute"). Among my fellow urchins, rationalizing Ted's behavior was an interruption to more agreeable pursuits, like casting the lead in "The Ted Williams Story."

After Williams Bendix starred in *The Babe Ruth Story*, we settled on Robert Ryan for the role, after many votes for John Wayne. The Duke might have been the right choice after all, for many years later, David Halberstam interviewed Ted and compared him to Wayne as an icon who lived up to his billing.

In the dismal 1960 season, I was among the Fenway faithful many times during the season, but passed up the final home game and the most impressive farewell performance since George Washington. Ted was heroic but the Red Sox were not, finishing 32 games out of first place. The presence of Williams in the fabled summer of '49 made stars seem brighter in his reflected glory. But '60 was different. Don Buddin reminded no one of Bobby Doerr. Willie Tasby was no Dom Di-Maggio.

Baseball is built on memories and Ted's stayed with me, even at the firing range in the Army. "You've got 20-10 vision, Ted Williams eyesight," the sergeant said, meaning that targets 500 yards away were easy to see. (Middle age took care of that distinction.)

The artistry of Williams, the perfectionism, was tested when he managed the Washington Senators in the late 1960s and early 1970s. I missed his final home run but I was there at RFK Stadium on Opening Day in 1969, when mellow, accommodating Teddy tipped his hat. That was news. He made hitters out of journeymen infielders Aurelio Rodriguez and Ed Brinkman, whose average plummeted 34 points after being traded to Detroit.

The legacy of every great baseball player is memories. In the Fenway area, the museum created by Theodore Samuel Williams is as impressive, eclectic, and enduring as the Isabella Stewart Gardner Museum. The phrase in Latin inscribed in St. Paul's Cathedral in London says, "*Si monumentum requiris circumspice.*" It is a tribute to the cathedral's architect, Sir Christopher Wren: "If you seek his monument, look about you."

Martin F. Nolan is editorial-page editor for the Boston Globe, *where he was a member of a team that won the Pulitzer Prize for Meritorious Public Service. As Washington bureau chief for the* Globe, *Nolan earned a spot on President Nixon's enemies list. His writings have appeared in* The Atlantic, The New York Times Book Review, National Review, *and* Washington Journalism Review.

THE FINAL SEASONS

The restoration of Ted Williams continued in the off-season. In 1957 *Look Magazine* assigned Tim Cohane to write a statistical analysis of Ted's career. Harold Kaese and Sy Siwoff of the Elias Sports Bureau were contacted to do research for the story.

When the analysis appeared late July of the 1957 season, it gave credence to the growing perception that Ted was one of the greatest hitters in the history of the game. What was most surprising, however, was that it revealed other factors that ran counter to the public perception of Williams. Williams, for example, hit more game-winning home runs than Babe Ruth.

Now armed with masses of statistical data, sportswriters began to consider Ted in his historical context. Suddenly his personality didn't seem to matter as much as his unparalleled record of performance. Not until January of 1958 did it become clear precisely how remarkable Williams had been in 1957. Three months after the season ended it was discovered Ted had broken a number of records. Williams's 3 pinch-hit home runs in September gave him a total of 7 for his career, then the American League record. He was walked

Accepting money for the Jimmy Fund with Mrs. Tom (Jean) Yawkey. Mrs. Yawkey has carried on for her late husband both in running the Red Sox and providing major support for the Jimmy Fund. She still attends every home game. (Courtesy of the Boston Globe)

intentionally 33 times in 1957, the highest figure ever recorded, although unofficially Babe Ruth may have been intentionally walked twice as many times in a season. Williams's total of 1,947 games played in a Red Sox uniform set a new team standard. Throughout the remainder of his career, Williams's watchers, particularly Kaese, would scramble to keep up with the records Ted was fast accumulating.

While Williams still spent the bulk of the winter fishing, he'd added other activities to ensure he would be in shape for the season ahead. Before going to bed, Ted spent a half-hour swinging a 50-ounce bat. He supplemented his fishing regimen with tennis. During the season Ted started to take naps before the Red Sox's increasing number of night games. He cut down on his movie watching, long a Williams staple, so his eyes wouldn't become strained. The Kid was serious about baseball.

In the off-season after 1957 Williams received more publicity, most of it favorable, than he had since the Sox glory years of the late 1940s. National magazines scrambled to produce profiles of the veteran slugger. His charity work, particularly for the Jimmy Fund, began to be recognized. Since 1956, Ted had served as a very active general chairman for the fund committee, which raised over four million dollars. One Boston paper even ran a series entitled "The Case for Ted Williams," an unthinkable notion only a few seasons earlier.

For twenty years Williams had been taken for granted and scrutinized by the press and public as if through a microscope. Now, with Williams on the verge of retirement, both stood back and looked at Ted from a distance. Everyone realized there was much more to Ted Williams than could be seen from up close. Even his personality, which so often had been described as boorish and selfish, was now seen as more an expression of Williams's own rugged individualism and determination.

In early February Ted returned to Boston and signed a contract for the 1958 season worth over $100,000. The Red Sox didn't expect a repeat of 1957, but they realized Ted was perhaps more valuable to the club than he had ever been. Fans were more excited about the prospect of seeing the great Ted Williams than they were about the not-always-so-great Red Sox. Ted had ruffled a few feathers a month before when he told an interviewer, "All the American League's got is me and the Yankees. When I leave, this league is going to be pretty damn dull." But he was right.

Signing a contract for $100,000, with Sox general manager Stanley (Bucky) Harris in 1959. (Courtesy of the Boston Red Sox)

In spring training Ted set his own pace, concentrating on getting his swing down, learning to wear a batting helmet for the first time, and waiting for an ankle, which he'd injured in the off-season, to heal. Then Ted pulled a muscle in his side, and was limited to pinch-hitting for most of the spring.

Although the injury healed, Ted wasn't in the Red Sox opening-day lineup. He was ill with a case of food poisoning from some bad oysters. A few days later he made his debut and got off to his usual slow start. By the end of April he was hitting only .219, his worst April ever, and the retirement talk started again. The Red Sox, too, were off to their worst start in twenty-five years at 4–10.

Williams would have none of it. As the weather warmed, so did he, hitting .287 in May. On May 22, Dave Egan died and the list of Williams's watchers grew shorter by one name.

In June Ted was rumored to be in line for the job of Red Sox manager. The team was struggling and Mike Higgins was in trouble. But Williams didn't want to be manager of the Red Sox. That would require talking with the press. Ted was content just as he was, swinging the bat and keeping to himself.

In a strange way Williams's approach to the game had returned to the way it had begun, in North Park in San Diego. Hitting was everything again. While Ted had long since become a more-than-adequate outfielder, particularly adept at playing the ball off Fenway's "green monster," he was no longer expected to perform miracles. With the Sox way ahead or way behind, Ted frequently left the game for a defensive replacement, which saved his energy for a more important contest. He was no longer expected to try to run the bases like a track star. Never fast, Williams had slowed considerably since returning from Korea and all an all-out effort was going to do was pull a muscle and put Ted on the bench. Hitting was his game again.

In July Williams tested the waters of controversy a final time, spitting toward the crowd in Kansas City. He was fined $250 by league president William Harridge. This time no one called for Williams to be outrighted to Siberia, and he apologized, after a fashion, saying, "I am principally sorry about the 250 dollars."

Batting second in the Red Sox batting order, just ahead of Williams, outfielder Pete Runnels took full advantage of Ted's presence in the lineup. By midseason Runnels was leading the league in hitting and looked like a shoo-in for the title.

Williams wasn't quite ready to give the award up. In August he came to life, hitting .371 to pull his average above .300 and into a virtual tie with Runnels. For most of September the two men vied for the lead game by game, at bat by at bat.

In late September Williams slumped. On September 21, the Sox hosted

Pete Runnels challenged Ted for the 1958 batting championship, falling just short at .322 to Williams's .328. (Photograph by Dick Darcy, courtesy of the photographer)

Washington at Fenway Park. Ted went hitless in his first at bat, turning an 0–7 slide into an 0–8 slump. With 2 strikes, Ted watched a Bill Fischer pitch across the heart of the plate. Williams hesitated and held up. Umpire Bill Summers called Ted out on strikes and the slump was now 0–9.

Angry at himself for not swinging, Williams turned toward the Red Sox dugout, kicking the ground and waving his hands in the air. He stopped and swung the bat again, as if going after a high fastball, and it slipped from his hands. The bat whipped boomeranglike 75 feet into the stands just to the left of the Sox dugout. The knob end struck an elderly woman squarely on the head.

Williams threw his hands into the air and raced over to the stunned woman, blubbering an apology. So, too, did Red Sox officials and medical

Ted flings his bat in response to umpire Bill Summers's calling him out on strikes, September 21, 1958. Once Williams discovered his bat had struck a lady in the third base stands, he rushed to her side and later wept in the dugout for his actions. (Courtesy of the Boston Red Sox)

Williams's bat struck Gladys Heffernan, Joe Cronin's sixty-year-old housekeeper. Fortunately for Williams, Heffernan was a big fan of his and forgave him for everything. (The Sporting News)

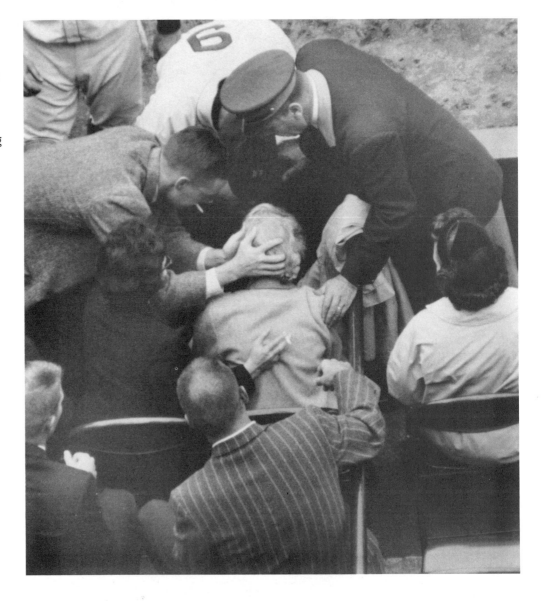

help. Bleeding from above the eye, the woman was helped from the stands and rushed to a hospital.

Williams was disconsolate. After being sent away from the stands by doctors, he sat in the dugout crying. Umpire Summers had to remind Ted to take the field. The crowd booed.

Fortunately for Williams, the woman, Gladys Heffernan, was not badly hurt, having sustained only a minor concussion. Even more fortunate was the fact that she was Joe Cronin's housekeeper and a rabid Ted Williams fan.

So what did Ted do in his next at bat? He gave Mrs. Heffernan, and everyone else, something to cheer about, smacking a long drive to the flagpole in center for a double, scoring Runnels and driving in the Sox's last run in a 2–0 win. Said the understanding Mrs. Heffernan from her hospital bed later that night, "He didn't mean it. I feel so bad for him because he's trying so hard. He's wonderful. I don't know why they booed him. Wasn't it wonderful we won the game?"

As he'd done so many times in the past, Williams used the incident for extra motivation. After striking Mrs. Heffernan, Ted hit .500 in his remaining 28 at bats for the season, including a remarkable 7 hits in his last 11 at bats. Runnels slipped to .322. Williams finished at .328 to win his sixth, and final, American League batting title.

The achievement moved Harold Kaese to write, "Aladdin had his wonderful lamp, King Arthur had Excalibur. And Ted Williams has his bat. If you are given a choice, take the bat. It is the magic wand of the century. There is

"Aladdin had his wonderful lamp, King Arthur had Excalibur. And Ted Williams has his bat."—Harold Kaese, 1958 (Photograph by Leslie Jones, Boston Public Library)

Two great hitters—Ted with Sugar Ray Robinson at a 1959 banquet. (Courtesy of The Boston Globe)

nothing fictitious or imaginary about its exploits. How often has the bat saved Williams after he has fallen overboard in public opinion? Maybe 25 or 30 times since he first joined the Sox in 1939. Williams . . . is one of the wonders of this age." Heffernan thought so, too, even before Ted sent her a $500 watch as an expression of his sorrow.

After the final game of the season Williams left for New Brunswick, where he hoped to catch the season's final hours of salmon fishing on the Miramichi River. He arrived at two-thirty in the afternoon the next day, rushed to the river, and started casting. Minutes later he hooked a twenty-pound hookbill, which he later called one of the most beautiful fish he'd ever caught. Nineteen fifty-eight was that kind of year.

As if the 40-year-old Kid were finally going to be reminded of his own mortality, 1959 was a disaster. Ted came to Boston in February for the sports show, signed a contract for $125,000, and in March headed to the Red Sox spring training camp in Scottsdale, Arizona.

His neck bothered him at the beginning of camp, but toward the end of

March started to feel better. Ted no longer made exhibition road trips, preferring to train on his own in the playgroundlike atmosphere of the practice diamonds. One day he felt so good he even volunteered to pitch batting practice. Three days later he could hardly move.

He had pinched a nerve in his neck and opened the season on the disabled list, not making an appearance until May 12. The neck wasn't right all year. Ted started out 0–7 and got worse. In June he was benched by manager Billy Jurges. The question became, as asked by Harold Kaese, "How will the Red Sox get rid of Ted Williams? . . . This is not an easy question, for such giants . . . are not easily brushed aside, even when they are age 40 and hitting around .200."

The Sox didn't know what to do. Williams pinch-hit, played against certain pitchers, and continued to struggle. By September he hardly played, collecting only 13 at bats for the month. Few expected him to return in 1960. Ted

Ted displays his Hollywood good looks at spring training. He was once approached to appear in a Hollywood western but never made the movie. (Photograph by Laban Whitaker, courtesy of the Whitaker family)

Ted and Ty Cobb discuss hitting at the Red Sox training camp at Scottsdale, Arizona. (Courtesy of the Boston Red Sox)

A pinched nerve sidelined Ted in 1959. (Courtesy of the Boston Globe)

finished the year with a .254 average, the only time in his career he hit below .317, with 10 home runs, and a slugging percentage of only .419. It looked as if the lights were ready to go out at the playground.

Tom Yawkey called Williams to his suite at the Ritz-Carlton and asked Ted what he wanted to do in 1960. Williams asked Yawkey what *he* wanted Williams to do. "I think you ought to quit," answered Yawkey.

This was not the right answer. Williams was miffed. He wanted to play but only if he was wanted. Ted spent the winter fishing and wondering what the hell was going on and what he was going to do. That Doris Williams had him back in court in an attempt to raise his child support payments didn't make him feel any better.

Ted went back to Boston in February for the Sportsman's Show unsure of the reception he would get at Fenway Park. When he met with Dick O'Connell, Ted found a contract was already filled out in his name.

Williams balked. Over the winter he'd had an idea. "I had a lousy year, the worst I ever had," he told O'Connell. "I don't deserve what I made last year. I've gone from nothing on this club to making $125,000 a year. I want to take the biggest cut ever given a player."

It was pure Teddy Ballgame, answering his own self-doubt, marching to his own beat, being his own person no matter what it cost. He signed a deferred contract, as he'd done the last several seasons, valued at $90,000.

The neck still bothered him, but Williams was on a mission. Everyone suspected this would be Ted's last year. His accomplishments took on special import. On opening day in Washington, Williams launched a 450-foot home run to center field off one of the best pitchers in the league, Camilio Pasqual. The home run was one of the longest of Williams's career and tied him with Lou Gehrig for fourth place on the all-time list with 493. The next day in Boston, Ted hit another off the Yankees' Jim Coates, passing Gehrig and setting a personal record by opening the season with home runs in both road and home openers.

Williams was 41 years old. Trotting around the bases, he pulled a muscle and missed nearly a month, then caught his annual virus. Williams contemplated retiring but couldn't. He didn't return to action until late May.

The rest of the 1960 season was a dream. Ted hit as though he were playing "Big League" again. While the Red Sox gave him plenty of rest, Williams hit home runs in bunches. On June 17 he smacked number 500 to left in Cleveland off Wynn Hawkins. By July 4, Ted was the league's hottest hitter. He belted a home run off Kansas City's Dick Hall to break a 1–1 tie and lead the Sox to a 13–2 win. The homer was his 12th in his last 80 at bats, the best sustained streak of his career.

Ted returned to action in May 1960, to finish his career with a flourish. (Courtesy of the Boston Red Sox)

By August Ted was pressing the leaders for the batting title, though it was obvious he'd lack the requisite number of plate appearances to qualify. Williams was playing a different game, one that was not defined by money, by wins and losses, or even by records. His game was greater. It was private and personal. He wasn't playing for a reason, he was playing for love of just being able to play, even if that love manifested itself, more often than not, in an equal measure of excruciating, physical labor. His shoulder bothered him and he thought about retiring again, but it was Ted's turn to hit and he didn't want to get out of the cage.

On August 10 in Cleveland, Williams hit home run number 512, third on the all-time list behind one man, Babe Ruth, whose picture once adorned Ted's bedroom wall, and another, Jimmie Foxx, whose muscles Ted had marveled at as a fresh rookie twenty-two years before.

Player of the Decade. Williams outpolled such stars as Willie Mays, Mickey Mantle, and Jackie Robinson.
(Courtesy of the San Diego Hall of Champions)

The Sporting News made a surprise announcement. It named Ted Williams baseball's "Player of the Decade." The award meant a lot to Williams. It made up for some of the MVP snubs and Ted took particular delight in the fact it came during the last half of his career. In 1951 people thought Ted would be too old to return after Korea. They had been wrong. The award meant Williams stood alone as the best player of a decade that featured Mickey Mantle, Eddie Mathews, Willie Mays, Hank Aaron, and Stan Musial.

In September, Ted belted a home run off Detroit's Don Lee. Twenty years before he'd homered off Lee's father, Thornton. A nice symmetry was taking hold.

Ted spurned various efforts to honor him as the Red Sox made their last circuit around the league. This was Ted's moment. There would be no time for front-runners.

On September 26, Red Sox publicist Jack Malaney read a statement by Tom Yawkey announcing Williams's retirement, effective at the end of the season. Ted delayed his final announcement until New York clinched the pennant over

Baltimore, not wanting the decision to have any impact on the pennant race. Yawkey stated Williams would attend spring training in 1961 as batting instructor under manager Mike Higgins, which confirmed that Higgins would remain as Sox manager.

Williams had no comment. He had hardly spoken to the press all year. That fact, combined with the Sox statement he would attend spring training, led many to believe Ted might remain active in 1961. The *Globe* ended its story on the announcement with a disclaimer, "That's what the announcement claims."

A few days earlier the Sox had actually offered Ted the position of Red Sox general manager, but Williams refused, unsure if he was qualified for the job or could stand doing it. The instructor's slot was a compromise.

On September 27, the Orioles came to Fenway Park for the last two home games of the Red Sox season. The club would finish with a three-game series in New York, and as far as anyone knew, so would Ted.

The Red Sox were terrible that day, losing 17–3. Ted came to bat three times, grounding out, popping up, and walking.

A few rushed plans took shape to give Ted a send-off the next day. Boston Mayor John Collins decided to declare "Ted Williams Day," and present several thousand dollars to the Jimmy Fund in Ted's honor, but that was about it. The Red Sox made no plans. As they had his entire career, the Sox front office provided little in the way of publicity help for Ted. That was Ted's concern, and Ted didn't care much for publicity.

Still, it is strange the Red Sox decided to wait until the very day of Wil-

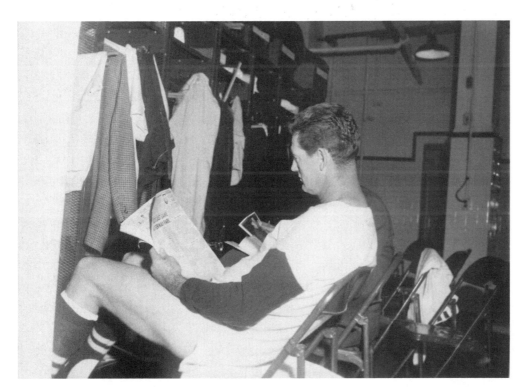

Ted reading a story on his retirement while sitting at his locker on his last day as a player. (Courtesy of The Brearley Collection)

liams's last appearance in Fenway Park to announce a major shake-up in the front office. On a day you'd expect the papers to be filled with Williams's tributes, the Sox blew Williams out of the headlines. Yawkey fired general manager Bucky Harris, gave manager Mike Higgins Harris's personnel duties, and named Dick O'Connell business manager.

Harris and Higgins hadn't gotten along since the spring of 1959, when Harris wanted Higgins to start the season with Elijah "Pumpsie" Green, the Sox first black player, at second base. Higgins refused. Harris took the heat from the press and never forgave Higgins. Yawkey apparently decided Higgins deserved a larger role.

At the same time the club announced outfielder Jackie Jensen would return in 1961. Despite leading the league in RBIs in 1958 and 1959, Jensen had retired in 1960 because of his fear of flying. That he decided to return at the precise time Williams decided to retire led some to falsely conclude the reason Jensen had left wasn't fear of air travel, but fear of Ted. On the morning of September 28, Ted Williams's last game was only the third biggest Red Sox story of the day.

The night before, Williams helped ex-Sox catcher Sammy White inaugurate a new bowling alley in Brighton, posing for a few photos, including one with White and Jackie Jensen, and bowling a few frames. Ted did nothing special on his last night as a player.

Williams was determined not to break character his last day in uniform. He would not be a front-runner, not even for himself. He got to the park early and chased out a few sportswriters who violated the pregame writers ban. He took his time, as he always did now, in preparing for the game, and emerged from the dugout at 12:25, only 35 minutes before the one o'clock start.

Fenway Park that day was anything but the "lyric little band-box of a ballpark . . . like the inside of an old-fashioned peeping type Easter egg," as later described by John Updike in his oft-quoted essay "Hub Fans Bid Kid Adieu." The sky was gray and low over the left-field wall, and the air was clammy but cool, a bit of Boston Harbor lapping at the edge of history. A few thousand early-arriving fans mulled around the grandstand, more packed into the section behind the Sox dugout. The bleachers were almost deserted. Only a couple of hundred Ted fanatics braved the elements behind "Williamsburg."

When Williams stepped from the dugout he was met with cheers from those few thousand, and a swirling mob of writers and photographers. Ted put them off with his best imitation of himself, snapping at reporters to leave him alone and refusing to pose for any pictures except for a few, favored photographers. The writers got nothing. Most got the message and went to Yawkey's office to get the official word about Jensen.

Williams did a brief television interview for a Boston television station and then started to warm up, tossing the ball back and forth a couple of dozen times with Pumpsie Green. Then Williams went into the dugout while a microphone was hurriedly placed on the field near home plate.

The stands were as full as they were going to get that day, although in time many thousands more would claim to have been in attendance. The weather, the uncertainty of Ted's retirement, and the weekday afternoon start combined to keep the crowd down. Most in the crowd were retirees, kids who'd cut school, and women. Some men may have found fault with Ted over the years, but to women, Williams still had the magnetism of a movie star.

The cheers started again as Williams and a small entourage gathered around the mike. Sox announcer Curt Gowdy spoke first. "As we all know," he said, his voice echoing oddly through the heavy air, "this is the final home game for—in my opinion and most of yours—the greatest hitter who ever lived, Ted Williams. Twenty years ago a skinny kid from San Diego came to the Red Sox camp. . . ."

Gowdy went on, detailing the highlights of Ted's career, while the crowd stood and watched the highlights in the mind's eye, the hits, the spits, the thrown bats, the home runs, the skinny kid loping through the outfield waving his cap at the crowd. The images flashed by quickly, too quickly, hardly seeming to share a place now with the looming, 42-year-old man standing on the field, motionless, the legendary, mystical number 9 on his back.

Continued Gowdy, "I don't think we'll ever see another one like him."

The Boston Chamber of Commerce presented Ted with another imitation Revere Bowl, just like the one he'd received before going to Korea. Boston Mayor John Collins officially proclaimed "Ted Williams Day," and gave Ted a check for the Jimmy Fund.

All the while, as if oblivious of the occasion, Baltimore starting pitcher Steve Barber played catch along the sidelines, trying to stay warm. Standing beside him was a messenger of the dark past, Baltimore coach Harry "the Cat" Brecheen, the man most often credited with collaring Ted in his lone World Series performance.

Gowdy stepped to the mike again and made his own proclamation. "Pride is what made him great," he said, then asked for one more ovation for "Number nine on his last game in Boston," as if the crowd could help it. They couldn't.

Williams took the mike and remembered to thank the Mayor for the contribution to the Jimmy Fund. Then he paused and spoke in the calm, clear, familiar voice the crowd had so often heard before. As always, Ted knew precisely what he felt and precisely what he wanted to say.

"Despite the fact of the disagreeable things that have been said about me—and I can't help thinking about it—by the Knights of the Keyboard out there," said Williams, jerking his head toward the press box in practiced disdain, "baseball has been the most wonderful thing in my life. If I were starting over

"If I were starting over again and someone asked me where is the one place I'd want to play, I would want it to be in Boston, with the greatest owner in baseball and the greatest fans in America."—September 28, 1960 (Courtesy of the Boston Red Sox)

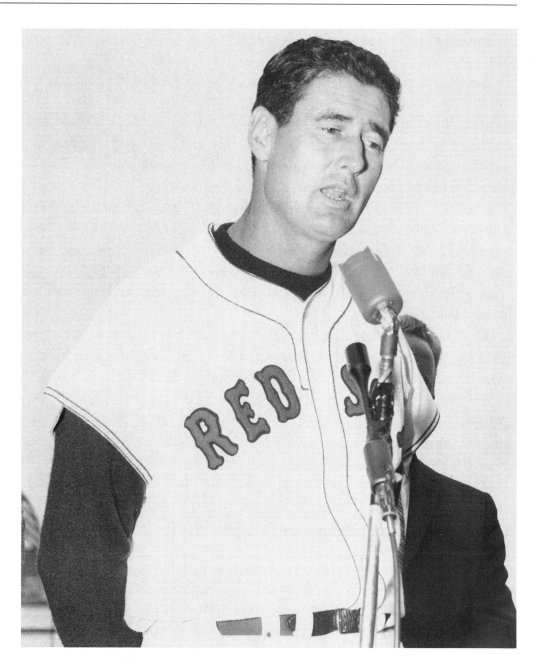

again and someone asked me where is the one place I would like to play, I would want it to be in Boston, with the greatest owner in baseball and the greatest fans in America. Thank you."

Fenway Park roared as best it could. Williams strolled to the dugout, tossed a wink to the crowd, and sat down. The last game was all that was left to be played.

In the Sox half of the first, Williams came up with 1 out and Willie Tasby on first. Oriole pitcher Steve Barber, who had been born a little over a week before Williams arrived at spring training his rookie year, walked Ted on 4 pitches.

Williams moved to third on a hit by Jim Pagliaroni and a passed ball. Lou

Clinton lined a pitch to center and Ted tagged up, sliding for the last time and easily beating the throw home.

Ted came up for the second time in the third inning, facing right-handed Jack Fisher, who was even ten days younger than Barber. With the count even at 1, Williams swung.

The ball soared, high and deep, but to the spacious expanses of center field. The crowd lurched to its feet, but settled back down as the ball came to rest in center fielder Jackie Brandt's glove. Moments later Jack Malaney announced over the public-address system that the Red Sox were retiring Williams's number 9 "after today's game." That meant Williams wasn't going to New York. That meant today was the end.

In the fifth inning Williams faced Fisher again. With 2 out and the Sox down by 2, Ted teed off. Again the crowd surged to its feet and watched the ball sail into right center. This time they remained standing.

Right fielder Al Pilarcik ran to the bull pen wall, well to the center field side of the 380 sign, and waited. The ball became a small black dot as it drifted down toward Pilarcik.

Ten thousand throats prepared to roar, then ten thousand throats were held in check as Pilarcik brought his hands to neck level, catching the ball and choking off the cheers. Williams simply stopped running and waited for someone to bring him his glove.

Williams's 521st, and last, home run, hit in his last at bat off Orioles pitcher Jack Fisher. (Courtesy of The Brearley Collection)

The lights were turned on in the sixth inning, as porchlights are sometimes turned on outside an empty house, as if by leaving them on the encroaching darkness is defeated and loneliness is somehow kept at bay. Fenway Park was certainly going to be a lonelier place without Ted Williams.

The Red Sox trailed 4–2 entering the eighth, but the game didn't matter, as so often those last few years it hadn't. Leading off, Willie Tasby stepped from the dugout and received the greatest ovation of his life. Williams was right behind him, on deck.

Crossing home plate to be greeted by teammate Jim Pagliaroni. (The Sporting News)

As Tasby stepped in, Williams crouched on one knee, genuflecting as he swung the barrel of a weighted bat back and forth. Tasby grounded out to short. Williams stood and walked to the plate.

The crowd stood *en masse,* like at the beginning of communion, praying to their private god and cheering for their public one. For a full two minutes they stood and cheered. Umpire Eddie Hurley called time. Williams waited in the box, expressionless, nervously swinging the bat. He was, as always, ready.

Twice before in his career he'd stood in the batter's box in a similar situation, once in his last game before going to Korea, and once in the seventh inning of the final game of the 1954 season. Each time he'd wondered if he'd ever step up to the plate again, and each time he'd hit a home run, answering uncertainty with another kind of wonder.

Fisher's first pitch was low, a ball, and quieted the crowd. The next pitch was higher, at the neck. Williams swung, twisting with the effort, and missed, but left no doubt that if it were his last swing, well, by God, he wasn't going to be cheated.

The next pitch—the last pitch—was buckle-high and over the plate. Williams swung.

This time the crowd did not wait to watch the outfielder, did not hold the roar of cheers in check, did not just stand, but began to leap and yell. In center field Jackie Brandt turned and loped toward the bull pen—toward Williamsburg—as if he, too, wanted one last look at the final moments of an extraordinary career.

There was no doubt. With Williams, there rarely was. The ball shot on a line—one bright moving object amidst the gray—far into right center and over the fence, then it clattered off the canopy above the bull pen bench, glanced off the wire fence that separates player from fan, and fell into the pen.

Trotting to left field one last time alongside rookie Marlan Coughtry. (Courtesy of the Boston Globe)

Carroll Hardy replaces Williams in the top of the ninth, as Ted leaves Fenway Park for the last time. (Courtesy of The Brearley Collection)

Ten thousand tongues applauded. Williams jogged quickly around the bases, number 9 on his farewell tour, his head down, his hat on, the bat finally taken from his hands. He crossed home plate, barely acknowledged Jim Pagliaroni on deck, and ducked into the dugout. It was over.

The crowd continued their emotive frenzy. Voices became hoarse, and hands became sore and numb from clapping before they settled into a rythmic chant, *"We Want Ted! We Want Ted! We Want Ted!"*

Williams stayed in the dugout, sitting by himself saying nothing, a secret grin on his lips. The first-base umpire motioned for Ted to acknowledge the cheers. Williams stayed put. There was no reason to move, no reason to do a goddamn thing. He had spoken to the crowd already, in the best way he knew. There was nothing more to add.

Four or five minutes later baseball resumed. The game was the same, but in Boston it had changed. The Red Sox went out quickly and Higgins ordered Williams to take left field.

Williams flashed Higgins an angry look but grabbed his glove and ran onto the field. The crowd roared again. Carrol Hardy followed Williams all the way out to left field, and when Ted noticed Hardy he realized Higgins's ruse and turned around, running hard this time, stepping on first base and making a beeline for the dugout. The cap stayed on and Ted kept going, down the runway toward the clubhouse, the cheers still audible as he walked away from the game he loved.

He was done.

SO, YOU'RE A SPORTSWRITER?

BY TIM HORGAN

The Knights of the Keyboard, he dubbed us, and it was the perfect sobriquet for the baseball writers of New England who jousted and dueled with Ted Williams for over twenty years.

The battle was joined, in fact, when Ted reported to his first Red Sox spring training in Sarasota, Florida, in 1938, and addressed everyone in camp, including manager Joe Cronin, as "Sport."

He was immediately labeled "brash," "irreverent," and "bush" by the heavy hitters of the Boston press—Dave Egan, Bill Cunningham, Austen Lake, Huck Finnegan, Mel Webb. And Ted seemed to go out of his way to live up to his billing when the heavy hitters were around.

The war was bitter and unceasing, if at times a bit lopsided, and it didn't end even when Ted retired. In his farewell address at Fenway Park on September 26, 1960, he said, with feeling, "Despite some of the terrible things written about me by the Knights of the Keyboard up there, and they were terrible things—I'd like to forget them but I can't—my stay in Boston has been the most wonderful part of my life."

I came late to the battle, but was embroiled in it soon enough. I began covering the Red Sox regularly for the now-defunct *Boston Traveler* in 1955. One afternoon early that season I was sitting at a table in the deserted Fenway Park clubhouse when Ted suddenly came clomping in his shower slippers. He cast a sidelong glance at me and had almost reached the shower when he called back, "Are you a writer?"

"Yes," I confessed.

A few minutes later, he came clomping by en route back to his locker at the far end of the room.

"What paper?"

"The *Herald Traveler*," I shuddered.

"That's good," Ted said. "As long as it isn't *The Record*."

"*Herald Traveler*," I reiterated, fully aware that Ted's mortal enemy, the bane of his existence, was Dave Egan, the sports columnist of the late Hearst tabloid whose nom de plume was The Colonel.

A few minutes later, Ted was back again. "I went to MIT today," he said, his words falling like raindrops upon a man parched for a story. And in those days just a single, exclusive, printable quote from Ted Williams was golden.

"A professor wanted to show me why a pitch curves," Ted went on. "He was all right. He knew his stuff."

For the next five minutes, Ted explained in scientific detail why a baseball curves, the essence of which was the more a pitcher spins the ball, the more it'll curve.

"So," said I, foolishly, "you should throw the ball underhand to make it curve more."

"Underhand!" Ted bellowed so the room echoed. "You've got to throw it *overhand!* Oh boy! Writers!"

That was the first time I heard Ted Williams use the word "writers" as an all-pupose expletive. He could say "writers" with such honest loathing, contempt, and disgust, that it became an obscenity.

For instance, during his final season, 1960, he'd walk into the dugout before a game, lift his head, sniff the air, and snarl, "I smell something. There must be a *writer* around here."

The great pity of Ted's war with the knights of the keyboard is that he was, on certain select occasions, a terrific interview. The best, in fact, in my forty years of experience. He was intelligent, enthusiastic, knowledgeable, and, by unpredictable turns, witty, charming, gracious, opinionated, belligerent, and almost eloquent.

"He even speaks in home runs," Jim Murray, the talented *Los Angeles Times* sports columnist, once wrote. This was where Ted had informed him that the greatest president in the United States history was Herbert Hoover.

"Who?" Murray blanched.

"Herbert by God Hoover!" Ted repeated.

I quickly learned two of the most important rules of war with Ted. On the average day, he'd talk about anything except baseball. Fishing and boxing were two of his favorite subjects, and I was covering boxing at the time. *Voila!*

One night before a game I bet Ted five dollars I could ill afford to lose that Archie Moore would beat heavyweight champion Rocky Marciano, who was Ted's particular favorite, by decision. During the game, however, I realized that the aging Moore's only chance was to catch Rocky with a lucky punch and knock him out, which he almost did. Almost.

After the game I decided to ask Ted to change the bet. Thus distracted, I forgot Rule 2: If Williams has a bad day at the plate, if he goes 0 for 4 and strikes out with the bases loaded three times, he'll at least be approachable. But if he has a good day, beware!

I was so distracted I forgot Ted had had a marvelous game. I didn't even notice that none of my fellow knights had gone within shouting distance of his locker. I strolled across the room and said, "Ted . . ."

I can't recall one word of the ensuing tirade, although it lasted a small eternity. The clubhouse was dead quiet and every eye was riveted on the rookie writer when I finally walked

away with my dignity in shreds. As I passed catcher Sammy White, sitting in front of a locker that bore a sign, NO WRITERS, he looked up, winked, and said, not unkindly, "Welcome to the big leagues, kid."

Looking back, some of the jousts with Williams now seem almost comic. There was, for instance, the Red Sox off-day when the late Hy Hurwitz of the *Boston Globe* and I, again desperate for a story, walked out of the club's offices into the left-field grandstand and heard gunfire. There was Ted standing in right field shooting pigeons as teammate Billy Goodman shooed them into the air. Pigeon corpses littered the right-field bleachers.

"What'll we do?" Hy Hurwitz asked, hunkering down so Ted wouldn't see and possibly shoot him.

"Are you a writer?" (Courtesy of The Brearley Collection)

"I'm calling the office," I said. And did. And told my sports editor, the late Arthur Siegel, who called the Society for the Prevention of Cruelty to Animals, who dispatched an agent to Fenway Park, who issued a citation to Ted, who was furious and who doesn't know to this day who blew the whistle on him.

My final battle with Ted erupted in Cooperstown, New York, when he was inducted into the Hall of Fame in 1965. He gave a superb speech, but you'd hardly know it reading the *Boston Traveler*'s account.

Just before Ted was introduced, a voice in the crowd yelled, "What would Dave Egan say now?"

"Bleep Dave Egan!" Ted retorted. Or words to that effect. Or so many of us, including several Red Sox officials and Boston sportswriters, thought. When I phoned in my account of the ceremonies I mentioned the incident, and the *Traveler* printed it under an eight-col-umn page-one streamer that read, "TED'S OBSCENITY MARS CEREMONY."

Four days later, I was told that Tom Yawkey, the Red Sox owner, wanted to see me in his office. I'd never met Mr. Yawkey. I didn't know where his office was. But I had a hunch I'd better go.

Mr. Yawkey had a tape of the Hall of Fame ceremonies, including Ted's response to the inquiry about Dave Egan. But the first word, the alleged obscenity, was unclear. I asked Mr. Yawkey to play it two or three more times, until he lost his patience. His tirade was in a class with Ted's locker room harangue. I'll omit the gory details, but he demanded a page-one retraction, which is a newspaperman's worst nightmare, but which the *Traveler* printed, although to this day I'm not convinced I was wrong.

"Ted *might* have said that," Mr. Yawkey admitted that day. "But he didn't." This was after the tirade had ended, and just before Mr. Yawkey put his arm around my shoulder and said, "Ted wanted to talk with you, but I asked him to let me handle this. If you'd done this to me, I wouldn't have said a word. But Ted is my friend, and I stick up for my friends. And this is the end of it. I give you Ted's word and mine that we will never mention this gain."

And they didn't. Neither one. I've talked to Ted many times over the past thirty years, and he's mellowed greatly. I'm not sure if he even likes writers now, but I wouldn't mind being his friend.

Tim Horgan is the dean of Boston sportswriters, having worked for the Boston Herald *since 1947. A graduate of Tufts University, he is an eight-time winner of the Massachusetts Sportswriter of the Year Award.*

THE LION IN WINTER

. . . .

W hen he walked off the field for the last time as a player, Ted Williams left behind one of the most remarkable records in the history of baseball. Over thirty years after Ted Williams swung at the final pitch of his career and knocked it over the fence for a home run, his performance at the plate seems as remarkable as it did the day he retired. In fact, Williams's final at bat was, in itself, something of a record.

Going into his last appearance, Williams was in ninth place, behind Tris Speaker, on the all-time list of major league hitters, .344322 to .344338. His final home run lifted Williams's average to .344407, past Speaker into eighth place.

His 521 home runs then placed him third, behind Ruth and Foxx, on the all-time list. His slugging average of .634, was 56 points behind Ruth's .690. His on-base percentage of .483 trailed no one. His career mark of 2,019 bases on balls was second to Ruth's 2,054. Except in those statistical categories based on longevity, Williams ranked in the top ten in virtually every significant offensive category. Had Williams not lost five seasons to World War II and

The final record places Williams above such .400 hitters as (left to right) Bill Terry, Rogers Hornsby, and George Sisler. His 521 career home runs far outdistance any hitter with similar batting averages, except for Babe Ruth. (The Sporting News)

Korea, he would likely rank either first or second in runs, runs batted in, total bases, and long hits. He'd likely have accumulated perhaps 3,500 hits instead of 2,654, and probably added another 150 to 200 home runs to his final total of 521.

Even so, by the time he retired Williams still set significant records, including most consecutive years leading in runs scored (5) and bases on balls (6), and most consecutive times reaching base safely (16). He accumulated six batting titles, missed an equal number by a hair, won two triple crowns, two MVP awards, four home run crowns, and four RBI titles. In addition to his Player of the Decade Award, *The Sporting News* named him Player of the Year five times. He made the All-Star team sixteen consecutive seasons.

Williams's real talent as a hitter defies any system of measure. It was not so much what Ted Williams did at the plate as when and how he did it, and what his presence in the lineup meant to a ballclub. Perhaps no other hitter showed such a predisposition to hit a home run at precisely the moment he needed to most. It was this propensity that made his failures—the 1946 Series, the 1948 play-off, the final two games of the 1949 season—loom so large. Williams's failures at these moments are glaring only because he succeeded so often at so many other times. Each of them took place in a game or series marked by underachievement by nearly the entire Red Sox team. When Williams failed, so did they, but he never alibied, and never put the blame somewhere else.

After his last home run Ted retreated to the Red Sox clubhouse. The Sox rallied to win, 5–4. The writers were forced to wait the usual fifteen minutes, and Williams was no more pleasant after the game than he had been before it. When pressed by *Sport* writer Ed Linn about how he felt, Ted groused, "Nothing. I felt nothing." Indeed, in light of his entire career, in the face of his final at bat, what, possibly, could there have been left for Williams to feel? Ted had never been one to spout the expected clichés, and he didn't do so now. He had done everything he could.

The burning question became what was Williams going to do without baseball? Ted left immediately to cover the World Series for *Life* magazine. Upon his return to Boston a few weeks later, he met with officials of Sears and Roebuck. Sears offered Williams a lucrative endorsement contract that required his active participation for only about two months a year. Williams's own fishing tackle business wasn't doing all that well, and he welcomed the opportunity to get more for doing less. Williams signed on.

There were other offers. The Tigers asked him to manage, but Ted turned them down. The Yankees offered Williams $125,000 to play one more season as a pinch hitter, but Williams refused. He had quit for good.

Ted returned to Islamorada, to the bonefish and tarpon, to talk tying flies rather than hitting them, and he began to decompress. Exhausted, Williams welcomed the chance to fish without worrying whether he was staying in shape or whether he was keeping his swing intact by swinging a leaded bat.

Even in retirement, Williams continued to fascinate the American public. On October 20, John Updike's essay on Williams's final day, "Hub Fans Bid Kid Adieu," appeared in the *New Yorker*. It was an instant classic, and the intelligentsia now swarmed to Ted; his importance as symbol almost overshadowed his actual ability. By becoming a part of American literature, Williams moved ever closer to a permanent slot in the realm of the immortal.

Updike didn't have an exclusive on Williams's final plate appearance. *Sport* magazine's Ed Linn also reported on Ted's last hurrah in a story that appeared in February 1961, "The Kid's Last Game." Linn's portrait, without passing judgment, manages to capture Williams's last few hours as a player with more precision and less flourish than Updike's story, with which it is often confused. Linn's piece ends, "And now Boston knows how England felt when it lost India." The two stories have made it impossible to forget Williams's last, remarkable moment as a hitter.

In the spring of 1961, as he earlier agreed, Williams again went to spring training with the Red Sox. Ted talked hitting to young ballplayers, conducted impromptu clinics in the batting cage, and dispensed various other baseball advice.

The Red Sox gave him the nondescript title of executive assistant, but neither Ted nor the Sox were ever quite sure precisely what that meant. He was not the team's official batting coach, and never would be. In 1961 that position was held by Rudy York. Williams's teachings were primarily limited to rookies and minor leaguers. Apart from his instructional duties, Ted occasionally evaluated talent, helped woo prospects, and appeared at charity functions. It was an awkward arrangement, and one that would prove increasingly uncomfortable for both parties.

Williams opened a summer baseball school in Lakeville, Massachusetts, and took pride in both its facilities and its instructional value. Unlike most similar camps, where star players jet in for a weekend clinic and autograph session, and leave the camp's operation to others, Ted spent most of the summer at his camp, actively teaching hitting to 12-year-olds.

On September 10, 1961, Williams married Lee Howard in an informal ceremony in East Cambridge. The marriage didn't last. Williams had never cared to answer to anyone. At Islamorada he was up at dawn to fish, or off at a moment's notice on some exotic hunting expedition. This life didn't appeal to the new, young Mrs. Williams, and in a short time the couple separated, finally divorcing five years later.

Ted's life followed a predictable pattern over the next several years: fishing most of the winter in Florida, attending spring training, doing promotional work for Sears, running the baseball camp, then off to New Brunswick for the salmon run before returning to Islamorada in the fall. In between, Ted made a few instructional baseball films, appeared on the odd television program—usually to talk fishing or hunting—and raised money for the Jimmy Fund.

The Jimmy Fund became increasingly more important to Ted. Started in 1948 by Boston Braves owner Lou Perini in memory of his father, and adopted by the Red Sox when the Braves left town, the program funds research into children's cancer. Williams's own brother, Danny, suffered from leukemia and died from the disease in 1960. As a child, Danny was the weaker of the brothers, often ill and unable to participate in the outdoor activities Ted loved so much. Williams and his brother were never close, and sometimes Ted was forced to bail his brother out from minor financial and legal problems. Ted blamed Danny's difficulties on his illness. Danny named his two sons Samuel and Ted, after his father and brother.

Danny Williams's illness made it easy for Ted to adopt the Jimmy Fund. He was the first Red Sox player to become involved with the charity, and over the years has personally raised millions of dollars on its behalf. As far as the Jimmy Fund is concerned, Williams has been anything but selfish.

In 1964, while on a flight from San Francisco, Williams spotted Dolores Wettach, a model. The two flirted, and Williams tossed her a note, asking who she was. She tossed one back, asking who he was. "Mr. Williams, fisherman," read Ted's response. Four years later, Dolores Wettach became the third Mrs. Williams.

But despite Williams's mocking self-assessment as "fisherman," baseball still held him in its grip. In February of 1966 the Red Sox tried to bring Ted

As a spring training hitting instructor, Williams has tutored the likes of Dick Stuart (in photo), Carl Yastrzemski, Fred Lynn, and Mike Greenwell. (Courtesy of the Boston Red Sox)

back in the fold, naming him executive vice-president. Tom Yawkey wanted Ted involved.

It didn't work. Williams's new position with the Sox was just as ill-defined as the old one. Most front office personnel from Williams's era were gone, and Sox general manager Dick O'Connell was building the club his way. There was a title for Ted, but no real place for him on the Red Sox.

In 1966, five years after his retirement, Ted Williams became eligible for the Baseball Hall of Fame. He had visited the Hall only once, in 1940, and wandered through the Museum in awe, wondering if he belonged with such luminaries as Ruth, Speaker, and Cobb. Then Ted had gone out and homered onto Susquehanna Avenue in the Red Sox exhibition game against the Cubs.

Williams was unsure about his prospects for election to the Hall. Players are selected by members of the Baseball Writers Association of America, and Williams feared, after his problems in MVP voting, the writers might be less than eager to see him gain admittance on the first ballot.

Ted's worries were unfounded. In January a record 302 electors gave Ted a record 282 votes. The twenty men who didn't vote for him didn't bother Ted. Even Ty Cobb and Babe Ruth had not been elected unanimously. It was Williams in a landslide.

Ted shared entry with Casey Stengel, who was selected by the Veterans Committee. Ted went to Cooperstown two days early to prepare his speech before the ceremony in front of the Baseball Library on July 25. The day was pure Ted.

Williams decided to keep his speech short and give Stengel, a Williams favorite and one of baseball's most entertaining speakers, more time. On a hot, sunny summer day, before a crowd of thousands, Ted, dressed in a sportcoat without a tie, accepted his plaque. Behind him on the platform was Baseball Commissioner William Eckert, Red Sox officials, and some Boston reporters. Ted pulled a copy of the speech from his coat pocket. As he stepped to the microphone someone yelled, "What do you think Dave Egan would think of this now?"

Ted was caught off guard. He muttered something under his breath, then started to speak. The crowd tittered. Guests on the platform behind Williams looked aghast. Red Sox officials shot worried looks at the sportswriters. The sportswriters took note and started scribbling in their notebooks.

There is no doubt that Ted said—something. The word "Egan" was heard by everyone. Precisely what he said before uttering Egan's name is another matter. According to some reports it was an indelicate comment about what Egan could do with himself. Williams denies uttering any profanity but claims he said, "Yeah, that Egan." Red Sox officials first confirmed a choicer interpretation, then pressured a Boston newspaper into printing a retraction.

Williams still had the ability to rise to the occasion and render any controversy moot. He delivered one of the more poignant acceptance speeches ever given by a player at the Hall of Fame.

"I guess every player thinks about going into the Hall of Fame. Now that the moment has come for me I find it difficult to say what is really in my heart. But I know it is the greatest thrill of my life. I received two hundred and eighty-odd votes from the writers. I know I didn't have two hundred and eighty-odd friends among the writers. I know they voted for me because they felt in their minds and in their hearts that I rated it, and I want to say to them: Thank you, from the bottom of my heart.

"Today I am thinking about a lot of things. I am thinking about my playground director in San Diego, Rodney Luscomb, my high school coach, Wos Caldwell, and my managers, who had so much patience with me—fellows like Frank Shellenback, Donie Bush, Joe Cronin, and Joe McCarthy. I am thinking of Eddie Collins, who had so much faith in me—and to be in the Hall with him particularly, as well as those other great players, is a great honor. I'm sorry Eddie isn't here today.

"I'm thinking of Tom Yawkey. I have always said it: Tom Yawkey is the greatest owner in baseball. I was lucky to have played on the club he owned, and I'm grateful to him for being here today.

"But I'd not be leveling if I left it at that. Ballplayers are not born great. They're not born great hitters or pitchers or managers, and luck isn't a big factor. No one has come up with a substitute for hard work. I've never met a great player who didn't have to work harder at learning to play ball than anything else he ever did. To me it was the greatest fun I ever had, which probably explains why today I feel both humility and pride, because God let me play the game and learn to be good at it.

"The other day Willie Mays hit his five hundred and twenty-second home run. He has gone past me, and he's pushing, and I say to him, 'go get 'em

Induction day, Cooperstown, 1966, with Casey Stengel and Commissioner William Eckert. (Courtesy of the Boston Red Sox)

Willie.' Baseball gives every American boy a chance to excel. Not just to be as good as anybody else, but to be better. This is the nature of man and the name of the game. I hope some day Satchel Paige and Josh Gibson will be voted into the Hall of Fame as symbols of the great Negro players who are not here only because they weren't given the chance.

"As time goes on I'll be thinking baseball, teaching baseball, and arguing for baseball to keep it right on top of American sports, just as it is in Japan, Mexico, Venezuela, and other Latin American and South American countries. I know Casey feels the same way. . . . I also know I'll lose a dear friend if I don't stop talking. I'm eating into his time, and that is unforgivable. So in closing, I am grateful and know how lucky I was to have been born an American and had the chance to play the game I love, the greatest game."

The speech was surprising in many respects. Not only did Williams hold out an olive branch to the writing fraternity, but his comments about black ballplayers and their right to be in the Hall shocked everyone. Ted was no politician, and 1966 was not the easiest time for a white baseball celebrity to take what was then a controversial stand on Hall of Fame racial policy. Williams didn't care. It was something he felt and he said it, years before others said it and deserving, old black ballplayers would finally gain admittance to the Hall. For maybe the fourth time in his career, Williams finished with a home run.

When the Red Sox fired manager Billy Herman in 1966, many thought Williams would become the manager in 1967. Williams did, but it was Dick Williams, the Sox AAA manager at Toronto, not Ted. Ted stayed in the background all season, particularly during the World Series. He didn't care to answer any more questions about the 1946 Series.

After the season he returned to Florida. *Sports Illustrated* writer John Underwood, who lived nearby, shared Williams's love of fishing. Although Ted's private life had always been off limits to reporters, Underwood convinced Ted that it was time for him to have his say. They began plans for Ted's autobiography and another book on Williams's theories of hitting.

Ever so slowly, baseball was again beckoning Ted Williams. In 1968 Bob Short purchased the Washington Senators. The Senators were awful and finished last in 1968 with the league's worst pitching and an anemic offensive attack. The club drew poorly and there was already speculation that the nation's capital was soon going to lose its franchise, not a good sign for the national pastime, particularly if Congress decided to remove baseball's exemption from antitrust laws.

Short asked Williams to be his manager in 1969. Williams refused, but Short was persistent. Then Joe Cronin got into the act. He called Williams and said, "Baseball needs you."

On February 21, 1969, Ted Williams became the manager of the Washing-

Williams's Hall of Fame Plaque. (Courtesy of the Boston Red Sox)

ton Senators. Short gave Williams a five-year contract worth $1,250,000, including stock in the club. Williams couldn't pass it up.

Other factors helped pull Williams back to baseball. His son, named John Henry because Williams thought the name sounded strong, was born in September of 1968, and Ted may have wanted him to grow up in a baseball atmosphere. The challenge also appealed to Ted, and the Washington Senators were nothing if not a challenge.

Babe Ruth had longed for the opportunity to manage, to show those who thought he was a brainless behemoth that he truly understood the game. Ted Williams may have felt the same way. He'd grown tired of hearing fairy tales about how his eyesight and reflexes made him a "natural" hitter, as if baseball had been easy for him. If Williams could improve the lowly Senators he could show everyone that Teddy Ballgame was no machine.

Ted won over the Washington press almost immediately, proving he'd learned a thing or two in retirement, and then set about to do the same thing with the Senators. Ted instituted Joe McCarthy's "Ten Commandment's of Baseball," although some cynically commented that as a player Ted hadn't paid much attention to more than four or five of them. When Williams talked, the Senators listened.

Ted's greatest success was with the team's hitters. The club batting average rose 25 points in 1969. His effect was particularly pronounced with slugger Frank Howard, who nearly doubled his walks, cut down on his strikeouts, raised his average almost 20 points, and increased production.

The Senators, and Williams, shocked everyone in 1969. The club climbed from the cellar to fourth place, only one game behind the Red Sox, at 86–76. Attendance climbed and Williams charmed everyone. He frequently appeared in public to help build interest in the club. At the end of the season he was named Manager of the Year.

But the club fell back in 1970 when the pitching fell apart. Williams grew impatient and by 1971 his wisdom was often falling on deaf ears or wasn't being spoken at all. Against his wishes the team traded half its infield for a washed up Denny Mclain. Attendance plummeted. In 1972, the team moved to Texas.

Ted hated Texas, although the 1972 Rangers did have the distinction of leading the American League in stolen bases. Who'd have ever thought a Ted Williams team could do that? Williams resigned after the season. He'd had enough of managing. Financially secure, Ted was ready to retire for good.

He and Dolores had another child, a daughter, Claudia, but soon divorced. Ted concluded he just wasn't cut out to be a family man.

Williams still had plenty to say about baseball. He published two books, *The Science of Hitting* and *My Turn at Bat,* his autobiography. *My Turn at Bat* appeared in 1968. One of the better books of the genre, it does a fine job of communicating Williams's voice and personality. Surprisingly frank in some areas, it leaves little doubt that apart from baseball and fishing, Ted Williams has never much been tempted by other interests. The irony of the book is that the persona Williams chose to show to the public differs very little from the persona created by a host of baseball writers who watched him his entire career. Ted always wore his heart, and his personality, on his sleeve.

The Science of Hitting appeared in 1971 and was an immediate success. For all the book's technical advice, it is most useful in its explanations of Williams's mental approach to the game. It destroys, once and for all, any lingering belief that his success was simply the product of random genetics. Perhaps no other hitter has thought as long and as hard about hitting as Ted Williams. Practice meant more than standing in the batting cage swinging at pitches. It meant *thinking* hitting—whether sitting in a hotel room or resting on a train or scanning the Atlantic for tarpon—thinking hitting all the time.

The new manager of the Washington Senators with his son John Henry Williams on Father's Day. (Photograph by Dick Darcy, courtesy of the photographer)

When Williams retired from the Rangers, he really retired. He became Ted Williams, fisherman. But he did not become a recluse. He added tennis and golf to his permanent off-season itinerary, and became good enough at each to routinely beat men half his age. Except for trips to New Brunswick for the annual salmon run, Islamorada was his permanent home. He felt at peace there. His friends in the local community respected his privacy. Trying to get Williams's phone number is like trying to dial the Oval Office. On occasion he'd invite friends from baseball to join him, where long days on the water would be followed by long nights talking fishing and hitting, with Ted surprising everyone with his expertise in the kitchen.

Williams could walk away from baseball, but he couldn't stay away. He still went to spring training, and despite his feelings to the contrary, granted the occasional press interview. In a telling 1974 interview, Williams admitted what many have always suspected. Despite his protestations that he felt "nothing" upon retirement and that managing was a "lousy job," when asked by James Kunen how he felt about baseball, Williams said, "It was always fun for me to play, I got to admit. Oh, God, baseball, I loved it so damn much."

In 1980 he accompanied Mrs. Tom Yawkey to Cooperstown for the late Tom Yawkey's induction into the Hall of Fame. It was an important moment for Ted. He had not been back to the Hall since his own induction, and didn't make many baseball appearances just for their own sake, preferring to limit himself to appearances for the Jimmy Fund, the occasional Old-Timers game, or spring training. Ted was surprised by the Cooperstown experience.

He enjoyed himself. The fans loved him, and there were no indelicate inquiries from the press. Ted walked the streets of Cooperstown, visited the Hall, signed autographs, and resumed the role of world's greatest hitter. It didn't matter that Ted couldn't do it on the field anymore. He was a bigger hit off the field.

Ted returns to Boston as manager of the Washington Senators on April 23, 1969. (Courtesy of The Brearley Collection)

It seems as if Ted has finally recognized his place in the game's history, and has realized that his continuing involvement is not only something baseball needs but something Ted Williams needs. He first gave himself to baseball on the rough, dirt diamonds of North Park, and over sixty years later finds he cannot, and does not want, to stay away.

Ted began to appear in public more frequently. The visits to the Hall became an almost annual occurrence. His contacts with the press have become civil, even friendly. In the early 1980s when the hitting theories of instructor Charlie Lau, popularized by Kansas City star George Brett, became the rage, Williams disagreed with them, loudly and publicly. Ted went on the stump for his own theories, but, this time, it was a friendly battle.

Williams has become more involved with the Hall of Fame. He is an active member of the Veterans Committee, helping select bypassed old-timers for admission. In 1985, Ted himself received another induction to the Hall.

Mrs. Yawkey commissioned a life-sized wooden statue of Ted from sculptor Armand LaMontagne. The artist's sculpture of Babe Ruth already had a place in the Hall. Williams spent hours with the artist, posing and discussing hitting to make certain the statue was perfect. The world's greatest hitter couldn't have it any other way, and neither could LaMontagne. Ted developed a deep appreciation of the sculptor's talent and craft, which LaMontagne practiced with a devotion similar to Ted's.

In 1985 the statue was unveiled and placed in the Hall, next to the statue of Ruth, the first thing a visitor sees upon entering. When Ted saw his statue side-by-side with Ruth's, he was moved to tears. It must have confirmed his boyhood dream to be "the greatest hitter who ever lived." The dream had come true and was recognized by everyone.

As the fiftieth anniversary of the 1941 season approached, Williams received renewed public acclaim. On Saturday, May 11, 1991, the Red Sox held Ted Williams Day at Fenway Park. In an on-field ceremony, Williams appeared genuinely touched by the outpouring of emotion that greeted him from the standing-room only crowd, which seemed to stand and cheer for him longer and harder than they ever had before. Boston Mayor Ray Flynn gave Williams a copy of a new street sign. The city of Boston renamed Lansdowne Street, which parallels Fenway's left field wall, "Ted Williams Way."

Before the ceremony, Williams worried about what he should say to the crowd. When he finally spoke, it was vintage Williams. "I realized far back I was playing for super great fans. I had a love affair with them but never showed it. When I finally consented to do this, I started to think, 'What am I gonna say?' Then I thought it might be nice if I tipped my hat. . . . Today I tip my hat to all the fans of New England—the greatest sports fans on Earth." With that Williams pulled a Red Sox cap from his back pocket—borrowed from Red Sox left fielder Mike Greenwell only moments before—and waved it to the crowd.

For one moment, Williams was a rookie again, and the men and women of his generation in the crowd were kids. Ted then continued, and turned his head to the press box. He couldn't let a moment like this pass without recognizing the press. He acknowledged the "knights of the keyboard," and thrilled every younger member of the press with the reference, happy now to be included in that select club with their forebears. Then Williams quipped, "And I still remember some of the things they wrote." But Williams's words contained little animosity and sounded more like blustery, playful banter between old friends. After the game, he was amused when reporters stood in line for his autograph.

The accolades continued. Later that year, Williams was awarded the Medal

In the decades since his retirement, Ted has remained a presence at spring training. He is still very much the man after whom men named their sons, women found irresistible, and pitchers had nightmares about. (Courtesy of the Boston Red Sox)

Ted joins Mrs. Yawkey and Bowie Kuhn in accepting the posthumous awarding of Tom Yawkey's Hall of Fame plaque in 1980. Yawkey loved Williams like the son he never had. (Courtesy of the Boston Red Sox)

No splinter, but still splendid—being outfitted for a uniform at spring training, Winter Haven, 1978. (Courtesy of the Boston Red Sox)

of Freedom, the nation's highest civilian honor, by President George Bush in a ceremony at the White House. It was an important day for Williams; he even wore a tie for the occasion.

Williams kept a grueling schedule in 1991, making appearance after appearance. It caught up with him on December 7, and Williams suffered a mild stroke. Hospitalized only two days, he traveled to Orono, Maine, two weeks later, to see his son graduate from the University of Maine.

The following January, Williams underwent surgery to relieve a blockage of his carotid artery, which precipitated the stroke. The surgery went well, and by midsummer Williams resumed his normal activities. He accepted an invitation to throw out the first ball at the 1992 All-Star game, played in his native San Diego. He enjoyed the trip immensely, visited with a number of boyhood friends, and even made a pilgrimage to the old house on Utah Avenue.

Williams, friend Brian Interland, and son John Henry formed Grand Slam Enterprises and started to produce baseball memorabilia, including a handsome set of classic baseball cards. To support the company, Williams made a number of appearances on television, hawking his wares directly to the public, answering questions from fans, and satisfying any lingering doubts about his health.

In the spring of 1993, plans were announced to build the Ted Williams Museum in Hernando, Florida, only the second, after the Babe Ruth Museum in Baltimore, to be built in honor of a baseball player. Williams was further honored in a ceremony at the Kennedy Center in Washington, D.C., as one of the first recipients of a National Sports Award. It is as if the applause that began in Fenway Park on Ted Williams Day has continued in a crescendo ever since.

Despite Williams's increasing ease in public, he has not changed. Ted was, and is, his own man. He continues to push himself to be the best. The same competitive fires that made him the game's greatest hitter has since made him perhaps the world's greatest fisherman. He is certainly the most famous.

Fishing now fulfills the same role in his life hitting once did. The parallels are obvious. Ted Williams fell in love with fishing at about the same age he fell in love with baseball, and his pursuit of the sport has followed a similar path. As a young man, Ted fished the way he hit; he couldn't get enough of it. If he caught ten fish, he wanted twenty; twenty, a hundred. It wasn't enough to get the fish; Ted wanted the biggest, most exotic, most difficult fish in the entire ocean. Marlin, barracuda, tuna, or bass: it didn't matter. It was fishing and he loved it.

It took Ted time, as it did with hitting, to appreciate the finer aspects of the sport. Just as he admitted in 1939 that "this baseball, it's one of the arts," so, too, would Ted eventually reach that conclusion about fishing. As he became more selective at the plate, he became more selective about fishing. It was the difference between being a glutton or connoisseur, a free-swinger or selective hitter, a simple fisherman or a sportsman. Ted is unquestionably a sportsman.

The transformation from fisherman to sportsman began when Ted started to spend time in Florida. The younger Williams thought he was an expert until he fished the warm Atlantic waters for game fish.

While stationed in Pensacola during World War II, Ted read an article about the snook, one of the best fighting fish, pound-for-pound, in the world. Williams and a companion saved gas ration stamps and drove to Everglades City. On Ted's second or third cast he came up with a 15-pound snook that

This sculpture of laminated basswood by Armand LaMontague was unveiled at the Baseball Hall of Fame in Cooperstown in August 1985. (Courtesy of Sherwin Kapstein)

Ted's daughter, Claudia, and son, John Henry. (Courtesy of John Henry Williams)

gave him a terrific fight. Williams and friend went wild, and caught 110 pounds of snook before giving up. Ted was hooked on fly fishing for game fish.

His forays into Florida took him farther and farther, until he traveled to the Keys. There he met men like Jimmie Albright, a consummate fisherman and guide, who was experimenting, and succeeding, with fishing for tarpon and bonefish with light casting equipment.

This was a different kind of fishing. The object was not how many fish but how they were caught. Now the sport became really fun. Equipment, technique, experience, and skill were all needed for a successful trip. Since neither the bonefish nor the tarpon are much worth eating, the goal becomes the larger experience, the science of fishing, the process.

Williams plunged into the sport wholeheartedly. Although baseball precluded active involvement in the sport during the season, Ted still found fishing useful. Nights in hotel rooms were spent reading about fish, for the literature of that sport is nearly as rich as that of baseball, tying flies, or dreaming of the turquoise waters, quiet, and solitude. For Williams, thinking about fishing became almost a meditational tool, allowing him to relax each evening before returning to baseball the next day.

Just as Ted carefully cleaned his bats with alcohol, honed them to perfection, selected the wood, and constantly checked their weights to see if a bat absorbed moisture and picked up half an ounce, so, too, did he learn to take care with his fishing gear. The rod and reel had to be top-notch, the flies tied perfectly, the line precise. Going fishing with Ted Williams and having poorly maintained equipment might put you in a league with Boston baseball writers in Ted's mind.

One doesn't, by the way, go fishing *with* Ted Williams. Instead, Williams *takes* you fishing, literally, almost physically. He rules the boat the same way he ruled the batting cage. It is his place, his sport, his theories, and he has his unmatched performance to back it up.

Just as hitting provides a series of numbers and feats to record and mull over that are fascinating, fishing provides the same kind of information. Each body of water is different, equipment changes, fish come in different sizes at different times, all requiring different strategies to catch.

The cast, like the swing, is the product of hours of practice, thousands of repetitions, training the body to produce precise and exact results from a violent and physical action. Just as Williams became the best hitter, hours of practice have made him perhaps the greatest fly caster of all time.

And patience. Fly casting is not throwing the line blindly into the water and hoping a hungry fish will wander past, any more than hitting is a random swing at an accidental pitch. The patience Williams showed at the plate while collecting over 2,000 walks is the same patience that allows him to stand for hours, scanning the water for the telltale movements of the fish. Getting a good ball to hit holds true in fly casting.

Ted casting for bass with friend and fellow fishing superstar Bud Leavitt and a fishing guide. Williams and Leavitt are now best known to New Englanders for their funny bread commercials on television. (Courtesy of Bud Leavitt)

In the last twenty years Williams has spent most of his time engaged in this parallel activity, substituting one discipline for the other, responding to the same secret dreams that first pulled him onto the baseball diamond and made him pick up a bat. There is one difference. Ted swung the bat from the left side. He casts from the right.

Winter through summer he is in Islamorada in the Florida Keys, fishing for tarpon and bonefish, although he has recently built a home in Citrus Hills. Early fall finds Ted in his camp in New Brunswick, along the Miramichi River, for the salmon run. Although he has fished for virtually every species of fish possible, today he concentrates on tarpon, bonefish, and salmon. Williams has caught over a thousand of each, and releases virtually every fish he catches. In 1982 he published a book on the subject, with John Underwood, *Ted Williams' Fishing the Big Three.* Each of the three fish is radically different; the pursuit of each appeals to something essential in the makeup of Ted Williams.

The tarpon is a large fish, little evolved from its prehistoric ancestors. It often weighs more than 50 pounds, but giants sometimes survive to weigh more than 250 pounds. From on board a 17-foot open boat, Williams scans the inlets and channel islands of the Keys, looking for what he terms "a fleet of small, gray submarines in the water" before launching the cast some 70 or 80 feet.

If the cast is right, Williams waits until the tarpon takes notice, then gives the line three or four bumps to make sure. The tarpon strikes harder than the salmon or bonefish, and once the hook is set, immediately starts to fight. The fish is a consummate leaper; Williams has had tarpon leap into the boat. Ted lands the fish as quickly as possible, believing this is the most humane approach, then releases it. Of the thousand plus he has caught, Williams has kept only a dozen. "Releasing a great fish," says Ted, "is about the greatest thrill I get from fishing."

The bonefish is a far different fish and requires a different approach. Only weighing six to twelve pounds, the bonefish is a skittish fish that noses through the shallows after crustaceans. Ted fishes for them from a skiff, poling it slowly and carefully through the shallows, looking for the tails of bonefish breaking the water. He tries to plant the fly a couple feet ahead, close enough to get the fish's attention but not close enough to scare it away.

The bonefish strikes gently, almost leisurely, then awakens and surges away with surprising power. For Ted, the excitement comes from the initial surge; the feeling of the fish on the line tests his ability to bring it back unscathed. As he does with the tarpon, Ted tries to land the fish as quickly as possible. After freeing the hook, he works the fish back and forth in the water, filling its gills, and giving it a chance to recover.

In midsummer Williams leaves Florida for his camp along the Miramichi, one of the best salmon rivers in the world. Over the past decade Williams has made conservation of the fish a personal crusade. Pollution, poaching, over-fishing, and ocean trawling have all placed the salmon at risk. Williams's concern is genuine. He can identify with the fish, finding the salmon's against-all-odds journey from freshwater to sea, then back upstream, a

"If I had to fish for only one fish it would be the Atlantic salmon."
(Courtesy of Bud Leavitt)

rough imitation of his own struggle to become the world's greatest hitter. The salmon is no easy catch. It resists the skills of even the best fisherman. Thousands of casts are sometimes required to catch a single fish. Yet, says Williams, if he had to fish for only one fish, it would be the Atlantic salmon.

This is where it's best to imagine Ted Williams today, along the Miramichi: the world's greatest hitter seeking the world's greatest fish. In the thousand casts before the salmon strikes, Williams is wholly and completely at ease, thoroughly enjoying himself, and savoring the challenge. Standing alone in midstream, the water sweeping around him, the sun glancing off the rocks along the bottom, the foliage on the shore moving gently in the wind. And Ted Williams in midcurrent, his mind clear and relaxed, the water rushing past and murmuring like the sound of the crowd in some imagined ballpark, his eyes narrow, focused on some place only he can see, his arms sweeping forward, the rod bending and the line playing out ahead, the fly following the same arc as so many hits and so many home runs, then becoming smaller and distant, finally dropping quietly into the water, and Ted Williams watching, ready, at home.

Still looking for a strike.

Ted Williams Day at Fenway Park, May 11, 1991: The Splendid Splinter tips his cap at last. (Courtesy of Dick Johnson)

AND HE CAN FISH, TOO!

BY BUD LEAVITT

The fiftieth-anniversary of his .406 season is upon him. His eyes are still quick and clear, his face still seems hewn from a granite quarry, his smile retains its luster, and serious autograph collectors still single him out. The Splendid Splinter is still splendid, still a phenomenal marquee attraction.

Hardly a week passes that I am not asked, "How good a fisherman is Ted Williams?" One morning at Islamorada in the Florida Keys, I overheard the answer to this oft-asked question. A longtime guide said, "He can kill a tarpon on a fly rod faster than any man who ever lived."

What makes Ted Williams, the fisherman, as powerful a force as he was on the baseball field? Guides will tell you, like measurers of batting skill, it's "the eyes and wrists." He can eyeball a fish before the ordinary mortal and, with those tremendously strong wrists, can cast an artificial fly into the area faster and farther than most human beings.

More than forty years ago, Ted Williams said, in one of our Fenway Park dugout conversations, "When I get through

playing baseball, I want to live and do the things Zane Grey did."

He has succeeded emulating his favorite author in many ways. Ted Williams's fishing diary has passages detailing the joys of muscling and landing a 1,230-pound marlin in thirty minutes down in Peru. Look closely and there are short paragraphs logging his experiences with tiger fish in Africa, sailfish in Florida, steelhead in Alaska, Atlantic salmon in Labrador and Ireland, and sessions on the bonefish flats, fighting muskellunge, trout, and bass.

Williams, the sports fisherman, is an extraordinary player—sharp, witty, intelligent, caustic, outspoken, profane, and certainly a world-class angler with an enormous enthusiasm and devotion that comes out of every pore in his body. No pretenses with this man. None of the irritating clichés. He speaks, whether it be on baseball, politics, or fishing, with nothing but the blunt truth.

"Somebody once wrote that I'd caught eleven hundred tarpon, one thousand bonefish, and one thousand Atlantic salmon. Well, the truth being, I've

caught more than twenty-five hundred bonefish, more than one thousand salmon, and fewer than five hundred tarpon."

Ted Williams remains totally impatient with continued mediocrity on the part of his angling acquaintances. Two years ago, a Florida banker, and friend of Williams's, appeared at Ted's home on Canada's Miramichi River. The Kid talked his guest into accompanying him downstream where several large salmon had been laying. The poor stiff, using a fly rod for the first time, managed several casts in the ten- to fifteen-foot range.

"Gene," barked a laughing Ted Williams, "take a seat on this rock while I tell you something about this fishing. To hook a salmon, you must present the fly properly. You are offering it improperly. There is the eating end of a fish and the other end. From now on, cast the goddamn fly to the eating end!"

During a post-dinner conversation, Ted expounded on his long love affair with the Atlantic salmon to the late, great sportswriter Red Smith and me, "After they are spawned," the Kid was saying, "they might go back down river more than two hundred miles to grow up. Then they fight their way back to the original spot where they were bred, by instinct alone, to spawn. This gorgeous fish battles river obstructions, lawbreakers, natural predators, and fishermen. It's a miracle this precious creature has lived to return another time around to spawn. The Atlantic salmon is something very, very special in my mind.

"The greatest single experience a fisherman can have is to hook an Atlantic salmon. There is nothing else in angling like it. One word tells it all—*anticipation*! One word—*anticipation*! You make five hundred, six hundred, and even one thousand casts a day and each time there is that moment of anticipation. Out of those five hundred, six hundred, or one thousand casts, you make the perfect one. *Bam!* Now it's the salmon and you . . . wow!

"Why does a salmon moving upstream," queried Red Smith, "take an artificial fly?"

"I believe the salmon takes the fly for the same reason a trout takes it—looks like food."

In the Kid's mind, fishing is not a game to be taken lightly— it is a life, an occupation, a totality of joy. He is my only angling companion who will make a federal case out of a single fishing knot or a simple leader splice.

Having spent over one hundred days and nights on some of the world's finest fishing grounds in Williams's company,

I can cite incident after incident of the Kid, bareheaded and towering over the surroundings, exuding the same awesome magnetism that dazzled you every time he went to bat.

We were once picking up our bags in an airport in Alaska. One Eskimo jostled another—"Know that big fella?"

"I sure do. It's Ted Williams, the big fisherman."

The Kid, The Fisherman, will bolt back into the limelight in

1991, marking the fiftieth anniversary of his .406 season.

If that doesn't make you feel old, you're Peter Pan.

Bud Leavitt and Ted Williams have fished the North American continent together for more than forty years. Leavitt has served as columnist and sports editor for the Bangor Daily News. *He appears regularly on public television and has his own radio program in Bangor, Maine.*

The inscription on this photograph reads, "To my real friend, Bud, two great fishermen and great profiles." (Courtesy of Bud Leavitt)

MY DINNER WITH THEODORE

BY DAVID HALBERSTAM

M y appointment with Mister Theodore Williams of the Islamorada, Florida, Williamses had been agreed on well in advance, though we had not yet talked to each other. That is normal in matters of this gravity, and our earlier arrangements had been conducted through intermediaries. My representative in this matter had been Mr. Robert M. Knight of Bloomington, Indiana, whose other job, in addition to being my occasional appointments secretary, is to coach the Indiana University basketball team. Mr. Knight has, on occasion, had troubles with members of the fourth estate himself, and was almost as celebrated as Mr. Williams in this regard.

It had taken no small amount of time to win over Mr. Knight's good opinion for, somewhat early in our relationship, I had failed him on a serious literary point. Mr. Knight, unbeknownst to many, is a literary man and I would not be amiss if I referred to him as a kind of literary executor for Mr. Williams albeit Mr. Williams is still alive. On that earlier occasion he had quizzed me on my qualifications

to write about Mr. Williams. I had done reasonably well until the final question. Mr. Knight had asked me to quote the final sentence of Mr. John Updike's famous *New Yorker* piece on Mr. Williams. I had not known and Mr. Knight had, with no small measure of disdain, pointed out that it said, "Gods do not answer letters." Still I had gradually managed to win my way back into Mr. Knight's good favor and the fact that someone like Mr. Knight recommended me as a worthy reporter-historian to Mr. Williams had weighed heavily in my favor, for Mr. Williams was reported to have said that if Mr. Knight gave his goddamn approval, why that was goddamn good enough for Mr. Williams.

I had arrived well in advance at the motel where Mr. Williams would call on me, and I was told he would come by at eight a.m. the next morning to summon me to our meeting. The motel itself was not exactly memorable. Simpler America, vintage 1950s southern Florida I would say, if architecture were my speciality, which it is not, but I do remember that the cost for a night was roughly what the

cost of orange juice is at any hotel in the city where I now live, New York. The next day, at exactly eight o'clock in the morning, there was an extremely loud knock on my door. I answered it, and there was Mr. Williams. He looked me over critically and then announced, "You look just like your goddamned pictures." So does, I might add, Mr. Williams. He has reached his seventies admirably tanned and handsome and boyish. He seems not to have aged, though he no longer, as he did in his playing days, looks undernourished.

Mr. Williams took me with him to his house and granted me the agreed upon interview. The interview, Mr. Williams being youthful and enthusiastic about whatever he undertakes, was exceptional. Not only did Mr. Williams answer my questions with great candor, but he also managed to give me several demonstrations of correct batting procedures. He emphasized that I should goddamn well swing *slightly up* since the mound was higher than the plate. Referring to his close friend, Mr. Robert Doerr of the Junction City, Oregon, Doerrs, with whom he had been negotiating this very point for some fifty years, he said, "I still can't get that goddamn Bobby Doerr to understand it." His advice was helpful, particularly since I, like him, bat left-handed, and for a moment I wondered whether, with coaching like this, I might make a belated attempt at a career as a designated hitter—I was, after all, a mere fifty-four at the time.

I found Mr. Williams on the whole to be joyous and warm-hearted. He had opinions on almost everything, and it was clear that he had loved playing professional baseball, and had stayed in touch with a large number of his teammates, which is unusual for a professional player some thirty or forty years after his career is over. Mr. Williams also sought to advise me about political developments in Salvador and Nicaragua. There seemed to be a considerable difference in our opinions on how best to bring a measure of happiness to those two countries, but Mr. Williams did not hold against me my lack of enthusiasm for greater military involvement. Late in our meeting Mr. Williams found out that I was a fisherman. It was not information I had volunteered readily since I was afraid that if Mr. Williams found me inadequately skilled with a fly rod, his judgment of me as a writer and interviewer would decline accordingly, and he might even report back unfavorably to Mr. Knight.

The interview took up most of the day, and that night Mr. Williams and his lady friend, Lou, took me to dinner. It was a wonderful dinner and Mr. Williams paid for us. We had been together some twelve hours and he was everything I had always hoped he would be. I consider it to be one of the happiest days of my life.

David Halberstam has won every major journalistic award in America, including the Pulitzer Prize. He is the author of eleven books, among them the highly acclaimed best-seller The Summer of '49.

The squire of Islamorada, with his son John Henry, at spring training. (Courtesy of Boston Red Sox)

APPENDIX

· · · · · · · · · · · · ·

TED WILLIAMS: THE RECORDS

Compiled from the Harold Kaese Archives
of the Boston Public Library

· · · · · · · · · · · · ·

Compiled and edited by
Mark Shreve and Dick Johnson

Harold Kaese probably knew more about Ted Williams, the hitter, than any man alive. From 1937 through 1973, first with the *Boston Transcript* and then with the *Globe,* Kaese authored a daily column, usually about baseball, often about Ted Williams. It is no accident, I think, that Kaese's writing career just so happened to begin one year before Williams officially became Red Sox property, and ended one year after Williams retired for good in 1972 as manager of the Texas Rangers. The opportunity to watch a ballplayer like Ted Williams comes along literally once in a lifetime. And when a writer has seen a ballplayer like Ted Williams, all that comes after must seem commonplace by comparison. Soon after Kaese stopped writing about Ted Williams, he stopped writing. His work was done.

Kaese was not Williams's favorite writer, but neither was he the most disliked. As a col-

umnist, he was not the most flamboyant, the most stylish, or the most popular. But he might be the best of all the writers who watched Williams over the years, for Kaese was, without qualification, the most accurate and thorough baseball writer of his generation. This book could not have been written without him.

Kaese knew sports, and knew baseball, far better than most imagined. Although born in Philadelphia, he grew up in Lynn, Massachusetts, and attended Lynn English and the Tilton School, where be became one of the best schoolboy athletes ever in a city renowned for producing athletes. He attended Tufts University, graduated magna cum laude, and captained the track, basketball, and baseball teams. He continued to compete in sports for the rest of his life and had an athlete's understanding of competition. In 1942 he was runner-up in National Squash Rackets; he was

named National Veteran Champion in both 1951 and 1952, Veteran Doubles Champion in 1962, and State Doubles Champion, with Roger Baker, for thirteen consecutive years.

Soon after graduation from Tufts, Kaese began writing for the *Transcript,* covering the Braves and the Red Sox. In spring training he'd travel back and forth between Sox headquarters in Sarasota, Florida, and the Braves camp in Bradenton, often filing, by mail, two stories a day. Some of his first bylines were for stories about Williams. On March 22, 1938, Kaese accurately noted, "You are justified in thinking that with Ted Williams, 20-year-old Red Sox outfielder, hitting is an obsession." Twenty years later, other writers were coming to the same conclusion and acting as if it were a revelation.

Like most other Boston writers, Kaese was enthralled with Williams. But while Williams's talent was undeniable, it was his personality that fired most writers' imaginations. Like other Boston writers, and like writers today, Kaese was drawn to Williams like the moth to the flame. They couldn't get close enough. But Williams the man was as elusive as Williams the hitter was obvious. Kaese, more than any other writer, saw the difference.

While others would constantly yammer about Ted's quirks, Kaese more often simply took note of them and moved on. When Kaese was wrong, he admitted it. In a 1940 analysis of Ted, Kaese wrote, "Can you imagine a kid, a nice kid with a nimble brain, not visiting his father and mother all last winter?" The comment infuriated Williams. But what Ted didn't know is that Kaese tried to have the comment excised from his story. It didn't appear in the first edition but was inserted, by accident, in later printings. Kaese apologized. He'd already decided the comment was "in bad taste" and felt worse over its appearance than Williams did.

More often, when other writers shot from the hip and lambasted Williams for his failure to hit in the clutch or for his stubbornness in trying to pull the ball against the shift. Kaese stood back, quietly accumulated data, and ended the argument. By the late 1940s, Kaese was keeping meticulous track of Williams's performance. By the 1950s, he'd begun a retrospective, cumulative analysis that, even with the aid of a computer, would be a challenge today.

At one point in the late 1940s, Kaese started an abortive biography of Williams entitled "Challenge Me." While he never completed the project, he must have remained intrigued. He began to collect newspaper reports and compile his notes on Ted with the same veracity with which he accumulated statistics. In the process, he assembled one of the most comprehensive collections of information on Williams ever compiled.

What Kaese learned occasionally leaked out in his columns, not as charts of mere numbers, but as a story explained and supported by cold, hard, irrefutable facts. He kept track of where, when, and against whom Ted hit home runs; how he performed on holidays, his birthday, and opening days; how he hit while injured, against each team, against left-handed starters who went nine innings, in the month of April, in the All-Star game, when he was hot, when he was not, and in a hundred other situations.

But there was not enough space, even in four or five weekly columns, to give those numbers full explication. Much of the information Kaese accumulated was never used. Nor could it be used today had not Kaese, perhaps looking ahead to the book he never had a chance to write, donated his complete clip file to the Boston Public Library.

Harold Kaese died on May 10, 1975. In a column written two days later, the late Ray Fitzgerald of the *Globe* began, "If Harold Kaese . . . had been granted one last wish to pass along to his newspaper colleagues, it might have been: 'Don't waste a lot of valuable space writing about me.' "

Fitzgerald gave Kaese his due, ending the column thusly: "After Harold retired and I began writing the morning column, a couple of people said, 'Hey, I see you've taken Harold Kaese's place.'

"Not true. I may occupy the same place in the paper but I didn't take his place. You don't replace a Harold Kaese."

Likewise, the pages that follow are surely neither a waste of valuable space nor an attempt to replace Harold Kaese. Reproduced are the results of Mr. Kaese's statistical research on Ted Williams. Some have been used to arrive at conclusions in the preceding text; others remain for the reader to discern his or her own meaning. Most lead to two inevitable conclusions: that Ted Williams was the greatest hitter who ever lived, and that we are fortunate that men like Harold Kaese were around to watch him perform.

To be sure, Ted Williams played the unforgettable music of his career. But on the following pages, Harold Kaese, one of the Knights of the Keyboard, wrote it down and made it possible to hear once more.

Note: *In the tables that follow, the incomplete nature of several categories (e.g., "Home Runs with Men on Base Through 1955") is due to the premature death of Mr. Kaese. Nevertheless, this compilation is the greatest statistical profile of a baseball player ever assembled.*

A reminder: Ted Williams was in the military during the 1943, 1944, and 1945 seasons, and again for large portions of the 1952 and 1953 seasons. In 1950, he fractured his elbow in the All-Star game and played in only 19 games during the rest of the season.

HOME RUNS
(Regular Season)

Home Runs off Opposing Pitchers

(Alphabetically)

A
Aber, Al 2
Abernathy, Ted 1
Aguirre, Hank 2
Anderson, Red 1
Appleton, Pete 1
Auker, Eldon 2

B
Bagby, Jim, Jr. 2
Bearden, Gene 2
Bell, Gary 2
Benton, Al 6
Berry, Joe 1
Bevens, Bill 2
Birrer, Babe 1
Bishop, Charlie 1
Black, Don 2
Bonham, Tiny 4
Boyer, Cloyd 1
Branca, Ralph 1
Breuer, Marv 1
Bridges, Tommy 2
Brissie, Lou 2
Broaca, Johnny 1
Brown, Hal 1
Brown, Walter 1
Bruce, Bob 1
Bunning, Jim 8
Burnette, Wally 1
Burtschy, Moe 1
Byerly, Bud 1
Byrd, Harry 5
Byrne, Tommy 1

C
Caldwell, Earl 1
Calvert, Paul 1
Carrasquel, Alex 2
Caster, George 2
Center, Pete 1
Chakales, Bob 3
Chandler, Spud 2
Christopher, Russ 4
Clevinger, Tex 1
Coates, Jim 1
Coleman, Joe 3
Cox, Bill 1

D
Daley, Bud 2
Dean, Chubby 3
Dietrich, Bill 2
Ditmar, Art 4
Dixon, Sonny 1
Dobson, Joe 2
Donald, Atley 2
Donovan, Dick 1

Dorish, Fritz 1
Drews, Karl 2

E
Eisenstat, Harry 2
Embree, Red 4
Estrada, Chuck 2

F
Fannin, Cliff 5
Feller, Bob 10
Ferrick, Tom 3
Fine, Tommy 1
Fischer, Bill 2
Fisher, Jack 1
Flores, Jesse 2
Ford, Whitey 1
Fornieles, Mike 1
Fowler, Dick 6
Foytack, Paul 4
Fricano, Marion 1
Fuchs, Charlie 1

G
Galehouse, Denny 3
Garcia, Mike 6
Garver, Ned 10
Gomez, Lefty 2
Gorman, Tom 4
Gorsica, Johnny 3
Grant, Jim 2
Gray, Johnny 1
Grba, Eli 1
Griggs, Hal 1
Gromek, Steve 6

H
Hadley, Bump 5
Harder, Mel 4
Harris, Bob 2
Harris, Lum 2
Harris, Mickey 1
Harrist, Earl 1
Hawkins, Wynn 1
Haynes, Joe 3
Hebert, Wally 5
Heving, Joe 1
Holcombe, Ken 3
Hollingsworth, Bonnie 2
Hooper, Bob 3
Host, Gene 1
Houtteman, Art 6
Hudson, Hal 1
Hudson, Sid 4
Humphries, Johnny 1
Hutchinson, Fred 8

J
Johnson, Connie 2
Johnson, Don 1
Judson, Howie 6

K
Keegan, Bob 7
Kellner, Alex 1
Kemmerer, Russ 1
Keriazakos, Nick 1
Kimberlin, Harry 2
Kinder, Ellis 2
Klippstein, Johnny 1
Knott, Jack 3
Krakauskas, Joe 2
Kramer, Jack 5
Kretlow, Lou 1
Kucab, John 1
Kucks, Johnny 2
Kuzava, Bob 2

L
Labine, Clem 1
LaPalme, Paul 1
Larsen, Don 3
Lary, Frank 1
Latman, Barry 2
Lawson, Roxie 2
Lee, Don 1
Lee, Thornton 1
Lemon, Bob 4
Leonard, Dutch 1
Linde, Lyman 1
Loes, Billy 1
Lopat, Eddie 2
Lyons, Ted 1

M
Maas, Duke 2
McCahan, Bill 1
McCrabb, Les 2
McDonald, Jim 2
McLish, Cal 2
Maltzberger, Gordon 1
Marchildon, Phil 5
Marrero, Connie 3
Martin, Morrie 2
Masterson, Walt 5
Miller, Ox 1
Miller, Stu 1
Milnar, Al 1
Moore, Ray 2
Moreno, Julio 1
Morgan, Tom 2
Mossi, Don 2
Moulder, Glen 1
Muncrief, Bob 6
Murphy, Johnny 2

Game-Winning Home Runs

1939

1. May 9 at St.L., with 2 on in the 10th off Harry Kimberlin to win 10–8.
2. July 2 vs. N.Y., with 2 on in the 7th off Lefty Gomez. Final score 7–3.
3. August 19 at Wash., grand slam in the 9th off Pete Appleton to win 8–6.
4. August 28 at Clev., with 2 on in the 8th off Mel Harder to win 6–5.
5. August 29 at Clev., grand slam in the 5th off Harry Eisenstat. Final score 7–4.
6. September 10 at Phil., with 1 on in the 9th off Chubby Dean. Final score 10–7.

1940

1. June 16 at Chi., solo HR in the 12th off Ted Lyons to win 4–3.
2. July 5 at Wash., with 1 on in the 5th off Walt Masterson to win 9–4.

1941

1. May 7 at Chi., solo HR in the 11th off Johnny Rigney to win 4–3.
2. May 27 vs. Phil., solo HR in the 3rd off Bump Hadley. Final score 5–2.
3. May 29 vs. Phil., with 1 on in the 7th off Jack Knott. Final score 6–4.
4. June 6 vs. Chi., with 1 on in the 3rd off Johnny Rigney to win 6–3.
5. June 12 at St.L., with 1 on in the 3rd off Johnny Niggeling to win 3–2.
6. August 31 vs. Phil., with 2 on in the 6th off Jack Knott. Final score 5–3.

1942

1. May 2 vs. St.L., with 1 on in the 9th off Eldon Auker to win 11–10.
2. May 16 at St.L., with 1 on in the 9th off Bob Muncrief to win 4–2.

3. May 29 at Phil., with 2 on in the 1st off Russ Christopher to win 14–2.
4. June 24 at Det., solo HR in the 7th off Virgil Trucks to win 1–0.
5. August 15 vs. Wash., with 1 on in the 3rd off Hal Hudson. Final score 2–1.
6. September 6 vs. Phil., with 1 on in the 8th off Lum Harris to win 8–7.
7. September 13 at Chi., with 1 on in the 7th off Buck Ross. Final score 6–1.

1946

1. May 2 vs. Det., solo HR in the 10th off Tommy Bridges to win 5–4.
2. May 22 at Clev., with 1 on in the 12th off Pete Center. Final score 7–4.
3. June 6 vs. St.L., with 1 on in the 7th off Ox Miller to win 5–4.
4. July 7 at Wash., with 1 on in the 3rd off Hal Hudson. Final score 11–1.
5. July 14 vs. Clev., with 2 on in the 8th off Joe Berry to win 11–10 (3rd HR of game).
6. July 30 at Clev., solo HR in the 4th off Steve Gromek to win 4–0.
7. September 13 at Clev., solo HR in the 1st off Red Embree to win 1–0.

1947

1. May 6 at St.L., with 2 on in the 11th off Fred Sanford to win 6–5 (HR off Jack Kramer tied score in 9th).
2. May 16 vs. St.L., grand slam in the 5th off Walter Brown. Final score 12–7.
3. May 18 vs. Det., with 1 on in the 9th off Virgil Trucks to win 5–4.
4. June 4 at St.L., solo HR in the 6th off Bob Muncrief. Final score 5–2.
5. July 16 at Chi., with 1 on in the 3rd off Red Ruffing. Final score 7–2.
6. July 26 vs. St.L., with 1 on in the 1st off Cliff Fannin. Final score 12–1.

7. August 2 vs. Det., with 1 on in the 1st off Virgil Trucks to win 2–1.
8. September 27 at Wash., with 2 on in the 1st off Walt Masterson to win 6–1.

1948

1. August 27 vs. Chi., with 2 on in the 6th off Marino Pieretti. Final score 10–5.
2. August 29 vs. St.L., with 2 on in the 1st off Karl Drews. Final score 10–2.
3. October 2 vs. N.Y., with 1 on in the 1st off Tommy Byrne. Final score 5–1.

1949

1. May 18 vs. Chi., with 1 on in the 3rd off Marino Pieretti. Final score 7–4.
2. May 28 vs. Wash., solo HR in the 5th off Dick Welteroth. Final score 5–4.
3. May 30 vs. Phil., with 1 on in the 8th off Carl Scheib. Final score 4–3.
4. June 24 vs. St.L., with 2 on in the 1st off Joe Ostrowski. Final score 21–2.
5. July 16 at Det., with 1 on in the 1st off Virgil Trucks. Final score 11–1.
6. September 21 vs. Clev., solo HR in the 7th off Steve Gromek. Final score 9–6.

1950

1. May 5 vs. Chi., with 1 on in the 7th off Billy Pierce. Final score 5–2.
2. May 16 at Det., with 1 on in the 3rd off Art Houtteman. Final score 6–1.
3. June 28 at Phil., with 1 on in the 8th off Lou Brissie. Final score 6–2.

1951

1. May 6 at St.L., solo HR in the 10th off Lou Sleater. Final score 5–4.

2. May 21 vs. Clev., with 1 on in the 7th off Gene Bearden. Final score 9–7.
3. May 27 vs. Wash., grand slam in the 3rd off Julio Moreno. Final score 7–1.
4. June 17 vs. St.L., with 1 on in the 1st off Al Widmar. Final score 3–0.
5. September 5 at N.Y., solo HR in the 3rd off Vic Raschi. Final score 4–2.
6. September 14 vs. St.L., with 1 on in the 2nd off Al Widmar. Final score 9–6.

1952

1. April 30 vs. Det., with 1 on in the 8th off Dizzy Trout. Final score 5–3 (Williams's farewell day before Korean War duty).

1953

1. August 19 vs. Phil., with 1 on in the 7th off Charlie Bishop. Final score 6–4.
2. August 31 at Clev., with 2 on in the 7th off Mike Garcia. Final score 6–4.
3. September 17 vs. Det., with 1 on in the 8th off Ned Garver. Final score 2–1.

1954

1. August 6 at Balt., with 1 on in the 10th off Bob Chakales. Final score 3–1.
2. August 11 vs. Wash., with 1 on in the 1st off Connie Marrero. Final score 10–1 (hit another in the 3rd).
3. September 3 at Phil., with 1 on in the 3rd off Arnie Portocarrero. Final score 11–1 (HR #362, which passed DiMaggio).

1955

1. June 10 at Det., with 1 on in the 3rd off Duke Maas. Final score 5–2 (hit HR in the 1st, also).
2. June 21 vs. Det., with 2 on in the 8th off Ned Garver. Final score 5–4.

3. July 29 vs. Det., solo HR in the 1st off Jim Bunning. Final score 5–0.
4. July 31 vs. Det., grand slam in the 4th off Ned Garver. Final score 8–3.
5. August 15 vs. Wash., grand slam in the 2nd off Ted Abernathy. Final score 8–4.
6. August 27 at Det., grand slam off Al Aber in the 9th to win 4–3.

1956

1. July 8 vs. Balt., with 1 on in the 1st off Ray Moore. Final score 9–0.
2. July 17 vs. K.C., solo HR in the 6th off Tom Gorman. Final score 1–0 (HR #400).
3. July 26 at K.C., with 1 on in the 10th off Bobby Shantz. Final score 5–3.
4. August 5 at Clev., solo HR in the 6th off Bob Lemon. Final score 2–1.
5. August 8 vs. Balt., solo HR in the 6th off Connie Johnson. Final score 7–2 (fined $5,000 for spitting the day before).
6. September 1 vs. Balt., with 1 on in the 8th off Morrie Martin. Final score 4–2.
7. September 8 at Balt., with 2 on in the 1st off Billy Loes. Final score 5–1.
8. September 11 at Chi., solo HR in the 5th off Bob Keegan. Final score 5–3.
9. September 25 vs. Wash., with 2 on in the 2nd off Pedro Ramos. Final score 10–4.

1957

1. May 7 at Chi., with 1 on in the 9th off Dick Donovan. Final score 4–3.
2. May 8 at Chi., solo HR in the 3rd off Bob Keegan. Final score 4–1.
3. June 2 at Wash., with 2 on in the 8th off Pedro Ramos. Final score 5–3.
4. June 13 at Clev., with 2 on in the 5th off Early Wynn. Final score 9–3.
5. July 14 vs. N.Y., with 2 on in the 2nd off Don Larsen. Final score 6–4.

6. July 28 at Det., solo HR in the 7th off Jim Bunning to win 1–0.
7. September 21 at N.Y., grand slam in the 2nd off Bob Turley. Final score 8–3.
8. September 24 at Wash., solo HR in the 4th off Hal Griggs. Final score 2–1.

1958

1. May 22 at K.C., grand slam in the 4th off Jack Urban. Final score 8–5.
2. June 26 at Clev., solo HR in the 9th off Cal McLish. Final score 2–1.
3. June 29 at Det., with 2 on in the 8th off Bill Fischer. Final score 10–7.
4. July 19 vs. Det., with 1 on in the 12th off Hank Aguirre to win 7–6.
5. July 29 at Det., with 2 on in the 11th off Bill Fischer. Final score 11–8.
6. August 8 at Clev., with 1 on in the 9th off Gary Bell. Final score 3–2.
7. September 28 at Wash., solo HR in the 7th off Pedro Ramos. Final score 6–4.

1959

1. May 30 vs. Balt., with 1 on in the 7th off Jerry Walker. Final score 8–3.
2. June 27 at Clev., with 1 on in the 5th off Jim Grant. Final score 6–4.
3. August 12 at Det., solo HR off Don Mossi in the 4th. Final score 7–1.

1960

1. June 17 at Clev., with 1 on in the 3rd off Wynn Hawkins. Final score 3–1 (HR #500).
2. June 19 at Clev., with 1 on in the 7th off Jim Perry. Final score 7–1.
3. August 20 vs. Balt., with 2 on in the 6th off Chuck Estrada. Final score 8–6.
4. September 17 at Wash., with 1 on in the 6th off Pedro Ramos. Final score 2–1.

Home Runs vs. Opponents

Year	G	Tot	H	A	at Balt.	at Chi.	at Cle.	at Det.	at K.C.	at N.Y.	at Phil.	at St.L.	at Wash.
1939	149	31	14	17	—	2	3	4	—	1	2	4	1
1940	144	23	9	14	—	3	1	1	—	4	2	2	1
1941	143	37	19	18	—	3	1	3	—	0	4	7	0
1942	150	36	16	20	—	1	2	5	—	4	4	4	0
1946	150	38	18	20	—	2	4	6	—	2	3	1	2
1947	156	32	16	16	—	1	0	1	—	2	5	5	2
1948	137	25	9	16	—	3	3	1	—	3	2	2	2
1949	155	43	23	20	—	6	2	6	—	1	1	4	0
1950	89	28	16	12	—	0	1	3	—	3	3	2	0
1951	148	30	18	12	—	1	1	1	—	1	4	2	2
1952	6	1	1	0	—	0	0	0	—	0	0	0	0
1953	37	13	8	5	—	0	2	0	—	0	1	0	2
1954	117	29	16	13	1	3	1	4	—	1	3	—	0
1955	98	28	15	13	2	1	2	4	2	1	—	—	1
1956	136	24	10	14	2	1	4	1	4	0	—	—	2
1957	132	38	12	26	0	5	6	5	4	3	—	—	3
1958	129	26	10	16	0	1	3	5	2	2	—	—	3
1959	103	10	3	7	0	2	2	2	1	0	—	—	0
1960	113	29	15	14	0	0	5	3	2	2	—	—	2
TOT.	2292	521	248	273	5	35	43	55	15	30	34	33	23

Climb to 500 Home Runs

#	Date	Pitcher	Opponent	Place
1	April 23, 1939	B. Thomas	Philadelphia	Boston
50	September 7, 1940	M. Russo	New York	Boston
100	May 21, 1942	J. Krakauskas	Cleveland	Cleveland
150	July 7, 1946	S. Hudson	Washington	Washington
200	April 29, 1948	W. McCahan	Philadelphia	Philadelphia
250	August 9, 1949	V. Raschi	New York	Boston
300	April 24, 1951	R. Kuzava	Washington	Boston
350	July 21, 1954	A. Houtteman	Cleveland	Boston
400	July 17, 1956	T. Gorman	Kansas City	Boston
450	August 27, 1957	P. Foytack	Detroit	Detroit
500	June 17, 1960	W. Hawkins	Cleveland	Cleveland
521	September 28, 1960	J. Fisher	Baltimore	Boston

Pinch-hit Home Runs

1. July 20, 1941, off Johnny Niggeling at St.L. with 2 on. Lost 6–3.
2. August 9, 1953, off Mike Garcia of Balt. at Bos. Solo HR. Lost 9–3.
3. September 14, 1953, off Mike Fornieles of Chi. at Bos. with 2 on. Lost 10–6.
4. June 25, 1954, off Bob Keegan at Chi. with 1 on in the 9th. Lost 6–4.
5. July 14, 1957, at Clev. off Stan Pitula with 1 on. Lost 17–4.
6. September 17, 1957, off Tom Morgan of K.C. at Bos. Solo HR in the 8th to tie. Lost in the 9th, 9–8.
7. September 20, 1957, off Whitey Ford at N.Y. Solo HR in the 9th. Lost 7–4.

NOTE: 1957—5 PH appearances, 2 BB, 3 HRs, 4 RBIs.

Home Runs with Men on Base Through 1955

	Men on Base				% with
Year	0	1	2	3	Men on
1939	8	12	9	2	74
1940	13	5	4	1	43
1941	16	16	4	1	57
1942	16	17	2	1	56
1946	21	12	3	2	45
1947	10	18	3	1	69
1948	13	8	4	0	48
1949	18	15	9	1	58
1950	10	13	4	1	64
1951	11	15	3	1	63
1952	0	1	0	0	100
1953	6	4	3	0	54
1954	11	13	5	0	62
1955	14	7	4	3	50
	167	156	57	14	58

Total Home Runs by Inning with Number of Men on Base Through 1955

On Base	1	2	3	4	5	6	7	8	9	10	11	12	13
0	22	8	14	25	22	24	17	19	11	2	1	2	0
1	32	1	26	11	12	15	25	15	16	1	0	1	1
2	14	3	5	4	4	6	7	9	3	1	1	0	0
3	0	1	2	1	4	1	1	2	2	0	0	0	0

Home Runs by Field at Fenway Park
(246 of 248 Career)

Left	Left-Center	Center	Right-Center	RF-pavilion	Right	RF-line
13	7	19	51	40	67	49

Home Runs by Inning, with Number of Men on Base

(Note: Numbers on same line as year indicate number of men on base for each home run.)

Year	1	2	3	4	5	6	7	8	9	Extra	
1939	122110	0	21211	110200	213	10	2	012	310	(10)2	
TOT. 31	6	1	5	6	3	2	1	3	3	1	
1940	00	—	2	001	130	11000	212	00	020	(12)0	
TOT. 23	2	0	1	3	3	5	3	2	3	1	
1941	01	0	001110	101	11000	000201	11132	012111	02	(11)0	
TOT. 37	2	1	6	3	5	6	5	6	2	1	
1942	2211000	0	0110	1100	10	010	101011	300	011111	—	
TOT. 36	7	1	4	4	2	3	6	3	6	0	
1946	01020	0	0101131	00010	3100	1000	1012	0021	0	(10)0	(12)10
TOT. 38	5	1	7	5	4	4	4	4	1	1	2
1947	1111112	0	11	010	2310	011	0111	00	10110	(11)2	
TOT. 32	7	1	2	3	4	3	4	2	5	1	
1948	1221	—	00	0	00110	0002	11	0201	010	—	
TOT. 25	4	0	2	1	5	4	2	4	3	0	
1949	0012121011	—	12110	201	2001	320	020100101	010020	201	—	
TOT. 43	10	0	5	3	4	3	9	6	3	0	
1950	20100	202	1111	20	010	01	0101	3111	1	—	
TOT. 28	5	3	4	2	3	2	4	4	1	0	
1951	111111001	001	320	020	0	11	11	0210	1	(10)0	(13)1
TOT. 30	9	3	3	3	1	2	2	4	1	1	1
1952	—	—	—	—	—	—	1	—	—	—	
TOT. 1	0	0	0	0	0	0	1	0	0	0	
1953	001	—	—	1	02	0	0112	2	1	—	
TOT. 13	3	0	0	1	2	1	4	1	1	0	
1954	2111	—	000111	00	—	0222110	000	1201	11	(10)1	
TOT. 29	4	0	6	2	0	7	3	4	2	1	
1955	2020	23	11	03000	001000	0110	01	12	3	—	
TOT. 28	4	2	2	5	6	4	2	2	1	0	
1956	1012102	2	11	—	0	000002	210	01	0	(10)1	
TOT. 24	7	1	2	0	1	6	3	2	1	1	
1957	00021000	23	021	00	021	0000	2010	001200	100000	—	
TOT. 38	8	2	3	2	3	4	4	6	6	0	
1958	1	2	013	0010	121	00	00	1200	1011	(11)2	(12)1
TOT. 26	1	1	3	4	3	2	2	4	4	1	1
1959	01	—	0	0	1	00	1	0	0	—	
TOT. 10	2	0	1	1	1	2	1	1	1	0	
1960	10	0	11	00020	10001	010121	2	010	0110	—	
TOT. 29	2	1	2	5	5	6	1	3	4	0	
TOT. 521	88	18	58	53	55	66	61	61	48	(10)5	
										(11)3	
										(12)4	
										(13)1	

BATTING

Career Batting Statistics

Year	G	AB	R	H	2B	3B	HR	RBI	AVG.	SP%	TB	Bases Per Hit	OBP%
1939	149	565	131	185	44	11	31	145	.327	.609	344	1.85	.436
1940	144	561	134	193	43	14	23	113	.344	.594	333	1.73	.442
1941	143	456	135	185	33	3	37	120	.406	.735	335	1.81	.551
1942	150	522	141	186	34	5	36	137	.356	.648	338	1.82	.499
1946	150	514	142	176	37	8	38	123	.342	.667	343	1.95	.497
1947	156	528	125	181	40	9	32	114	.343	.634	335	1.85	.499
1948	137	509	124	188	44	3	25	127	.369	.615	313	1.67	.497
1949	155	566	150	194	39	3	43	159	.343	.650	368	1.89	.490
1950	89	334	82	106	24	1	28	97	.317	.647	216	2.04	.452
1951	148	531	109	169	28	4	30	126	.318	.556	295	1.75	.464
1952	6	10	2	4	0	1	1	3	.400	.900	9	2.25	.500
1953	37	91	17	37	6	0	13	34	.407	.901	82	2.21	.509
1954	117	386	93	133	23	1	29	89	.345	.635	245	1.84	.516
1955	98	320	77	114	21	3	28	83	.356	.703	225	1.98	.501
1956	136	400	71	138	28	2	24	82	.345	.605	242	1.75	.479
1957	132	420	96	163	28	1	38	87	.388	.731	307	1.88	.528
1958	129	411	81	135	23	2	26	85	.328	.584	240	1.78	.462
1959	103	272	32	69	15	0	10	43	.254	.419	114	1.65	.377
1960	113	310	56	98	15	0	29	72	.316	.645	200	2.04	.454
TOT.	2292	7706	1798	2654	525	71	521	1839	.344	.634	4884	1.881	.483

Career Batting Statistics
(cont.)

Year	G	BB	HP	SO	SAC(f)	SB	CS	DP
1939	149	107	2	64	3	2	1	0
1940	144	96	3	54	1	4	4	13
1941	143	145	3	27	0	2	4	10
1942	150	145	4	51	0	3	2	12
1946	150	156	2	44	0	0	0	12
1947	156	162	2	47	1	0	1	10
1948	137	126	3	41	0	4	0	10
1949	155	162	2	48	0	1	1	22
1950	89	82	0	21	0	3	0	12
1951	148	144	0	45	0	1	1	10
1952	6	2	0	2	0	0	0	0
1953	37	19	0	10	0	0	1	1
1954	117	136	1	32	0(3f)	0	0	10
1955	98	91	2	24	0(4f)	2	0	8
1956	136	102	1	39	0	0	0	13
1957	132	119	5	43	0(2f)	0	1	11
1958	129	98	4	49	0(4f)	1	0	19
1959	103	52	2	27	0(5f)	0	0	8
1960	113	75	3	41	0(2f)	1	1	7
TOT.	2292	2019	39	709	25	24	17	188

Career Batting at Fenway Park

Year	G	AB	R	H	TB	2B	3B	HR	RBI	BB	HPB	AVG.	OBP%
1939	75	277	74	95	169	22	5	14	68	52	2	.343	.450
1940	76	297	69	101	166	28	5	9	60	47	2	.340	.434
1941	75	243	72	104	186	21	2	19	62	80	3	.428	.574
1942	75	261	73	93	168	21	3	16	68	64	2	.356	.486
1946	76	266	74	98	181	21	4	18	69	73	0	.368	.504
1947	81	277	67	92	176	24	6	16	63	84	2	.332	.490
1948	66	239	57	88	140	23	1	9	66	66	3	.368	.510
1949	77	272	87	95	193	27	1	23	86	91	0	.349	.512
1950	43	160	50	57	118	13	0	16	56	41	0	.356	.488
1951	73	268	69	108	190	22	3	18	81	64	0	.403	.518
1952	4	6	1	3	6	0	0	1	3	1	0	.500	.571
1953	19	47	10	17	45	4	0	8	18	10	0	.362	.474
1954	58	186	48	69	129	12	0	16	39	72	1	.371	.548
1955	54	172	48	67	125	11	1	15	47	52	1	.390	.533
1956	72	205	39	74	127	19	2	10	43	59	0	.361	.504
1957	63	206	42	83	138	19	0	12	36	52	2	.403	.527
1958	66	207	47	68	116	14	2	10	41	57	3	.329	.479
1959	52	134	14	37	56	10	0	3	21	20	1	.276	.374
1960	60	164	32	54	107	8	0	15	38	47	0	.329	.479
TOT.	1165	3887	973	1403	2536	319	35	248	965	1032	22	.361	.497

Career Batting on the Road

Year	G	AB	R	H	TB	2B	3B	HR	RBI	BB	HPB	AVG.	OBP%
1939	74	288	57	90	175	22	6	17	77	55	0	.313	.423
1940	68	264	65	92	167	15	9	14	53	49	1	.348	.452
1941	68	213	63	81	149	12	1	18	58	65	0	.380	.525
1942	75	261	68	93	170	13	2	20	69	81	2	.356	.512
1946	74	248	68	78	162	16	4	20	54	83	2	.315	.489
1947	75	251	58	89	159	16	3	16	51	78	0	.355	.508
1948	71	270	67	100	173	21	2	16	61	60	0	.370	.485
1949	78	294	63	99	175	12	2	20	73	71	2	.337	.469
1950	46	174	32	49	98	11	1	12	41	41	0	.282	.419
1951	75	263	40	61	105	6	1	12	45	80	0	.232	.411
1952	2	4	1	1	3	0	1	0	0	1	0	.250	.400
1953	18	44	7	20	37	2	0	5	16	9	0	.455	.547
1954	59	200	45	64	116	11	1	13	50	64	0	.320	.485
1955	44	148	29	47	100	10	2	13	36	39	1	.318	.463
1956	64	195	32	64	115	9	0	14	39	43	1	.328	.452
1957	69	214	54	80	169	9	1	26	51	67	3	.374	.528
1958	63	204	34	67	124	9	0	16	44	41	1	.328	.443
1959	51	138	18	32	58	5	0	7	22	32	1	.232	.380
1960	53	146	24	44	93	7	0	14	34	28	3	.301	.424
TOT.	1127	3819	825	1251	2348	296	36	273	874	987	17	.328	.468

Career Batting vs. Opponents

Chicago White Sox

			Total					Home					Away		
Year	AB	R	H	HR	RBI	AB	R	H	HR	RBI	AB	R	H	HR	RBI
1939	84	13	24	2	9	40	9	13	1	2	44	4	11	1	7
1940	88	23	30	3	13	44	10	14	0	2	44	13	16	3	11
1941	69	17	26	7	17	42	11	17	4	9	27	6	9	3	8
1942	71	8	17	2	13	40	3	9	1	7	31	5	8	1	6
1946	76	13	22	2	14	40	5	12	0	8	36	8	10	2	6
1947	80	20	29	6	15	44	12	13	3	10	36	8	16	1	5
1948	58	10	27	4	31	29	4	13	1	18	29	6	14	3	13
1949	87	30	31	12	39	36	14	12	6	21	51	16	19	6	18
1950	44	14	15	3	10	19	10	9	3	10	25	4	6	0	0
1951	73	18	25	5	18	42	13	20	4	15	31	5	5	1	3
1952	Did not play														
1953	18	4	8	1	5	7	2	4	1	3	11	2	4	0	2
1954	60	9	19	5	12	32	6	12	2	4	28	3	7	3	8
1955	38	7	12	1	8	12	4	5	0	1	26	3	7	1	7
1956	55	6	19	1	6	24	2	8	0	2	31	4	11	1	4
1957	63	9	21	6	13	25	3	11	1	4	38	6	10	5	9
1958	68	12	21	2	9	31	8	11	1	4	37	4	10	1	5
1959	46	3	8	2	5	18	1	4	0	2	28	2	4	2	3
1960	47	8	10	3	7	23	3	6	3	4	24	5	4	0	3
TOT.	1125	124	364	65	244	548	120	193	31	126	573	104	166	34	116
			AVG. .324					AVG. .352					AVG. .290		

St. Louis Browns

(1939–1953)

			Total					Home					Away		
Year	AB	R	H	HR	RBI	AB	R	H	HR	RBI	AB	R	H	HR	RBI
1939	91	20	32	5	32	41	8	12	1	9	50	12	20	4	23
1940	89	20	29	3	13	45	11	12	1	7	44	9	17	2	6
1941	61	17	26	9	26	33	7	13	2	11	28	10	13	7	15
1942	75	21	34	6	23	41	13	18	2	15	34	8	16	4	8
1946	72	22	34	5	18	47	13	27	4	12	25	9	7	1	6
1947	82	31	39	11	33	48	17	22	6	19	34	14	17	5	14
1948	62	20	26	4	13	20	7	7	2	4	42	13	19	2	9
1949	79	20	28	6	26	38	10	13	2	15	41	10	15	4	11
1950	60	17	24	6	23	22	9	9	4	12	38	8	15	2	11
1951	74	18	24	5	16	34	13	13	3	11	40	5	11	2	5
1952	Did not play														
1953	9	0	0	0	0	9	0	0	0	0					
TOT.	754	186	296	60	223	378	108	146	27	115	376	98	150	33	108
			AVG. .393					AVG. .386					AVG. .399		

Baltimore Orioles
(1954–1960)

Year	AB	R	Total H	HR	RBI	AB	R	Home H	HR	RBI	AB	R	Away H	HR	RBI
1954	44	8	11	5	8	20	6	7	4	6	24	2	4	1	2
1955	32	9	10	5	10	18	7	6	3	8	14	2	4	2	2
1956	65	17	26	5	21	32	11	16	3	11	33	6	10	2	10
1957	66	8	23	1	7	27	5	9	1	4	39	3	14	0	3
1958	43	6	11	0	4	24	5	5	0	2	19	1	6	0	2
1959	26	4	10	1	6	12	3	5	1	3	14	1	5	0	3
1960	34	8	11	3	11	24	5	8	3	9	10	3	3	0	2
TOT.	310	60	102	20	67	157	42	56	15	43	153	18	46	5	24
			AVG. .329					AVG. .357					AVG. .301		

Cleveland Indians

Year	AB	R	Total H	HR	RBI	AB	R	Home H	HR	RBI	AB	R	Away H	HR	RBI
1939	77	14	18	4	23	41	8	7	1	11	36	6	11	3	12
1940	77	17	23	3	17	39	10	14	2	12	38	7	9	1	5
1941	58	22	24	3	9	38	14	18	2	6	20	8	8	1	3
1942	71	27	25	4	20	34	13	10	2	8	37	14	15	2	12
1946	78	20	30	11	28	39	13	20	7	18	39	7	10	4	10
1947	66	15	18	0	4	34	8	6	0	3	32	7	12	0	1
1948	87	23	33	5	23	43	12	15	2	12	44	11	18	3	11
1949	81	11	25	3	18	38	8	14	1	10	43	3	11	2	8
1950	44	8	11	4	10	20	6	7	3	5	24	2	4	1	5
1951	94	12	24	3	19	52	8	16	2	11	42	4	8	1	8
1952	Did not play														
1953	14	6	5	5	9	8	3	3	3	5	6	3	2	2	4
1954	47	7	16	3	9	24	4	10	6	6	23	3	6	1	3
1955	56	9	12	5	15	34	4	8	3	6	22	5	4	2	9
1956	56	16	22	4	15	37	11	15	0	6	19	5	7	4	9
1957	57	22	27	9	20	30	11	14	3	8	27	11	13	6	12
1958	69	10	22	3	7	34	5	12	0	3	35	5	10	3	4
1959	41	5	8	2	3	20	1	3	0	0	21	4	5	2	3
1960	54	9	18	8	16	32	5	10	3	6	22	4	8	5	10
TOT.	1127	253	361	79	265	597	144	202	36	137	530	109	161	43	129
			AVG. .320					AVG. .338					AVG. .304		

Detroit Tigers

Year	AB	R	Total H	HR	RBI	AB	R	Home H	HR	RBI	AB	R	Away H	HR	RBI
1939	80	19	24	4	21	36	7	10	0	7	44	12	14	4	14
1940	73	18	27	1	15	45	10	17	0	8	28	8	10	1	7
1941	74	21	25	5	19	36	7	12	2	9	38	14	13	3	10
1942	80	20	31	7	22	37	9	16	2	9	43	11	15	5	13
1946	77	28	30	10	21	39	16	12	4	7	38	12	18	6	14
1947	82	13	27	4	19	40	7	15	3	9	42	6	12	1	10
1948	66	17	20	2	12	29	9	12	1	5	37	8	8	1	7
1949	96	32	33	10	25	46	15	16	4	13	50	17	17	6	12
1950	49	10	12	5	14	26	3	7	2	7	23	7	5	3	7
1951	76	10	19	2	12	39	3	12	1	7	37	7	7	1	5
1952	3	1	2	1	2	3	1	2	1	2					
1953	8	1	3	1	3	4	1	1	1	2	4	0	2	0	1
1954	58	15	19	5	16	28	7	6	1	3	30	8	13	4	13
1955	53	20	22	8	24	27	12	11	4	13	26	8	11	4	11
1956	60	8	19	2	8	32	3	10	1	4	28	5	9	1	4
1957	64	16	23	6	11	36	7	13	1	4	28	9	10	5	7
1958	63	15	16	6	15	28	8	7	1	2	35	7	9	5	13
1959	46	7	11	3	11	23	2	4	1	3	23	5	7	2	8
1960	59	10	23	6	13	28	3	10	3	7	31	7	13	3	6
TOT.	1167	281	386	88	283	582	130	193	33	111	585	151	193	55	162
			AVG. .331					AVG. .332					AVG. .330		

Kansas City Athletics
(1955–1960)

Year	AB	R	Total H	HR	RBI	AB	R	Home H	HR	RBI	AB	R	Away H	HR	RBI
1955	58	14	26	4	12	29	7	14	2	8	29	7	12	2	4
1956	57	10	21	6	13	27	3	8	2	4	30	7	13	4	9
1957	60	19	26	7	14	28	8	13	3	8	32	11	13	4	6
1958	66	10	23	4	16	30	6	9	2	9	36	4	14	2	7
1959	47	4	12	1	6	25	1	6	0	1	22	3	6	1	5
1960	39	8	12	3	13	13	5	5	1	7	26	3	7	2	6
TOT.	327	65	120	25	74	152	30	55	10	37	175	35	65	15	37
			AVG. .367					AVG. .362					AVG. .371		

New York Yankees

Year	AB	R	Total H	HR	RBI	AB	R	Home H	HR	RBI	AB	R	Away H	HR	RBI
1939	60	19	21	6	17	30	14	11	5	12	30	5	10	1	5
1940	68	17	24	6	14	32	8	13	2	5	36	9	11	4	9
1941	68	23	32	2	14	35	13	16	2	6	33	10	16	0	8
1942	77	14	23	6	16	39	6	11	2	7	38	8	12	4	9
1946	69	18	13	3	10	35	11	8	1	5	34	7	5	2	5
1947	74	11	17	2	7	38	8	8	0	3	36	3	9	2	4
1948	83	16	29	5	30	42	8	16	2	21	41	8	13	3	9
1949	78	17	30	5	18	43	11	17	4	10	35	6	13	1	8
1950	59	18	20	4	16	31	12	13	1	10	28	6	7	3	6
1951	67	12	24	3	13	45	9	18	2	11	22	3	6	1	2
1952	Did not play														
1953	17	2	8	1	6	10	2	5	1	5	7	0	3	0	1
1954	57	18	23	3	15	24	9	9	2	8	33	9	14	1	7
1955	36	4	13	2	4	15	2	7	1	3	21	2	6	1	1
1956	56	3	11	1	6	31	3	8	1	5	25	0	3	0	1
1957	53	10	24	6	13	32	6	17	3	6	21	4	7	3	7
1958	42	10	19	3	13	28	6	12	1	7	14	4	7	2	6
1959	31	5	12	1	8	20	3	10	1	8	11	2	2	0	2
1960	40	7	14	3	9	30	4	11	1	5	10	3	3	2	4
TOT.	1035	224	357	62	229	560	135	210	32	135	475	89	147	30	94
			AVG. .345					AVG. .375					AVG. .309		

Philadelphia Athletics
(1939–1954)

Year	AB	R	Total H	HR	RBI	AB	R	Home H	HR	RBI	AB	R	Away H	HR	RBI
1939	83	28	39	6	24	46	15	23	3	15	37	13	16	3	9
1940	90	23	33	4	23	48	12	17	2	13	42	11	16	2	10
1941	63	19	28	8	22	28	9	13	4	11	35	10	15	4	11
1942	75	21	21	10	29	35	11	11	6	15	40	10	10	4	14
1946	70	17	19	3	13	29	4	5	0	4	41	13	14	3	9
1947	69	22	22	9	22	34	9	12	4	12	35	13	10	5	10
1948	69	15	25	2	9	39	8	14	0	3	30	7	11	2	6
1949	76	19	26	5	20	35	14	11	4	14	41	5	15	1	6
1950	31	10	13	5	18	9	5	5	2	7	22	5	8	3	11
1951	69	18	26	7	24	31	13	12	3	12	48	5	14	4	12
1952	1	0	0	0	0	1	0	0	0	0					
1953	9	2	4	2	3	5	1	2	1	2	4	1	2	1	1
1954	63	20	25	5	17	29	8	12	2	7	34	12	13	3	10
TOT.	768	214	281	66	224	369	109	137	31	115	409	105	144	35	109
			AVG. .366					AVG. .371					AVG. .352		

Washington Senators

Year	AB	R	Total H	HR	RBI	AB	R	Home H	HR	RBI	AB	R	Away H	HR	RBI
1939	90	18	27	4	19	43	13	19	3	13	47	5	8	1	6
1940	76	14	27	3	18	44	7	14	2	13	32	7	13	1	5
1941	63	16	24	3	13	31	11	15	3	10	32	5	9	0	3
1942	73	28	35	1	14	35	16	18	1	7	38	12	17	0	7
1946	72	24	28	4	19	37	12	14	2	10	35	12	14	2	9
1947	75	13	29	2	14	38	6	16	0	8	37	7	13	2	6
1948	84	23	28	3	9	37	9	11	1	3	47	14	17	2	6
1949	69	21	21	2	13	36	13	12	2	8	33	8	9	0	5
1950	47	5	11	1	6	33	4	7	1	5	14	1	4	0	1
1951	78	21	27	5	24	34	11	17	3	14	44	10	10	2	10
1952	6	1	2	0	1	2	0	1	0	1	4	1	1	0	0
1953	16	3	9	3	8	4	1	2	1	1	12	2	7	2	7
1954	57	16	20	3	11	29	8	13	3	6	28	8	7	0	5
1955	47	13	19	3	10	37	11	16	2	8	10	2	3	1	2
1956	51	11	20	5	13	22	6	9	3	11	29	5	11	2	2
1957	57	12	19	3	10	28	2	6	0	3	29	10	13	3	7
1958	60	12	23	8	21	32	9	12	5	14	28	3	11	3	7
1959	35	3	8	0	4	16	2	5	0	4	19	1	3	0	0
1960	37	8	10	3	4	14	4	4	1	1	23	4	6	2	3
TOT.	1093	172	387	56	231	552	145	211	33	140	541	117	176	23	91
			AVG. .354					AVG. .382					AVG. .325		

Career Home and Away Totals

	AB	H	HR	RBI	AVG.
Home	3887	1403	248	965	.361
Away	3819	1251	273	874	.328

Harold Kaese, baseball writer extraordinaire and compiler of the most comprehensive statistical record ever assembled on the career of one ballplayer. (Courtesy of the Boston Globe)

Pinch-hitting Totals

Year	AB	H	HR	RBI	AVG.
1940	0	0	0	0	.000
1941	9	3	1	5	.333
1948	2	0	0	0	.000
1950	1	1	0	1	1.000
1951	0	0	0	0	.000
1952	4	1	0	1	.250
1953	10	2	2	5	.200
1954	4	2	1	3	.500
1955	2	1	0	2	.500
1956	20	5	0	4	.250
1957	5	3	3	4	.750
1958	11	3	0	2	.273
1959	24	11	0	5	.458
1960	19	1	0	2	.052
TOT.	111	33	7	34	.297

Worst Slumps Through 1956

1939: 2–21; 1–19, Aug. 2–19
1940: 2–25 (included 0–19 stretch), June.
1941: 0–7, July.
1942: 1–19 (included 0–15 stretch), May (avg. from .342 to .295); 0–11, Aug.
1946: 2–18 (included 0–12 stretch).
1948: 0–10.
1951: 7–37 (included 0–12 stretch), May (avg. from .256 to .216); 2–22 (included 0–14 stretch), July (avg. from .333 to .320).
1954: 0–17, Aug. (avg. from .354 to .336); 3–34 (included 0–13 stretch), Sept. (avg. from .361 to .332).
1955: 13–63 (included 0–10 stretch), July.
1956: 2–12, pinch-hitting; 2–14, July; 0–9, Aug.; 1–12, Aug.

Williams on Holidays

x indicates an away game

Year	Memorial Day					July 4th					Labor Day				
	AB	R	H	RBI		AB	R	H	RBI		AB	R	H	RBI	
1939	9	2	2	4		8	5	3	3		6	2	2	1	(Wash.)
1940	4	2	1	1		8	2	4	0		9	1	4	0	(Wash.x)
1941	5	1	3	1		. . . .					5	5	3	5	(Wash.)
1942	7	2	2	2		6	2	3	3		3	4	2	1	(Wash.x)
1946	7	3	2	2		8	3	3	4		7	1	2	0	(N.Y.x)
1947	5	0	1	1	(Wash.x)	7	1	3	1	(Phil.)	5	1	0	0	(N.Y.)
1948	7	2	2	3	(Phil.x)	7	0	0	2	(N.Y.)	9	2	3	0	(Wash.)
1949	7	3	1	2	(Chi.)	7	0	3	1	(N.Y.x)	6	3	3	0	(Wash.)
1950	8	2	2	2	(N.Y.x)	. . . . .rain.					. . . . bad elbow				(Wash.x)
1951	13	3	7	5	(N.Y.)	7	0	0	0	(Phil.x)	. . . . . cold.				(Wash.)
1952	. . . .					. . . .					. . . .				
1953	. . . .					. . . .					5	1	2	4	(N.Y.)
1954	6	3	3	4	(Phil.)	5	2	2	1	(Wash.x)	9	3	6	2	(N.Y.x)
1955	4	2	1	3	(Balt.)	4	1	2	1	(N.Y.x)	8	1	3	0	(Wash.)
1956	6	1	2	3	(Balt.x)	4	1	1	0	(N.Y.)	4	1	1	0	(Wash.x)
1957	5	1	2	1	(Balt.)	4	0	0	0	(Balt.)	. . . . . cold.				
1958	3	1	2	0	(Balt.x)	4	1	1	0	(Balt.)	. . . . . cold.				
1959	8	3	4	2	(Balt.)	5	1	2	0	(Balt.x)	. . . . . cold.				
1960	. . . . . .cold.					7	1	2	2	(Balt.)	3	0	0	0	
TOT.	104	31	37	36	9HR	91	20	29	18	4HR	79	25	31	13	4HR
	AVG .356					AVG .319					AVG .392				

Year	Season Openers						His Birthday (8/30)					
	AB	R	H	RBI	HR		AB	R	H	RBI	HR	
1939	4	0	1	0		(N.Y.x)	4	1	1	3		(Det.)
1940	4	0	2	0		(Wash.x)	5	1	2	1		(Phil.)
1941	1	0	1	1		(Wash.)	3	3	2	2	1	(Phil.)
1942	4	1	3	5	1	(Phil.)	9	2	5	1		(St.L.)
1946	5	1	1	1		(Wash.x)	6	2	1	1		(Phil.)
1947	4	0	2	2		(Wash.)	4	0	1	0		(Phil.)
1948	4	0	1	0		(Phil.)	. . . .					
1949	3	0	2	1		(Phil.x)	3	0	0	0		(Det.)
1950	3	3	2	2		(N.Y.)	. . . . did not play					
1951	3	0	1	0		(N.Y.x)	4	0	0	0		(Det.x)
1952	3	1	1	0		(Wash.x)	. . . . rain					
1953	. . . . . . did not play						2	2	1	1	1	(Clev.x)
1954	. . . . . . did not play						4	0	0	0		(Clev.)
1955	. . . . . . did not play						2	1	2	2		(Chi.x)
1956	4	1	3	1		(Balt.)	. . . . .no game					
1957	5	1	1	0		(Balt.x)	. . . . sick					
1958	. . . . . . did not play						. . . . sick					
1959	. . . . . . did not play						. . . . sick					
1960	2	1	1	1	1	(Wash.x)	. . . . .no game					
TOT.	49	9	22	14	2		46	12	15	11	2	
	AVG. 449						AVG. .326					

Season Home/Away Averages and Miscellaneous Season Highs

Year		HR	AVG	Hit Streak (Games)	Hitless Streak (Games)	High RBI	Hits (Single Game)	Perfect Days AB	Grand Slams
1939	H	14	.343	12	4	6	4(3×)	5	2
	A	17	.313						
1940	H	9	.340	11	3 (0-19)	4	4(2×)	4	1
	A	14	.348						
1941	H	19	.428	23	2 (0-7)	4	4(4×)	8	1
	A	18	.380						
1942	H	16	.356	15	4 (0-15)	7	3(17×)	5	1
	A	20	.356						
1946	H	18	.368	10	4 (0-12)	8	4(2×)	8	2
	A	20	.315						
1947	H	16	.332	9	4	5(2×)	5	8	1
	A	16	.355						
1948	H	9	.368	16	3 (0-10)	7	5	9	0
	A	16	.370						

Season Home/Away Averages and Miscellaneous Season Highs

Year		HR	AVG	Hit Streak (Games)	Hitless Streak (Games)	High RBI	Hits (Single Game)	Perfect Days AB	Grand Slams
1949	H	23	.349	12	2 (3×)	7	4	1	1
	A	20	.337						
1950	H	16	.356	12(2×)	3	7	4(2×)	1	1
	A	12	.282						
1951	H	18	.403	10	4 (0-14)	5	4(3×)	2	1
	A	12	.232						
1952	H	1	.500	—	—	—	2	1	0
	A	0	.250						
1953	H	8	.362	12	3 (ph)	4(2×)	4	5	0
	A	5	.455						
1954	H	16	.371	14	4 (0-17)	5	5	7	0
	A	13	.320						
1955	H	15	.390	9	3 (0-10)	6	4	3	3
	A	13	.318						
1956	H	10	.361	7(3×)	3 (5 ph)	4(4×)	4(2×)	10	0
	A	14	.328						
1957	H	12	.403	17	2	5	4	11	1
	A	26	.374						
1958	H	10	.329	6	3 (0-9)	7	4	4	2
	A	16	.328						
1959	H	3	.276	4	4 (0-17)	3	3	11	0
	A	7	.232						
1960	H	15	.329	7(ph)	6	6	3(6×)	2	0
	A	14	.301	2(st)					

Batting Average vs. the Yearly Batting Champion

1939	Joe DiMaggio	.381
	Jimmie Foxx	.360
	Luke Appling	.348
	Bob Johnson	.338
	Hal Trosky	.335
	Charlie Keller	.334
	Red Rolfe	.328
	TED WILLIAMS	.327
1940	Joe DiMaggio	.352
	Luke Appling	.348
	TED WILLIAMS	.344
1941	TED WILLIAMS	.406
1942	TED WILLIAMS	.356
1946	Mickey Vernon	.353
	TED WILLIAMS	.342
1947	TED WILLIAMS	.343
1948	TED WILLIAMS	.369
1949	George Kell	.3429
	TED WILLIAMS	.3427
1950	Billy Goodman	.354
	TED WILLIAMS	.317 (89G, 106–334, DNQ)
1951	Ferris Fain	.344
	Minnie Minoso	.326
	George Kell	.319
	TED WILLIAMS	.317
1952	Ferris Fain	.327
	TED WILLIAMS	.400 (6g, 4–10, DNQ)
1953	Mickey Vernon	.337
	TED WILLIAMS	.407 (37g, 37–91, DNQ)
1954	Bobby Avila†	.341
	TED WILLIAMS	.345 (117g, 133–386, DNQ)
1955	Al Kaline	.340
	TED WILLIAMS	.356 (98g, 114–320, DNQ)
1956	Mickey Mantle	.353
	TED WILLIAMS	.345
1957	TED WILLIAMS	.388
1958	TED WILLIAMS	.328
1959	Harvey Kuenn	.353
	TED WILLIAMS	.254 (69–272, DNQ)
1960	Pete Runnells	.320
	TED WILLIAMS	.316 (98–310, DNQ)

Years qualified for the title	12
Years as batting champion	6
Second	3
Third	1
Fourth	1
Seventh	1
Disqualified from	7

When he qualified he was only beaten out by twelve players in his career.

†*Total Baseball* credits Williams, not Avila, with the 1954 title.

Best Doubleheaders
(Through 1956)

	AB	R	H	RBI	HR	Two-Game Totals				
						AB	R	H	RBI	HR
1939										
July 18	5	1	3	3	0					
at Chi.	5	1	3	1	0	8	2	6	4	0
Aug. 13	3	2	3	1	0					
Wash.	3	2	3	1	0	6	4	6	2	0
Sept. 10	4	3	3	2	0					
at Phil.	3	2	2	1	0	7	5	5	3	0
1940										
July 17	4	2	3	1	0					
Det.	4	1	2	1	0	8	3	5	2	0
1941										
Aug. 19	3	1	1	1	1					
at St. L.	5	2	4	3	2	8	3	5	4	3
Sept. 8	5	2	4	2	1					
at Phil.	3	0	2	0	0	8	2	6	2	1
1942										
June 30	5	2	2	0	0					
Wash.	4	1	3	1	0	9	3	5	1	0
Aug. 20	4	0	2	1	0					
St. L.	3	2	3	0	0	9	2	5	1	0
Sept. 2	4	1	3	1	0					
Det.	4	0	2	3	0	8	1	5	4	0
1946										
May 6	4	1	3	2	0					
St. L.	3	1	3	0	0	7	2	6	2	0
July 14	5	4	4	8	3					
Chi.	2	2	1	0	0	7	6	5	8	3
July 21	4	0	3	1	0					
St. L.	5	2	4	2	1	9	2	7	3	1
1947										
Aug. 22	3	1	2	1	0					
at Chi.	4	2	4	0	0	7	3	6	1	0
1948										
May 29	4	2	2	1	0					
at Wash.	4	2	3	2	1	8	4	5	3	1
June 1	3	2	1	0	0					
Det.	5	2	4	3	1	8	4	5	3	1
1949										
Aug. 24	5	2	3	2	0					
at Chi.	6	2	3	2	0	11	4	6	4	0
1951										
May 20	8	2	4	2	1					
N.Y.	5	1	2	3	0	13	3	7	5	1
1954										
May 16	4	1	3	2	0					
at Det.*	5	2	5	5	2	9	3	8	7	2
1956										
July 8	3	2	3	4	1					
Balt.	5	1	1	1	0	8	3	4	5	1

*6 hits in a row.

Batting by Month

	April					May					June				
Year	AB	H	RBI	HR	AVG.	AB	H	RBI	HR	AVG.	AB	H	RBI	HR	AVG.
1939	32	11	5	1	.344	101	26	31	7	.257	88	28	22	2	.318
1940	43	13	5	1	.302	76	31	16	3	.408	109	32	23	5	.294
1941	18	7	5	1	.389	101	44	22	6	.436	94	35	29	8	.372
1942	52	14	14	3	.269	101	38	41	12	.376	86	28	18	2	.326
1946	52	18	10	1	.346	93	32	27	8	.344	103	38	27	11	.369
1947	38	13	9	3	.342	81	22	20	8	.272	83	24	13	2	.289
1948	32	11	6	3	.344	107	41	36	8	.383	87	40	28	4	.460
1949	36	11	9	1	.306	102	35	32	11	.304	115	35	38	7	.304
1950	20	9	12	3	.450	113	32	29	9	.283	116	40	40	12	.345
1951	37	11	10	4	.297	97	32	32	7	.330	102	37	28	3	.363
1952	10	4	3	1	.400	. . . .					. . . .				
1953	. . . .					. . . .					. . . .				
1954	. . . .					49	20	15	4	.408	38	9	7	2	.237
1955	. . . .					12	4	4	1	.333	63	25	20	8	.397
1956	10	5	3	0	.500	21	5	3	0	.238	91	33	14	2	.363
1957	47	20	8	4	.426	82	33	14	7	.402	95	28	21	9	.295
1958	32	7	7	3	.219	87	25	13	3	.287	84	29	16	5	.345
1959	. . . .					63	12	5	1	.190	70	16	10	4	.229
1960	9	2	2	2	.222	11	4	1	0	.364	76	25	24	11	.329
TOT.	468	156	108	31	.333	1297	436	341	95	.336	1500	502	378	97	.335

	July					August					September				
Year	AB	H	RBI	HR	AVG.	AB	H	RBI	HR	AVG.	AB	H	RBI	HR	AVG.
1939	129	48	28	6	.372	121	35	36	6	.289	94	37	23	9	.394
1940	125	42	21	5	.336	99	35	25	4	.353	109	40	23	5	.367
1941	63	27	19	6	.429	107	43	26	10	.402	73	29	19	6	.397
1942	103	40	15	6	.388	115	38	29	4	.330	65	28	20	9	.431
1946	103	36	29	8	.350	103	28	21	6	.272	60	24	9	4	.400
1947	115	44	29	10	.383	107	41	18	4	.383	104	37	25	5	.356
1948	63	20	12	1	.317	100	32	20	7	.320	110	39	21	1	.355
1949	106	41	25	7	.387	116	47	34	10	.405	86	24	21	7	.279
1950	19	5	2	1	.263	. . . .					61	16	11	3	.262
1951	99	30	20	7	.303	119	36	18	6	.303	77	23	18	3	.299
1952	. . . .					. . . .					. . . .				
1953	. . . .					42	18	17	7	.429	49	19	17	6	.388
1954	104	40	29	11	.385	99	33	24	7	.333	96	31	14	5	.323
1955	92	27	23	10	.293	88	34	26	6	.386	65	24	10	3	.369
1956	102	36	23	7	.353	88	29	15	8	.330	88	30	24	7	.341
1957	84	37	21	9	.391	93	33	14	4	.355	19	12	9	5	.632
1958	90	28	21	6	.311	62	23	15	4	.371	56	23	13	5	.411
1959	71	21	16	3	.296	55	13	9	2	.236	13	7	3	0	.538
1960	73	23	12	5	.315	83	26	20	6	.313	58	18	13	5	.310
TOT.	1541	545	345	108	.354	1597	544	367	101	.341	1283	461	293	88	.359

	October				
Year	AB	H	RBI	HR	AVG.
1948	10	5	4	1	.500
1949	5	1	0	0	.200
1950	5	4	3	0	.800
TOT.	20	10	7	1	.500

Career Batting Before and After the All-Star Break

	Before						After				
Year	AB	H	HR	RBI	AVG		AB	H	HR	RBI	AVG
1939	258	79	12	70	.306		307	106	19	75	.345
1940	267	92	11	52	.345		294	101	12	61	.344
1941	237	96	16	62	.405		219	89	21	58	.406
1942	262	91	18	80	.347		260	95	18	57	.365
1946	274	95	23	71	.347		240	81	15	52	.338
1947	225	69	15	48	.307		303	112	17	66	.370
1948	263	102	16	72	.388		246	86	9	55	.350
1949	289	94	20	85	.325		277	100	23	74	.361
1950	268	86	25	83	.321		66	20	3	14	.303
1951	267	91	16	76	.341		264	78	14	50	.295
1952	10	4	3	1	.400				Did not play		
1953			Did not play				91	37	13	34	.407
1954	120	44	8	34	.367		266	89	21	55	.394
1955	99	39	12	30	.394		221	75	16	50	.339
1956	155	57	5	30	.368		245	81	19	52	.331
1957	248	85	20	45	.343		172	78	18	42	.454
1958	226	71	14	45	.314		185	64	12	40	.346
1959	152	33	5	18	.217		120	36	5	25	.300
1960	123	42	14	33	.341		187	56	15	39	.299
TOT.	3743	1270	251	937	.339		3963	1384	270	902	.349

Williams vs. Left-handed Pitchers Pitching Complete Games

Date	Pitcher, Team		AB	R	H	RBI	
1939							
April 25	Joe Krakauskas, Wash.		4	1	1	0	
July 1	Marius Russo, N.Y.		4	2	1	0	
July 2(1)	Lefty Gomez, N.Y.		3	2	1	3	HR
July 20	Thornton Lee, Chi.		4	0	1	0	
July 26	Thornton Lee, Chi.		4	0	2	0	
Aug. 19(2)	Ken Chase, Wash.		4	0	0	0	
Sept. 6	Lefty Gomez, N.Y.		4	0	1	0	
Sept. 17(1)	Thornton Lee, Chi.		3	1	1	1	HR
		TOT.	30	6	8	4	2 HR
			AVG. .267				
1940							
June 6	Emil Bildilli, St. L.		4	1	0	0	
June 7	Hal Newhouser, Det.		3	0	0	0	
June 21	Al Milnar, Clev.		4	1	1	3	HR
June 23(1)	Al Smith, Clev.		4	0	1	0	
July 4(2)	Marius Russo, N.Y.		4	1	3	0	
July 6	Ken Chase, Wash.		4	0	0	0	
July 7(2)	Rene Monteagudo, Wash.		5	0	2	1	
Aug. 13(1)	Marius Russo, N.Y.		3	0	0	0	
Sept. 2(2)	Ken Chase, Wash.		3	1	2	0	
Sept. 7	Marius Russo, N.Y.		4	1	2	3	
Sept. 13	Al Milnar, Clev.		4	0	0	0	
Sept. 22	Marius Russo, N.Y.		4	1	1	1	HR
Sept. 28(1)	Chubby Dean, Phil.		4	4	4	2	
		TOT.	50	10	16	10	2 HR
			AVG. .308				
1941							
April 23	Lefty Gomez, N.Y.		0	0	0	0	
April 24	Marius Russo, N.Y.	(ph)	1	0	0	0	
May 3	Al Milnar, Clev.		3	0	1	0	
June 7	Al Smith, Clev.		4	1	1	0	
June 8(2)	Thornton Lee, Chi.		3	1	0	0	
June 14	Al Smith, Clev.		4	2	2	2	HR
July 23	Thornton Lee, Chi.		5	1	2	0	
Aug. 24	Al Smith, Clev.		3	0	0	0	
Sept. 14(2)	Thornton Lee, Chi.		4	1	1	1	
Sept. 20	Marius Russo, N.Y.		4	0	2	0	
		TOT.	31	6	9	3	1 HR
			AVG. .333				
1942							
June 19	Eddie Smith, Chi.		1	0	0	0	
July 9	Hal Newhouser, Det.		5	0	1	0	
July 15	Eddie Smith, Chi.		5	0	2	2	
		TOT.	11	0	3	2	
			AVG. .273				

1946

Date	Pitcher	AB	R	H	RBI	
April 30	Hal Newhouser, Det.	3	1	0	0	
May 14(2)	Hal Newhouser, Det.	4	0	1	0	
May 26(2)	Joe Page, N.Y.	3	0	0	0	
June 20	Sam Zoldak, St. L.	2	0	0	0	
June 26(1)	Hal Newhouser, Det.	2	1	1	1	HR
June 30(2)	Mickey Haefner, Wash.	4	0	0	0	
July 6	Mickey Haefner, Wash.	4	0	0	0	
July 17(1)	Eddie Lopat, Chi.	3	0	1	1	
Aug. 11(2)	Joe Page, N.Y.	3	0	0	0	
Aug. 18(2)	Joe Page, N.Y.	4	2	2	0	
Aug. 24(2)	Frank Papish, Chi.	4	0	0	0	
TOT.		36	4	5	2	1 HR
	AVG. .139					

1947

Date	Pitcher	AB	R	H	RBI	
June 8	Hal Newhouser, Det.	2	0	0	0	
June 25	Hal Newhouser, Det.	3	1	2	0	
June 27	Mickey Haefner, Wash.	4	0	0	0	
July 10	Hal Newhouser, Det.	2	0	1	0	
July 11(2)	Stubby Overmire, Det.	3	0	0	0	
July 15	Frank Papish, Chi.	2	0	1	0	
July 22	Eddie Lopat, Chi.	4	1	2	0	
Aug. 3	Hal Newhouser, Det.	5	0	1	1	
Aug. 6	Mickey Haefner, Wash.	4	0	0	0	
Aug. 11	Mickey Haefner, Wash.	4	0	2	0	
Aug. 27(1)	Stubby Overmire, Det.	4	0	0	0	
Sept. 14	Eddie Lopat, Chi.	2	0	0	0	
Sept. 16(1)	Frank Papish, Chi.	4	0	1	0	
Sept. 28	Mickey Haefner, Wash.	4	0	2	0	
TOT.		47	2	12	1	
	AVG. .255					

1948

Date	Pitcher	AB	R	H	RBI	
April 19(2)	Lou Brissie, Phil.	4	0	1	1	
May 19	Hal Newhouser, Det.	3	0	0	0	
May 22	Gene Bearden, Clev.	3	0	1	0	
May 29(1)	Mickey Haefner, Wash.	4	2	2	1	
June 8	Gene Bearden, Clev.	3	0	0	0	
June 24(1)	Bill Wight, Chi.	3	0	1	0	
June 29	Eddie Lopat, Chi.	4	0	1	0	
July 2	Lou Brissie, Phil.	4	0	1	0	
Aug. 1(2)	Sam Zoldak, St. L.	4	1	2	1	HR
Sept. 26	Tommy Byrne, N.Y.	4	1	1	0	
Oct. 4	Gene Bearden, Clev.	4	1	1	0	
TOT.		40	5	11	3	1 HR
	AVG. .275					

1949

Date	Pitcher	AB	R	H	RBI	
April 16	Lou Brissie, Phil.	3	0	2	1	
May 16	Rickey Haefner, Wash.	3	0	2	1	
July 1	Lou Brissie, Phil.	4	1	1	1	
July 3	Alex Kellner, Phil.	2	0	0	0	
July 20	Bob Kuzava, Chi.	5	2	2	3	HR
Aug. 25	Billy Pierce, Chi.	4	0	0	0	
Sept. 24	Eddie Lopat, Chi.	2	1	1	1	HR
TOT.		23	4	8	7	2 HR
	AVG. .348					

1950

Date	Pitcher	AB	R	H	RBI	
April 26	Eddie Lopat, Chi.	4	0	0	0	
May 17	Ted Gray, Det.	3	0	0	0	
May 21(1)	Bill Wight, Chi.	5	0	1	0	
May 21(2)	Billy Pierce, Chi.	3	0	1	0	
June 11(1)	Hal Newhouser, Det.	3	2	0	0	
June 16	Hal Newhouser, Det.	2	0	0	0	
June 17	Ted Gray, Det.	2	0	0	0	
June 20	Bill Wight, Chi.	4	1	1	0	
June 21	Billy Pierce, Chi.	4	0	0	0	
June 28	Lou Brissie, Phil.	3	1	1	2	HR
July 9	Eddie Lopat, Chi.	4	0	0	0	
Sept. 23	Eddie Lopat, Chi.	4	0	1	0	
Sept. 27(2)	Gene Bearden, Clev.	5	0	0	0	
TOT.		46	4	5	2	1 HR
	AVG. .109					

1951

Date	Pitcher	AB	R	H	RBI	
April 18	Vic Raschi, N.Y.	4	1	1	0	
April 20	Alex Kellner, Phil.	4	0	1	1	
April 24	Bob Kuzava, Chi.	4	1	2	1	HR
May 4	Hal Newhouser, Det.	3	0	0	0	
May 6(1)	Lou Sleater, St. L.	4	1	1	1	HR
May 20	Hal Newhouser, Det.	4	0	0	0	

Date	Pitcher		AB	R	H	RBI	
June 4(1)	Billy Pierce, Chi.		4	1	3	2	
June 7	Ted Gray, Det.		3	2	1	0	
June 12	Ted Gray, Det.		4	1	1	0	
July 1	Eddie Lopat, Chi.		3	0	0	0	
Aug. 9(2)	Alex Kellner, Phil.		4	1	1	1	
Aug. 16	Bobby Shantz, Phil.		4	0	1	0	
Sept. 7(2)	Alex Kellner, Phil.		4	0	1	0	
Sept. 9(2)	Bobby Shantz, Phil.		4	0	1	1	
Sept. 12	Ted Gray, Det.		2	0	0	0	
		TOT.	55	8	14	7	2 HR
			AVG. .255				

1952—did not face a left-hander who pitched a complete game.

1953

Date	Pitcher		AB	R	H	RBI	
April 21(1)	Chuck Stobbs, Wash.		3	0	1	0	
Sept. 16	Ted Gray, Det.		4	1	1	0	
Sept. 27	Whitey Ford, N.Y.		3	1	1	0	
		TOT.	10	2	3	0	
			AVG. .300				

1954

Date	Pitcher		AB	R	H	RBI	
July 3	Alex Kellner, Phil.		2	1	1	0	
July 5	Chuck Stobbs, Wash.		3	0	0	0	
July 9	Alex Kellner, Phil.		2	1	0	0	
July 25(1)	Jack Harshman, Chi.		3	1	0	0	
Aug. 3	Jack Harshman, Chi.		4	0	1	0	
Aug. 12(1)	Chuck Stobbs, Wash.		3	1	0	0	
Aug. 17	Whitey Ford, N.Y.		4	1	2	0	
Sept. 4	Ted Gray, Det.		4	0	0	0	
Sept. 17	Dean Stone, Wash.		4	0	0	0	
Sept. 24	Chuck Stobbs, Wash.		4	0	3	0	
		TOT.	33	5	7	0	
			AVG. .242				

1955

Date	Pitcher		AB	R	H	RBI	
July 24(1)	Billy Pierce, Chi.		3	0	1	0	
July 31(2)	Billy Hoeft, Det.		2	0	0	0	
Aug. 9	Whitey Ford, N.Y.		3	0	0	0	
Aug. 26	Billy Hoeft, Det.		4	0	2	1	
Sept. 17	Tommy Byrne, Wash.		4	0	1	0	
Sept. 20(1)	Bill Wight, Chi.		3	1	2	1	HR
		TOT.	19	1	6	2	1 HR
			AVG. .316				

1956

Date	Pitcher		AB	R	H	RBI	
May 5	Billy Hoeft, Det.	(ph)	1	0	1	0	
May 26	Chuck Stobbs, Wash.	(ph)	1	0	1	1	
June 10	Billy Pierce, Chi.		2	0	1	0	
June 24	Alex Kellner, Phil.		3	1	2	1	HR
June 26	Jack Harshman, Chi.		4	0	0	0	
July 5	Whitey Ford, N.Y.		3	0	0	0	
July 12	Jack Harshman, Chi.		3	0	0	0	
July 29	Billy Pierce, Chi.		3	0	1	0	
Aug. 10	Chuck Stobbs, Wash.		4	1	1	1	HR
Aug. 19	Chuck Stobbs, Wash.		3	1	1	0	
Sept. 5	Whitey Ford, N.Y.		4	0	3	0	
Sept. 13	Billy Pierce, Chi.		4	0	1	0	
Sept. 14	Herb Score, Clev.		2	2	2	1	HR
		TOT.	37	5	14	4	3 HR
			AVG. .378				

1957

Date	Pitcher		AB	R	H	RBI	
April 27	Bobby Shantz, Phil		3	0	1	1	
June 4	Billy Pierce, Chi.		4	0	0	0	
June 12	Don Mossi, Clev.		4	0	1	0	
Aug. 23	Billy Pierce, Chi.		4	0	0	0	
		TOT.	15	0	2	1	
			AVG. .133				

1958

Date	Pitcher		AB	R	H	RBI	
May 10	Jack Harshman, Balt.		4	0	1	0	
May 17(1)	Jack Harshman, Balt.		4	0	0	0	
May 21	Dick Tomanek, Clev.		5	0	0	0	
May 25(2)	Billy Pierce, Chi.	(ph)	1	0	0	0	
June 8(1)	Billy Pierce, Chi.		3	1	0	0	
June 17	Billy Pierce, Chi.		4	0	0	0	
Aug. 1(2)	Hal Woodeshick, Clev.	(ph)	0	0	0	0	
Sept. 10	Billy Pierce, Chi.		3	0	1	0	
Sept. 18	Bud Daley, K.C.		3	0	1	0	
		TOT.	27	1	3	0	
			AVG. .111				

1959							
June 21	Billy Pierce, Chi.	(ph)	1	0	1	0
July 28(2)	Herb Score, Clev.	(ph)	1	0	0	0
Aug. 1	Don Mossi, Det.		4	1	1	1
Aug. 19	Bud Daley, K.C.		4	0	0	0
Sept. 19	Whitey Ford, N.Y.	(ph)	1	0	0	0
		TOT.	11	1	2	1
		AVG. .182				

1960							
June 28	Don Mossi, Det.	(ph)	1	0	1	0
July 6	Jack Kralick, Wash.	(ph)	1	0	0	0
July 15	Bud Daley, K.C.		4	1	1	0
July 18	Herb Score, Clev.		4	0	0	0
July 19	Billy Pierce, Chi.		4	0	1	0
Aug. 26	Frank Baumann, Chi.		2	0	0	0
Sept. 9	Bud Daley, K.C.	(ph)	1	0	0	0
		TOT.	17	1	3	0
		AVG. .176				

Game-by-Game Account of the 1941 Season

		Game	Opponent	RBI	R	AVG	Totals
April	15	1–1 (pinch hit single)	Wash.	1		1.000	1–1
April	16	0–1 (ph)	Wash.			.500	1–2
April	17	Rained out vs. Washington at Boston					
April	18	1–1 (pinch hit single)	at Phil.			.667	2–3
April	19	DNP	at Phil.				
April	20	0–1 (pinch hitter)	at Wash.			.500	2–4
April	21	0–1 (pinch hitter)	at Wash.			.400	2–5
April	22	2–4 (single, double, 1st start)	at Wash.	2	1	.444	4–9
April	23	DNP	at N.Y.				
April	24	0–1 (pinch hitter)	at N.Y.			.400	4–10
April	25	DNP	Phil.				
April	26	DNP	Phil.				
April	27	Rained out vs. Phil. at Boston					
April	28	Day off					
April	29	2–3 (HR, double)	at Det.	1	2	.462	6–13
April	30	1–5 (single)	at Det.	1		.389	7–18
May	1	1–5 (single)	at Det.	1	2	.348	8–23
May	2	0–3	at Clev.			.308	8–26
May	3	1–3 (single)	at Clev.			.310	9–29
May	4	2–5 (2 singles)	at St. L.	2	1	.324	11–34
May	5, 6	Rained out at St. Louis					
May	7	3–4 (2 HR, single)	at Chi.	3	2	.368	14–38
May	8	Rained out at Chicago					
May	9	Day off					
May	10	Rained out vs. N.Y. at Boston					
May	11	3–6 (2 singles, double)	N.Y.	1	2	.386	17–44
May	12	1–3 (single)	N.Y.		2	.383	18–47
May	13	1–4 (HR)	Chi.	1	1	.373	19–51
May	14	0–5	Chi.			.336	19–56
May	15	1–3 (single)	Clev.		2	.339	20–59
May	16	1–4 (single)	Clev.		1	.333	21–63
May	17	3–5 (2 doubles, single)	Clev.	1	1	.353	24–68
May	18	1–4 (single)	Det.			.347	25–72
May	19	1–4 (HR)	Det.	2	1	.342	26–76
May	20	1–3 (single)	Det.		1	.341	27–79
May	21	4–5 (3 singles, double)	St. L.	1		.369	31–84
May	22	2–4 (2 singles)	St. L.			.375	33–88
May	23	1–3 (single)	at N.Y.	3		.374	34–91
May	24	2–3 (2 singles)	at N.Y.		3	.383	36–94
May	25	4–5 (3 singles, double)	at N.Y.	2	2	.404	40–99
May	26	Day off					
May	27	1–2 (HR)	Phil.	2	1	.406	41–101
	27	1–4 (single)	Phil.			.400	42–105
May	28	3–5 (2 singles, double)	Phil.		1	.409	45–110
May	29	3–4 (HR, 2 singles)	Phil.	2	2	.421	48–114
May	30	1–2 (double)	N.Y.		2	.422	49–116
	30	2–3 (2 singles)	N.Y.	1	2	.429	51–119
May	31	Rained out at Detroit					
June	1	2–4 (double, single)	at Det.	1	2	.431	53–123
	1	2–5 (HR, single)	at Det.	3	2	.430	55–128
June	2	1–4 (single)	at Det.	1	2	.424	56–132
June	3, 4	Rained out at Cleveland					
June	5	3–4 (HR, 2 singles)	at Clev.	3	4	.434	59–136
June	6	2–4 (HR, double)	at Chi.	2	2	.436	61–140
June	7	1–4 (single)	at Chi.		1	.431	62–144
June	8	0–2	at Chi.	1		.425	62–146
	8	0–3	at Chi.		1	.416	62–149

June	9	Exhibition game at Indianapolis						
June	10, 11	Rained out at St. Louis						
June	12	1–5 (single)	at St. L.				.409	63–154
	12	1–2 (HR)	at St. L.	2	1		.410	64–156
June	13	Day off						
June	14	3–5 (double, 2 singles)	Chi.				.416	67–161
June	15	2–3 (single, HR)	Chi.	1	2		.421	69–164
	15	2–3 (2 singles)	Chi.	1	2		.425	71–167
June	16	Day off						
June	17	1–4 (HR)	Det.	2	1		.421	72–171
	17	1–1 (double)	Det.		2		.424	73–172
June	18	0–3	Det.				.417	73–175
June	19	1–3 (single)	Det.	2			.416	74–178
June	20	2–3 (single, double)	St. L.	2	1		.420	76–181
June	21	0–2	St. L.		1		.415	76–183
June	22	1–3 (single)	St. L.	2	1		.414	77–186
	22	0–3	St. L.				.407	77–189
June	23	Day off						
June	24	0–2	Clev.		2		.403	77–191
June	25	2–3 (HR, single)	Clev.	2	2		.407	79–194
June	26	3–5 (3 singles)	Clev.	1	2		.412	82–199
June	27	1–3 (single)	at Wash.				.411	83–202
June	28	1–3 (single)	at Wash.				.410	84–205
June	29	2–4 (HR, single)	at Phil.	2	2		.410	86–209
	29	0–4	at Phil.	1			.404	86–213
June	30	Day off						
July	1	1–4 (single)	at N.Y.				.401	87–217
	1	1–2 (single)	at N.Y.		1		.402	88–219
July	2	1–3 (single; DiMag. stk. at 45)	at N.Y.		1		.401	89–222
July	3	2–4 (HR, single)	at Phil.	2	2		.403	91–226
July	4	Rained out at Phil.						
July	5	1–3 (double)	Wash.	1	1		.402	92–229
July	6	1–4 (single)	Wash.	1			.399	93–233
	6	3–4 (2 doubles, single)	Wash.	2	2		.405	96–237
July	7, 8, 9	All-Star break						
July	10	Rained out at Detroit						
July	11	0–4	at Det.				.398	96–241
July	12	0–1	at Det.		2		.397	96–242
	12	DNP	at Det.					
July	13	DNP	at Clev.					
July	14	DNP (injured ankle)	at Clev.					
July	15	DNP	at Clev.					
July	16	0–1 (sacrifice fly)	at Chi.	1			.395	96–243
July	17	DNP	at Chi.					
July	18	DNP	at Chi.					
July	19	0–1	at St. L.				.393	96–244
	19	0–0 (walk)	at St. L.					
July	20	1–1 (ph HR)	at St. L.	3	1		.396	97–245
	20	DNP	at St. L.					
July	21	Day off						
July	22	1–2 (HR)	Chi.	1	1		.397	98–247
July	23	2–5 (double, single)	Chi.		1		.397	100–252
July	24	2–5 (2 singles)	Chi.		1		.397	102–257
July	25	2–3 (HR, single)	Clev.	2	3		.400	104–260
July	26	3–4 (3 singles)	Clev.		1		.405	107–264
July	27	2–3 (single, double)	Clev.				.408	109–267
July	28	Day off						
July	29	1–3 (HR)	St. L.	2	1		.407	110–270
July	30	Rained out vs. St. Louis at Boston						
July	31	2–3 (grand slam, single)	St. L.	4	2		.410	112–273
	31	1–3 (double)	St. L.				.409	113–276
Aug.	1	Day off (Ted catches 374-pound tuna)						
Aug.	2	2–3 (double, single)	Det.		1		.412	115–279
Aug.	3	1–4 (single)	Det.				.410	116–283
Aug.	4	0–2	Phil.				.407	116–285
Aug.	5	2–4 (double, single)	Phil.	2	1		.408	118–289
Aug.	6	1–3 (single)	N.Y.				.408	119–292
	6	0–3	N.Y.				.403	119–295
Aug.	7	3–4 (HR, 2 singles)	N.Y.	2	3		.408	122–299
Aug.	8	1–3 (single)	Wash.		2		.407	123–302
Aug.	9	1–3 (single)	Wash.		1		.407	124–305
Aug.	10	3–4 (2 singles, triple)	Wash.				.411	127–309
	10	1–3 (single)	Wash.				.410	128–312
Aug.	11	1–1 (single)	at N.Y.	1	1		.412	129–313
Aug.	12	1–3 (single)	at N.Y.				.411	130–316
Aug.	13	1–1 (double)	at Phil.	1			.413	131–317
Aug.	14	1–5 (HR)	at Phil.	3	2		.410	132–322
	14	1–4 (single)	at Phil.		1		.408	133–326
Aug.	15	0–2	at Wash.				.405	133–328
Aug.	16	3–5 (double, 2 singles)	at Wash.	1	2		.408	136–333
Aug.	17	0–3	at Wash.				.405	136–336
Aug.	18	Rained out at St. Louis						
Aug.	19	1–3 (HR)	at St. L.	1	1		.404	137–339
	19	4–5 (2 HR, 2 singles)	at St. L.	3	2		.410	141–344

Aug.	20	2–4 (HR, single)	at St. L.	2	3	.411	143–348
	20	1–2 (HR)	at St. L.	2	1	.411	144–350
Aug.	21	2–3 (2 singles)	at Chi.		2	.414	146–353
Aug.	22	0–2	at Chi.	1		.411	146–355
Aug.	23	1–4 (single)	at Chi.			.409	147–359
Aug.	24	1–4 (single)	at Clev.		1	.408	148–363
	24	0–3	at Clev.			.404	148–366
Aug.	25	0–2	at Clev.		1	.402	148–368
Aug.	26	1–1 (single)	at Clev.			.404	149–369
Aug.	27	2–4 (2 singles)	at Det.	1		.405	151–373
Aug.	28	2–3 (HR, triple)	at Det.	1	2	.407	153–376
Aug.	29	Day off					
Aug.	30	2–3 (HR, single)	Phil.	2	3	.409	155–379
Aug.	31	1–3 (HR)	Phil.	3	1	.408	156–382
	31	0–1	Phil.			.407	156–383
Sept.	1	2–3 (2 HR)	Wash.	4	2	.409	158–386
	1	1–2 (HR)	Wash.	1	3	.410	159–388
Sept.	2	Day off					
Sept.	3	1–3 (single)	N.Y.			.409	160–391
Sept.	4	1–1 (single)	N.Y.		1	.411	161–392
Sept.	5	Day off					
Sept.	6	1–4 (single)	at N.Y.	1	1	.409	162–396
Sept.	7	3–4 (2 doubles, single)	at N.Y.	1	1	.413	165–400
Sept.	8	Day off					
Sept.	9	1–3 (single)	Det.			.412	166–403
Sept.	10	2–4 (double, single)	Det.	3	1	.413	168–407
Sept.	11	Day off					
Sept.	12	0–3	St. L.		1	.410	168–410
Sept.	13	0–1	St. L.			.409	168–411
Sept.	14	2–3 (double, single)	Chi.	1	1	.411	170–414
	14	1–4 (triple)	Chi.	1	1	.409	171–418
Sept.	15	1–3 (HR)	Chi.	3	1	.409	172–421
Sept.	16	Day off					
Sept.	17	1–3 (double)	Clev.			.408	173–424
Sept.	18	0–3	Clev.			.405	173–427
Sept.	19	Day off					
Sept.	20	2–4 (2 singles)	N.Y.			.406	175–431
Sept.	21	1–3 (HR)	N.Y.	2	1	.406	176–434
Sept.	22	Day off					
Sept.	23	1–3 (double)	at Wash.		1	.405	177–437
Sept.	24	0–3	at Wash.			.402	177–440
	24	1–4 (single)	at Wash.		1	.401	178–444
Sept. 25, 26		Days off					
Sept.	27	1–4 (double)	at Phil.		1	.400	179–448
Sept.	28	4–5 (HR, 3 singles)	at Phil.	2	2	.404	183–453
	28	2–3 (double, single)	at Phil.			.406	185–456

SEASON TOTALS: AB—456; R—135; H—185; 2B—33; 3B—3; HR—37; RBI—120; SP%—.735; AVG.—.406

NOTE: His longest hitless streak of the season was 0–7 over 4 games. He is the youngest player ever to hit .400 in a season, turning 23 during the season. Others who hit .400 at a young age were:

Ty Cobb at 24 hit .420 in 1911.
Joe Jackson at 24 hit .408 in 1911.
Nap Lajoie at 26 hit .422 in 1901.
Rogers Hornsby at 26 hit .401 in 1922.
George Sisler at 27 hit .407 in 1920.
Harry Heilmann at 29 hit .403 in 1923.
Bill Terry at 31 hit .401 in 1930.

OTHER NOTABLE STATISTICS

Career Firsts

First game: at New York, April 20, 1939.
First walk: vs. Joe Krakauskas on 26th at bat.
First strikeout: vs. Charles Ruffing at N.Y., 2nd inning, 1st at bat, April 20, 1939.
First hit: vs. Ruffing at N.Y., 4th inning, 2nd at bat, triple to right-center, April 20, 1939.
First HR: April 23, 1939 (3rd game) at Fenway vs. Philadelphia A's pitcher Luther Thomas, 1 on in 1st inning, hit to right-center (lost 12–8).

First 2 HR game: May 4, 1939, at Detroit, off Roxie Lawson and Robert Harris (Harris's HR over press box).
First HR off an LHP: May 27, 1939, at Wash. off Joe Krakauskas.
First grand slam: August 19, 1939, at Wash. off Pete Appleton in 9th inning to win game 8–6.
First over LF fence at Fenway: May 13, 1947, vs. Chicago off Earl Harrist.

First inside-the-park HR: September 13, 1946, at Clev. off Red Embree. Won 1–0 to clinch pennant (also only inside-park homer during Williams's career).

First extra-inning HR: May 9, 1939, at St.L. off Harry Kimberlin, 3-run HR to win game 10–8, in Williams's 14th game.

First pinch-hit HR: July 20, 1941, off Johnny Niggeling at St.L. with 2 on in 9th inning. Red Sox lost 6–3.

First pinch-hit appearance: August 2, 1940, at Detroit. Walked and scored as Sox won 12–9.

First opening day HR: April 14, 1942, at Fenway vs. Phil., 3-run HR off Phil Marchildon in 1st inning.

First run scored: April 21, 1939. Scored from 3rd in 7th inning on a passed ball by Hayes of the Athletics.

First single: April 21, 1939, vs. Phil. off Roy Parmelee in 7th inning.

First RBI: April 21, 1939, vs. Phil. off Parmelee in 7th inning, scored Joe Cronin from 2nd.

First hit to CF fence at Fenway: April 22, 1939, a triple leading off the 2nd inning off the Athletics' Lee Ross.

First DP: April 24, 1939, 5th inning vs. Wash., grounded to 2B Charlie Myer with Jim Tabor on 1st.

First bunt: April 25, 1939, with Cronin on 2nd and Tabor on 1st in 9th inning; game tied 5–5 vs. Wash. off Joe Krakauskas, popped to Ossie Bluege at 2nd (Foxx HR won it in 11th inning).

First put out: April 20, 1939, caught Gehrig line drive in RF with 2 on, 2 out.

First HR he saw in majors: Over his head by Bill Dickey off Lefty Grove in N.Y., April 20, 1939.

Career All-Star Summary

1940 at St. Louis Final: NL 4–AL 0
Batted 7th behind Jimmie Foxx and played left field.
Walked by Paul Derringer in the 1st.
4-3 groundout off Bucky Walters in the 3rd.
4-3 groundout off Whit Wyatt in the 6th.
Replaced in 7th by Hank Greenberg.

1941 at Detroit Final: AL 7–NL 5
Batted 4th behind Joe DiMaggio and played left field.
Walked by Whit Wyatt in 2nd.
Doubled off Paul Derringer to score Cecil Travis in the 4th.
Flied to center off Bucky Walters in the 6th.
Struck out looking off Claude Passeau with 1 on in the 8th.
Home run off Claude Passeau on a 2–1 pitch with Joe Gordon on 3rd and Joe DiMaggio on 1st with 2 out in the 9th to win game 7–5.

1942 at the Polo Grounds Final: AL 3–NL 1
Batted 3rd behind Tommy Henrich.
Flied to left field off Mort Cooper in the 1st with 1 on.
Singled off Cooper in the 3rd.
Flied to center off Johnny Vander Meer in the 6th.
Flied to center off Claude Passeau in the 8th.

1946 at Fenway Park Final: AL 12–NL 0
Batted 3rd behind Johnny Pesky.
Walked in the 1st off Claude Passeau and scored on Charlie Keller HR.
Solo HR ("wind blown") in the 4th off Kirby Higbe.
Singled in the 5th off Higbe with 2 on scoring Dom DiMaggio.
Singled in the 7th off Ewell Blackwell.
3-run HR off Rip Sewell in the 8th into the bull pen.

1947 at Wrigley Field Final: AL 2–NL 1
Batted 3rd behind Buddy Lewis.
Struck out looking off Ewell Blackwell in the 1st.
Doubled off Harry Brecheen to right field in the 4th.
Singled off Brecheen in the 6th sending Luke Appling to 3rd.
4-3 groundout in the 8th off Warren Spahn.

1948 at St. Louis Final: AL 5–NL 2
Playing with a rib injury.
Walked off Ewell Blackwell in the 6th as a pinch-hitter. Hal Newhouser pinch-ran for him at first.

1949 at Brooklyn Final: AL 11–NL 7
Batted 3rd behind George Kell.

Struck out against Warren Spahn with 1 on in the 1st.
Walked in the 2nd off Spahn.
Walked in the 4th off Don Newcombe.
Flied to center in the 6th off Vern Bickford.
Made a good catch off Newcombe in 2nd.
Replaced by Dale Mitchell in bottom of 6th.

1950 at Comiskey Park Final: NL 4–AL 3
(14 innings)
Batted 4th behind George Kell.
Grounder to 1st off Robin Roberts with 1 on in the 1st.
Flied to left off Roberts with 1 on.
Singled in the 5th off Don Newcombe, scoring Larry Doby.
Struck out looking off Larry Jansen in the 7th.
Hurt left elbow on Ralph Kiner fly, replaced by Dom DiMaggio in 9th.

1951 at Detroit Final: NL 8–AL 3
Batted 4th behind George Kell.
Popped to Bob Elliot off Robin Roberts with 1 on in the 1st.
Struck out in 3rd off Sal Maglie with Nellie Fox on 2nd.
Walked in the 5th off Maglie after a George Kell HR.
Tripled in 8th off Don Newcombe with none out—did not score.

1953 at Cincinnati
Did not play. Wore marine captain uniform.

1954 at Cleveland Final: AL 11–NL 9
Team was picked up by Manager Casey Stengel, not voted.
Struck out off Johnny Antonelli in the 4th. Pinch-hitting for Bob Lemon with a man on 1st, played LF and batted 9th.
Walked in the 6th off Warren Spahn on 4 pitches. Scored on Bobby Avila single for an 8–7 lead.
Struck out off Marv Grissom (screwball).

1955 at Milwaukee Final: NL 6–AL 5
Walked in 1st off Robin Roberts after Harvey Kuenn and Nellie Fox, scored on a Mickey Mantle HR.
Singled 3rd off Robin Roberts to start inning. Out on Yogi Berra DP grounder.
1-3 groundout in 5th for 3rd out off Harvey Haddix.
Flied to center in 8th to Willie Mays off Don Newcombe (near HR).

1956 at Washington Final: NL 7–AL 3
Struck out off Bob Friend in the 1st.
Grounded to 1st off Friend in the 3rd—left 2 on.
HR off Warren Spahn in the 6th over 400 feet with
Nellie Fox on 1st.
Flied to Ken Boyer in left off Johnny Antonelli in
8th.

1957 at St. Louis Final: AL 6–NL 5
Batted 5th behind Mantle (4) and Kaline (3).
Walked off Curt Simmons in 2nd and scored on a
Harvey Kuenn double.
Grounded to 1st off Lew Burdette in 3rd.
Flied to left off Jack Sanford in the 6th.
Flied to Willie Mays in center off Larry Jackson.

1958 at Baltimore Final: AL 4–NL 3
Pinch-hit for Luis Aparicio in the 6th. Played LF
until 9th.
Reached base in the 6th on 3B Frank Thomas error
off Bob Friend.

Struck out in the 8th on a 3–2 pitch by Turk
Farrell.

1959 at Pittsburgh Final: NL 5–AL 4
Pinch-hit for Rocky Colavito and walked in the 8th.
Walked off Roy Face to load the bases and was
replaced by PR Gil McDougald.

1959 All-Star #2 at LA Final: AL 5–NL 3
Grounded to Stan Musial at 1st off Don Drysdale.
Flied to center off Don Drysdale.
Struck out in 5th off Gene Conley.

1960 at Kansas City Final: NL 5–AL 3
Grounded out 4–3 pinch-hitting for Bill Monbou-
quette vs. Bob Friend with a runner on 1st in the
2nd.

1960 at New York
PH for Minnie Minoso in the 7th and singled off
Larry Jackson. Brooks Robinson replaced him as
a pinch-runner.

All-Star Totals

Year	POS	AVG.	AB	R	H	2B	3B	HR	RBI	BB	SO	E	PO	A
1940	LF	.000	2	0	0	0	0	0	0	1	0	0	3	0
1941	LF	.500	4	1	2	1	0	1	4	1	1	1	3	0
1942	LF	.250	4	0	1	0	0	0	0	0	0	0	0	0
1946	LF	1.000	4	4	4	0	0	2	5	1	0	0	1	0
1947	LF	.500	4	0	2	1	0	0	0	0	1	0	3	0
1948	PH	—	0	0	0	0	0	0	0	1	0	0	0	0
1949	LF	.000	2	1	0	0	0	0	0	2	1	0	1	0
1950	LF	.250	4	0	1	0	0	0	1	0	1	0	2	0
1951	LF	.333	3	0	1	0	1	0	0	1	1	0	3	0
1954	PH-LF	.000	2	1	0	0	0	0	0	1	2	0	2	0
1955	LF	.333	3	1	1	0	0	0	0	1	0	0	1	0
1956	LF	.250	4	1	1	0	0	1	2	0	1	0	2	0
1957	LF	.000	3	1	0	0	0	0	0	1	0	0	2	0
1958	PH-LF	.000	2	0	0	0	0	0	0	0	1	0	1	0
1959	PH	—	0	0	0	0	0	0	0	1	0	0	0	0
1959	LF	.000	3	0	0	0	0	0	0	0	0	0	0	0
1960	PH	.000	1	0	0	0	0	0	0	0	0	0	0	0
1960	PH	1.000	1	0	1	0	0	0	0	0	0	0	0	0
TOT.		.304	46	10	14	2	1	4	12	11	9	1	24	0

1946 World Series Totals

	AVG.	G	AB	R	H	2B	3B	HR	RBI	BB	SO	E
1946	.200	7	25	2	5	0	0	0	1	5	5	0

Pitching Record

August 24, 1940
8th inning:
Frank Croucher (ss) singled (to third).
Tommy Bridges (p) bunted to Williams, who forced
Croucher at 2nd.
Pete Fox (of) grounded to Finney at 1st, who forced
Bridges at 2nd.
Barney McCoskey (of) flied out to Doc Kramer in
CF.
9th inning:
Mike Higgins (3B) singled to left.
Hank Greenberg (of) singled to right.
Rudy York (1B) took called 3rd strike.
Dutch Meyer (2B) grounded to 3rd for out with
Higgins scoring.
Birdie Tebbetts (c) grounded back to Williams to
end inning.

IP	H	R	ER	BB	SO	ERA
2.0	3	1	1	0	1	4.50

Minor League Career

December 7, 1937: Purchased from San Diego for $25,000 plus OFs Dom Dallessandro and Spencer Harris and INFs Al Niemiec and Bunny Griffiths.

Year	Club	AVG.	G	AB	R	H	2B	3B	HR	TB	RBI	BB	SO	SB
1936	San Diego	.271	42	107	18	29	8	2	0	41	11	0	0	2
1937	San Diego	.291	138	454	66	132	24	2	23	229	98	0	0	1
1938	Minneapolis	.366	148	528	130	193	30	9	43	370	142	114	75	6

Notable Achievements

AL MVP	1946, 1949	

AL Batting Champion	1941	.406
	1942	.356
	1947	.343
	1948	.369
	1957	.388
	1958	.328

AL Home Run Champion	1941	37
	1942	36
	1947	32
	1949	43

		AVG	HR	RBI
Triple Crown Winner	1942	.356	36	137
	1947	.343	32	114

Entered the military in the fall of 1942.
Entered the military again April 30, 1952, and
   returned to baseball August 6, 1953.

Career Fielding Statistics

Year	G	PO	A	E	TC	DP	Pct
1939	149	318	11	19	348	3	.945
1940	144	302	15	13	328	2	.961
1941	143	262	11	11	284	2	.961
1942	150	313	15	4	332	4	.988
1946	150	325	7	10	330	2	.971
1947	156	347	10	9	366	2	.975
1948	137	289	9	5	303	2	.983
1949	155	337	12	6	355	3	.983
1950	89	165	7	8	180	0	.956
1951	148	315	12	4	331	6	.988
1952	6	4	0	0	4	0	1.000
1953	37	31	1	1	33	1	.970
1954	117	213	5	4	222	0	.982
1955	98	170	5	2	177	0	.989
1956	136	174	7	5	186	2	.973
1957	132	215	2	1	218	0	.995
1958	129	154	3	7	164	0	.970
1959	103	94	4	3	101	0	.990
1960	113	131	6	1	138	1	.993
TOT.	2292	4159	142	113	4414	30	.974

Career MVP Balloting

1939
J. DiMaggio, N.Y.	280
J. Foxx, Bos.	170
B. Feller, Clev.	155
TED WILLIAMS	126

1940
H. Greenberg, Det.	292
B. Feller, Clev.	222
J. DiMaggio, N.Y.	151
B. Newsom, Det.	120
L. Boudreau, Clev.	119
J. Foxx, Bos.	110
TED WILLIAMS (15th)	16

1941
| J. DiMaggio, N.Y. | 291 |
| TED WILLIAMS | 254 |

1942
| J. Gordon, N.Y. | 270 |
| TED WILLIAMS | 249 |

1946
| WILLIAMS WINS MVP | 224 |

1947
| J. DiMaggio, N.Y. | 202 |
| TED WILLIAMS | 201 |

1948	
L. Boudreau, Clev.	324
J. DiMaggio, N.Y.	213
TED WILLIAMS	171

1949	
WILLIAMS WINS MVP	272

1950	
P. Rizzuto, N.Y.	284
B. Goodman, Bos.	180
Y. Berra, N.Y.	146
G. Kell, Det.	127
B. Lemon, Clev.	102
TED WILLIAMS (23rd)	7

1951	
Y. Berra, N.Y.	184
N. Garver, St.L.	157
A. Reynolds, N.Y.	125
M. Minoso, Chi.	120
B. Feller, Clev.	118
TED WILLIAMS (13th)	35

1952	
DID NOT RECEIVE A VOTE	

1953	
A. Rosen, Clev.	336
Y. Berra, N.Y.	167
M. Vernon, Wash.	162
M. Minoso, Chi.	100
V. Trucks, Chi.	81
TED WILLIAMS (26th)	1

1954	
Y. Berra, N.Y.	230
L. Doby, Clev.	210
B. Avila, Clev.	203
M. Minoso, Chi.	186
B. Lemon, Clev.	179
E. Wynn, Clev.	72
TED WILLIAMS	65

1955	
Y. Berra, N.Y.	218
A. Kaline, Det.	201
A. Smith, Clev.	200
TED WILLIAMS	143

1956	
M. Mantle, N.Y.	336
Y. Berra, N.Y.	186
A. Kaline, Det.	142
H. Kuenn, Det.	80
B. Pierce, Chi.	75
TED WILLIAMS	70

1957	
M. Mantle, N.Y.	233
TED WILLIAMS	209

1958	
J. Jenson, Bos.	233
B. Turley, N.Y.	191
R. Colavito, Clev.	181
B. Cerv, K.C.	164
M. Mantle, N.Y.	127
R. Sievers, Wash.	95
TED WILLIAMS	89

1959	
N. Fox, Chi.	295
L. Aparicio, Chi.	255
E. Wynn, Chi.	123
R. Colavito, Clev.	117
T. Francona, Clev.	102
TED WILLIAMS (26th)	2

1960	
R. Maris, N.Y.	225
M. Mantle, N.Y.	222
B. Robinson, Balt.	211
M. Minoso, Chi.	141
R. Hansen, Balt.	110
TED WILLIAMS (13th)	25

Projected Career Statistics

Had Williams played in the 727 games he missed while in the Marines his career totals and all-time rank would be as follows:

	Career Total	Career Rank	Projected Total	Projected Rank
Games	2,292	63rd	3,017	6th
At Bats	7,706	100th	10,149	12th
Runs	1,798	13th	2,301	1st
Hits	2,654	48th	3,496	6th
Doubles	525	19th	692	5th
Triples	71	—	93	—
Home Runs	521	10th	686	3rd
Extra Base Hits	1,117	10th	1,471	2nd, by 6
RBIs	1,839	11th	2,242	2nd
Total Bases	4,884	13th	6,433	2nd
Walks	2,019	2nd	2,659	1st
Strikeouts	709	—	934	99th
Stolen Bases	24	—	32	—
Grand Slams	17	—	22	2nd
Average	.344	6th		
On Base Percentage	.483	1st		
Slugging Percentage	.634	2nd		

SELECTED BIBLIOGRAPHY

Books
Linn, Ed. *Ted Williams: The Eternal Kid*. New York: Bartholomew House, 1961.
Pope, Edwin. *Ted Williams: The Golden Year*. Englewood Cliffs, NJ: Prentice-Hall, 1970.
Robinson, Ray. *Ted Williams*. New York: G. P. Putnam, 1962.
Sampson, Arthur. *Ted Williams: A Biography of The Kid*. New York: A. S. Barnes, 1950.
Schoor, Gene, and Henry Guilfond. *The Ted Williams Story*. New York: Julian Messner, 1954.
Williams, Ted, and John Underwood. *My Turn at Bat*. New York: Simon and Schuster, 1969.
————. *Fishing the Big Three*. New York: Simon and Schuster, 1982.
————. *The Science of Hitting*. New York: Fireside Books (rev. ed.), 1986.

Selected Articles
Amory, Cleveland. "Young Ted Williams: 'I Wanna Be an Immortal.'" *Sport USA*. New York: Nelson, 1961: 334–338.
Broeg, Bob. "Ted Williams." *Super Stars of Baseball*. St. Louis: The Sporting News, 1971: 271–280.
Daley, Arthur. "The Fabulous Career of Tempestuous, Terrific Ted." *Baseball Register, 1961*. St. Louis: The Sporting News, 1961: 2–18.
Hano, Arnold. "Sport's Hall of Fame: Ted Williams' Wild Career." *Sport* (September 1964): 24–27.
Linn Ed. "The Kid's Last Game." *Sport* (February 1961): 52–63.
Updike, John. "The Last Game of Ted Williams." *New Yorker* (October 22, 1960): 109–110.
Williams, Ted (as told to Joseph Reichler). "This Is My Last Year." *Saturday Evening Post* (April 10–24, 1954): 17–19, 24–25, 31.
"Williams of the Red Sox Is Best Hitter." *Life* (September 1, 1941): 43–44.

Other Sources
Newspapers: *The Boston American, The Boston Daily Record, The Boston Globe, The Boston Herald, The Boston Post, The Boston Sunday Advertiser, The Boston Traveller, The Boston Transcript*.
Hirshberg, Al. Al Hirshberg Collection. Microfilm. Boston Public Library.
Kaese, Harold. Columns of Harold Kaese. Microfilm. Boston Public Library.
Harold Kaese Archives from "The Boston Tradition in Sports" collection, Boston Public Library.

INDEX